A Practical Guide for Company Directors

A Practical Guide for Company Directors

David W. Duffy

and

Anne McFarland

Published in 2017 by
Chartered Accountants Ireland
Chartered Accountants House
47–49 Pearse Street
Dublin 2
www.charteredaccountants.ie

© The Institute of Chartered Accountants in Ireland 2017

Copyright in this publication is owned by The Institute of Chartered Accountants in Ireland. All rights reserved. No part of this text may be reproduced or transmitted or communicated to the public in any form or by any means, including photocopying, Internet or e-mail dissemination, without the written permission of The Institute of Chartered Accountants in Ireland. Such written permission must also be obtained before any part of this document is stored in a retrieval system of any nature.

This publication is designed to provide accurate and authoritative information in regard to the subject matter covered. It is provided on the understanding that The Institute of Chartered Accountants in Ireland is not engaged in rendering professional services. The Institute of Chartered Accountants in Ireland disclaims all liability for any reliance placed on the information contained within this publication and recommends that if professional advice or other expert assistance is required, the services of a competent professional should be sought.

ISBN 978-1-910374-01-6

Typeset by Datapage
Printed by Turner's Printing Company, Longford, Ireland

For Ena, Benjamin, Rachel and Gavin

Contents

Preface	xiii

Part I   The Director

1.	**Corporate Governance**	3
	Introduction	5
	Background to Corporate Governance	5
	'Hard' vs. 'Soft' Law	8
	The Companies Act 2014	10
	Conclusion	10
2.	**What is a Company?**	13
	Introduction	15
	The Company as a Separate Legal Entity	15
	Types of Company	17
	Conclusion	23
3.	**The Company Director**	25
	Introduction	27
	Why Become a Company Director?	27
	Who Can be a Company Director?	27
	What is a Company Director?	28
	Types of Director	28
	Due Diligence and the Appointment of Directors	32
	Removal of Directors	35
	Conclusion	36
4.	**Duties of a Director**	39
	Introduction	41
	A Director's Duties are Owed to the Company	41
	Principal Fiduciary Duties of Directors	42
	Other Duties of a Director	51
	Directors' Duties to Other Stakeholders	52
	Breach of Directors' Duties	55
	Conclusion	60

5.	**Conflicts of Interest and Restricted Activities**	63
	Introduction	65
	Areas of Conflict of Interest	65
	Connected Persons and Loans	70
	The Summary Approval Procedure	72
	Conclusion	74
6.	**Directors' Responsibilities: What Directors Need to Know**	77
	Introduction	79
	Strategy	79
	Finance	82
	Risk Management	89
	Internal Control	93
	Information Communications Technology (ICT)	95
	Insurance	97
	Conclusion	99
7.	**Regulatory Environment**	101
	Introduction	103
	The Registrar of Companies	103
	Office of the Director of Corporate Enforcement	104
	Competition Law	106
	Money Laundering	108
	Bribery and Corruption	109
	Environmental Protection	109
	Relevant Foreign Legislation	110
	Conclusion	113

Part II The Board

8.	**Ethics**	117
	Introduction	119
	Ethics and the Role of the Board	119
	Ethics in Practice	120
	Ethical Challenges	123
	Good Faith Reporting	124
	Conclusion	127

9. The Role of the Board and of Individual Directors — 129

Introduction — 131
The Board of Directors — 131
The Chairman — 138
The Chief Executive Officer (CEO) — 141
Non-Executive Directors — 142
The Company Secretary — 148
Conclusion — 151

10. How the Board Works — 153

Introduction — 155
Composition of the Board — 155
The Board as a Team — 159
Proceedings of Directors — 160
The Board Workplan — 162
Agendas for Board Meetings — 162
Chairing and Conducting the Board Meeting — 163
Minutes of Board Meetings — 164
Board 'Away Days' — 166
Confidentiality — 166
Information for the Board — 166
Evaluating the Board — 168
Conclusion — 170

11. Board Committees — 173

Introduction — 175
The Purpose of Board Committees — 175
The Audit Committee — 176
The Nomination Committee — 181
The Remuneration Committee — 184
Conclusion — 188

12. General Meetings, Resolutions and Registers — 191

Introduction — 193
Meetings of the Members — 193
Resolutions — 198

Written Resolutions	199
Rights of Members	200
Registers and Letterheads	200
Conclusion	201

PART III   PRACTICAL ISSUES FOR DIRECTORS

13. Financial Matters — 207

Introduction	209
Statutory Accounting Requirements	209
Directors' Duties with regard to Financial Matters	211
Directors' Duties to Keep Adequate Accounting Records	212
A Company's 'Accounts'	213
Management Accounts	215
Statutory Financial Statements	215
The Importance of 'True and Fair View'	216
Further Requirements for Statutory Financial Statements	217
Directors' Approval of the Statutory Financial Statements	221
Obligation to have Statutory Financial Statements Audited	221
Specific Considerations for Transactions involving Directors for Statutory Financial Statements	222
Conclusion	223
Appendix 13.1: Profit and Loss Account – Sample Format	225
Appendix 13.2: Balance Sheet – Sample Format	226
Appendix 13.3: Cash-flow Statement – Sample Format	229
Appendix 13.4: Statement of Changes In Equity – Sample Format	231

14. The Audit of Statutory Financial Statements and Internal Audit — 233

Introduction	235
Statutory Audits and Auditors	235
Appointment of Statutory Auditors	236
What do Statutory Auditors Do during the Audit?	237
Audit Rotation	238
Removal of Auditors	239
Resignation of Auditors	239

	The Rights of Auditors	240
	The Auditor's Report	240
	Other Reporting by Statutory Auditors	243
	Audit Exemption	244
	Internal Audit	246
	Conclusion	248
15.	**Employer Responsibilities**	**249**
	Introduction	251
	Employment Law	251
	Pensions	256
	Health & Safety	257
	Conclusion	263
16.	**Directors' Remuneration**	**265**
	Introduction	267
	Developments in Executive Director Remuneration	267
	Performance-related Pay	271
	The Components of Remuneration	273
	Remuneration of Non-executive Directors	280
	Conclusion	282

Part IV Financial Difficulty and Winding up

17.	**Financial Difficulty and Insolvency**	**285**
	Introduction	287
	Financial Difficulty	287
	Going Concern	289
	Fraudulent Acts, Fraudulent Trading and Reckless Trading	295
	Examinership and Receivership	297
	Conclusion	301
18.	**Winding Up: Processes and Options**	**303**
	Introduction	305
	Strike Off	306
	Members' Voluntary Winding Up	307
	Creditors' Voluntary Winding Up	309
	Winding Up by the Court	310

Duties of Company Directors in a Winding Up	311
Liquidators	311
Dissolution	312
Restriction and Disqualification of Directors	312
Conclusion	315
Index	**317**

Preface

> "If you don't see the book you want on the shelf, write it."
> *Beverly Cleary*

With the commencement of the Companies Act 2014, it struck us that there is a need for a guide for existing and aspiring company directors to help them understand the new Companies Act and their duties under it, other relevant legislation, guidance and best practice. This book is intended as a unique resource for those who want to know more about what it means to be a company director in Ireland and the myriad of related responsibilities, and who want to contribute to the improvement of corporate governance in their organisations.

The focus of the Companies Act 2014 is on private rather than public companies, which is the converse of the Companies Act 1963. This makes sense, as private companies make up the vast majority of incorporated entities in this country. The 2014 Act has clarified director's responsibilities for the first time and simplified many matters, such as setting up a company, which can only be good for entrepreneurship and the economy.

Finally, as practitioners in corporate governance, we have tried to present the contents in a form that makes this guide an accessible and valuable resource, which is easy to read, practical and readily applicable. We have also attempted to provide a balance between information that is a critical to know and guidance for those who want to know more about any particular topic. We hope we have succeeded and that you find it useful.

David W. Duffy and Anne McFarland
August 2017

Part I

THE DIRECTOR

To be a company director does not require any qualifications except that one needs to be at least 18 years of age. Nevertheless, on becoming a director, a person acquires considerable responsibilities and may be held personally liable for decisions taken. It is therefore essential that directors have a good understanding of their role and statutory duties.

A company director **cannot** be: 1. an undischarged bankrupt (breach is classed as a Category 2 offence); 2. a corporate body; 3. the auditor of the company or its related companies; 4. a disqualified person; and 6. a restricted person (in certain situations).

Many of the duties and responsibilities of a director are set out in the Companies Act 2014 (CA 2014). An important innovation in the Act is that it codifies, i.e. writes into statute, for the first time directors' duties, although case law remains important. The Act emphasises that a director owes his or her duties to the company and not to the shareholders: "a director of a company shall owe the duties … to the company (and the company alone)".[1] This is not a new principle but one not often appreciated by directors. The Act also covers in detail areas where the director may be exposed to a conflict of interests.

A director's role is not governed by company law alone. Corporate governance codes also set out and provide mandatory and non-mandatory guidance on how a company should be directed and controlled. Of particular relevance is the *UK Corporate Governance Code*, which, although aimed at listed companies, is a useful, concise guide that is relevant to all directors. In addition, the Code has set the context for the development of other, more sector-specific codes, such as the code for the voluntary sector in Ireland.[2]

Finally, directors' duties are also provided for in statutes other than the Companies Act 2014; for example, responsibilities under health and safety legislation. To be effective, the company director needs:
- an understanding of other relevant laws, e.g. competition, contract, health and safety, employment, etc.;
- to have the knowledge and skills to perform the responsibilities of the role, e.g. finance, strategy, risk, etc.; and
- to be aware of other elements of the regulatory environment, e.g. requirements of the Registrar at the Companies Registration Office (CRO) and the Office of the Director of Corporate Enforcement (ODCE).

Thus, although being a director does not require any formal qualifications, the amount of knowledge required to be an effective director is considerable. In this Part I, therefore, we will look at:

1. Corporate Governance
2. What is a Company?
3. The Company Director
4. Duties of a Director
5. Conflicts of Interest, Compliance and Restricted Activities
6. Directors' Responsibilities
7. Other Elements of the Regulatory Environment.

[1] Section 227(1) CA 2014.
[2] *A Code of Governance for Voluntary, Charitable and Community Organisations* (2012).

1.
Corporate Governance

- Introduction
- Background to Corporate Governance
- 'Hard' vs. 'Soft' Law
- The Companies Act 2014
- Conclusion
- Key Points

Introduction

In this chapter we will examine the context for the development of corporate governance generally and its evolution in Ireland. The governance failures in many Irish organisations that became manifest during and since the financial crisis have accelerated the general adoption of corporate governance principles as well as the development of new codes of governance for specific sectors of the economy, such as financial services, state-funded organisations and charities.

Background to Corporate Governance

According to Sir Adrian Cadbury, a pioneer of governance, corporate governance is "the system by which companies are directed and controlled".[1]

Governance is an important issue in all companies, which is highlighted by the problems exposed in the governance of banks, public sector bodies and voluntary organisations over the past decade in Ireland. Governance did not get sufficient attention and priority until the very recent public failures. While good governance seldom comes into the public gaze, poor governance can often have a disproportionate impact when a serious issue is exposed. For example, the lack of transparency on top executive salaries in large charities in Ireland resulted in a negative impact on fundraising not only on the large charities themselves, but also in the wider charity sector.

The foundation stone in the governance of a company is its board of directors, a group of people generally appointed (or in some cases elected) by the company's shareholders to govern the company and oversee the performance of the executive.

Corporate governance is not just about:
- having independent directors on a board;
- separating the roles of the chair and chief executive for the sake of good practice;
- establishing remuneration, audit and other committees; or
- well-meaning statements in the organisation's annual report or on its website.

---

[1] *Report of the Committee on the Financial Aspects of Corporate Governance* ('The Cadbury Report' (Gee Publishing, 1992)), para 2.5.

Corporate governance is more specifically about:
- setting the 'tone from the top' on the ethical values of the organisation;
- the board's oversight of the executive, together with the supporting processes (e.g. ensuring that the board is supplied with timely and accurate information to enable it to do its job);
- regulating the relationships between the company, its shareholders, directors and the executive management team.

The UK Corporate Governance Code

The *UK Corporate Governance Code*[2], as supplemented by the "Irish Corporate Governance Annex"[3], underpins and informs much of the approach to corporate governance in Ireland. It addresses governance under the following headings:
- leadership;
- effectiveness;
- accountability;
- remuneration; and
- relations with shareholders.

Although the *UK Corporate Governance Code* reflects governance practices that are relevant in the context of listed companies, i.e. companies with a full listing on the Irish or London Stock Exchanges, it is recommended that all directors take time to familiarise themselves with its key principles. The concepts underlying these principles can be used for other types of entity, such as a private company limited by shares.

Though the specific provisions of the *UK Corporate Governance Code* may not be applicable to smaller or non-profit entities, the Code may be used to help inform the development of governance structures that respond to the expectations of finance providers and stakeholders. As a useful reference for corporate governance, the Code is a short document that is easy to read and understand.

What is Corporate Governance?

Good corporate governance is important for directors as it lays down the principles of how to run a company effectively. Rather than being about making the 'correct' decision, good governance involves having the best processes in place for making those decisions.

---

[2] Financial Reporting Council, *UK Corporate Governance Code* (FRC, April 2016).
[3] Irish Stock Exchange, *Main Securities Market Listing Rules and Admission to Trading Rules*, Appendix 4, "Irish Corporate Governance Annex" (ISE, 2011).

Characteristics of good corporate governance include:
- accountability;
- openness and transparency;
- responsiveness;
- effectiveness and efficiency; and
- compliance with the law.

A well-governed and well-managed company should be more sustainable and resilient. It gives the executive and staff confidence in the leadership and values of the organisation, which is very important if the company has to navigate through tough times. The more transparent the governance, the more confidence it creates.

Stakeholders are also interested in well-run companies. A stakeholder might be an investor, a lending institution, a government agency, debtor, creditor or even a potential purchaser. Their assessment of the robustness of the governance of a company will influence how they view and assess the organisation for their own specific purposes.

Corporate governance should be proportionate to the size of the organisation. The running of a company with a single shareholder is different from that of one with 100 shareholders, or indeed a non-profit organisation. There is a cost to governance, and a board has to strike a balance between the cost and the benefits. It is the role of the board to ensure that the appropriate governance structures are put in place as a company develops. All companies have different heritages and cultures, which make them unique, but the approach to good governance should have similar characteristics, with clear leadership and strong accountability.

Corporate Governance Codes in Ireland

There are different governance codes for certain sectors. Some of the more important ones in Ireland are:
- *The Code of Practice for the Governance of State Bodies* (Revised and Updated August 2016)[4];
- *Corporate Governance Code for Credit Institutions and Insurance Undertakings* (2013)[5];

---
[4] See www.per.gov.ie/en/revised-code-of-practice-for-the-governance-of-state-bodies/
[5] See www.centralbank.ie

- *A Code of Governance for Voluntary, Charitable and Community Organisations* (2012)[6];
- *Irish Development NGOs Code of Corporate Governance* (2008).[7]

The first two of these codes are mandatory corporate governance codes, while the last two are voluntary.

If there is no mandatory corporate governance code or code of practice, it is the responsibility of the directors to discuss, develop and document the appropriate code of governance for their company.

Mandatory codes set out rules for the appropriate governance for the type of organisations to which they are relevant. These codes can be enforced by law, if necessary, and directors can be held to account.

Given the recent financial crisis, it is difficult to argue against mandatory codes being applied to large financial institutions, while there is also a trend towards more 'hard' law approaches. However, such mandatory codes can suffer from being inflexible.

'Hard' vs. 'Soft' Law

'Hard' law has its basis in legislation, such as the Companies Act 2014, while mandatory governance codes have the backing of the Stock Exchange or the regulator. 'Soft' law has its basis in non-mandatory codes, such as the *UK Corporate Governance Code*, and other codes that provide guidance on best practice but are not enforceable by law.

The advantages and disadvantages of hard law versus soft law can be debated. Hard law brings a unilateral set of requirements, with rules that can be enforced and for which there are specific consequences for particular breaches of the law. However, as a conceptual framework for resolving issues, the soft law approach has the advantage of flexibility and the ability to cope with unforeseen circumstances that have not been anticipated in the law.

It can be tempting to codify everything and limit the room for interpretation. However, a rules-based approach is no guarantee of better governance. A proportionate combination of both approaches is probably the preferred solution.

---

[6] See www.governancecode.ie
[7] See www.dochas.ie

'Comply or Explain'

The concept of 'comply or explain', when correctly applied, is a good example of an effective 'soft' law approach.

The *UK Corporate Governance Code* is made up of broad principles and specific provisions, which in turn illustrate and amplify each principle. While the Code requires that the broad **principle** be complied with, the more specific **provisions** need not be complied with. However, if a listed company chooses not to comply with a provision, it must explain why; this explanation should be sufficient to let investors and shareholders make a judgement as to whether the company is being well run and whether the principles of the Code are being properly applied. This is the concept of 'comply or explain'. If the shareholders are dissatisfied with the explanations given, they may move to dismiss the directors and/or sell their shares. Thus, there is a market sanction for non-compliance.

Rejecting a box-ticking approach, 'comply or explain' allows for the company diversity where 'one size does not fit all'. While it ensures that the key principles of corporate governance are observed, it allows the more specific provisions to be adapted, providing a clear explanation is given. For example, while a company may not have had an audit committee for a period of time, it can explain that the work of the audit committee was covered using the internal audit department and the external auditors as appropriate for that period.

Comply or explain is reflected in many mandatory and non-mandatory governance codes in Ireland, the UK and across the world in countries such as Germany, The Netherlands, South Africa and Singapore.

The *UK Corporate Governance Code* is not a legal obligation for listed companies, but adherence to it is essential if a company is to be listed or to continue to be listed on the London Stock Exchange (LSE). If a listed company goes against the principles of the Code, it may face sanctions by the LSE, such as censure of the company or directors, suspension of shares or even being delisted.

Similarly, as mentioned above, there is no legal compunction for smaller companies to adhere to the *UK Corporate Governance Code*, but it is good practice and should enhance the confidence of investors, stakeholders and creditors. Companies should take advantage of the option to explain when they have practices that do not comply with the Code. This could relate to disclosure requirements for executive remuneration.

As we have seen, the aftermath of the financial crash has resulted in a move to make more codes mandatory and offending directors accountable before the law. The desire for legally enforceable governance has grown and the Companies Act 2014 in Ireland reflects this with its clear description of penalties if the law is breached.

The Companies Act 2014

The Companies Act 2014 has contributed and is contributing to improving corporate governance in Ireland by clearly setting out the consequences of not complying with company law and by simplifying certain aspects of governance. The Act came into force on 1 June 2015, replacing all previous Companies Acts. It presents a new, simplified form of private company limited by shares (LTD), and this is the basis for the Act.

Changes Incorporated in the Companies Act 2014

Although CA 2014 is really a consolidation of previous company law, it also includes a number of important changes. The rationale for these changes includes:
- simplifying the management of companies, for example a LTD company can now have just one director and one shareholder;
- simplifying procedures for complying with the law, for example the introduction of a new 'Summary Approval Procedure' in place of having to apply to court for permission to undertake certain activities; and
- improving governance by clarifying penalties and by codifying directors' duties.

Conclusion

This chapter discussed the background to corporate governance, highlighted the influence of the *UK Corporate Governance Code* on our thinking in Ireland and on the codes that have been developed since the advent of what is arguably the first corporate governance code, the *Cadbury Report* in 1992.

The importance of directors in fulfilling their governance function in a company was emphasised. The concept of 'comply or explain', which underlies the *UK Corporate Governance Code*, was examined, as well as the advantages of the 'soft' law approach. The chapter concluded by examining the main changes to the 'hard' law around corporate governance in Ireland with the introduction of the Companies Act 2014.

In the next chapter we will consider the company as a separate legal entity.

10 Key Points: Corporate Governance

1. Corporate governance is defined in the *Cadbury Report* as "the system by which companies are directed and controlled".
2. Corporate governance regulates the relationships between the company, shareholders, directors and the executive management team.
3. The *UK Corporate Governance Code*, while aimed at listed companies, is a concise summary of corporate governance principles, which is useful to all companies. It underpins many of the approaches to corporate governance in Ireland.
4. Governance codes for different sectors may be mandatory or voluntary. For instance, the *Code of Practice for the Governance of State Bodies* (2016) is mandatory, while others, such as *A Code of Governance for Voluntary, Charitable and Community Organisations* (2012), are simply guidelines.
5. 'Hard' law, involving legislation and mandatory codes, brings a unilateral set of requirements with rules that can be enforced by law and for which there are specific consequences for breaches of the rules.
6. 'Soft' law, based on guidance and voluntary codes, has the advantage of flexibility and the ability to cope with unforeseen circumstances that the law cannot anticipate. It provides a conceptual framework for decision-making and resolving issues.
7. 'Comply or explain' means that if a company does not comply with the provisions of the *UK Corporate Governance Code* it must explain why. If a company has decided that it wants to comply with the Code, however, its broad underlying principles must always be complied with.
8. The Companies Act 2014 is a consolidation of previous Companies Acts and other, secondary legislation, as well as common law principles.
9. The focus of the Companies Act 2014 is the simplified private company limited by shares (the LTD), which is now classed as the model company in Ireland, rather than the PLC as in previous Companies Acts.
10. The Companies Act 2014 encourages better corporate governance by clarifying penalties and by codifying directors' duties. It emphasises the accountability of directors.

2.
What is a Company?

- Introduction
- The Company as a Separate Legal Entity
- Types of Company
- Conclusion
- Key Points

Introduction

The previous chapter outlined the background to good corporate governance and recent developments. It explained that the Companies Act 2014 (CA 2014) focuses on the private company limited by shares (LTD), as the majority of companies in Ireland are SMEs.[1] In this chapter we will look at what a company is and the main types of company set out in CA 2014.

The Company as a Separate Legal Entity

The limited liability company was created so that shareholders could take risks, the principle being that once shareholders have paid up their share capital they have no further liability.

A company exists separately in law from its owners and directors. In the case of *Salomon v. Salomon and Co Ltd*,[2] it was confirmed that a company "must be treated like any other independent person with its rights and liabilities appropriate to itself".[3] In this case, though Mr Salomon was the major shareholder, a director, an employee and a creditor of the company he created, the company was held to be a separate legal entity.

Thus, a company:
- contracts in its own name;
- has property rights;
- can employ staff;
- can sue and be sued, or be criminally prosecuted;
- can buy other companies;
- enjoys perpetual succession, i.e. it is theoretically everlasting; and
- can be established for a particular purpose and then liquidated when that purpose is complete.

The *Foss v. Harbottle* case[4] illustrated that the company is separate from its shareholders. In this case it was judged that the proper claimant in an action in respect of a wrong done to a company is the company itself, not the shareholders. It is important to remember that a company is not the same as its shareholders.

---

[1] According to the Central Statistics Office (CSO), there were 237,753 small medium-sized enterprises active in Ireland in 2014.
[2] Lord Halsbury in *Salomon v. Salomon and Co Ltd* [1897] A.C. 22.
[3] *Ibid.* at 30.
[4] *Foss v. Harbottle* (1843) 67 E.R. 189.

The shareholders provide capital to a company and appoint the directors to govern it. Neither the directors nor the shareholders own the assets of the company. These are owned by the company. A shareholder's stake in a company is determined by the number of ordinary shares they have and the value attributed to each share. A company may be limited by guarantee, in which case it has 'members' rather than shareholders. Thus, 'members' is a broader term than 'shareholders' for the owners of a company.

In law, the company, being a separate legal entity, has certain obligations. These include:
- Keeping adequate accounting records[5] and preparing financial statements. A company must correctly record and explain all transactions that enable its financial position to be determined with reasonable accuracy.[6]
- Holding an annual general meeting[7]: all companies, except for private limited companies (LTDs),[8] must hold an annual general meeting.
- Keeping registers of directors and secretaries[9] and members.[10]
- Sending certain documentation to the Companies Registration Office (CRO). This information is available to the public and includes the company's financial statements,[11] any notices of change of office, director or Company Secretary, or any mortgages or charges on the company's property.

The 'Veil of Incorporation'

As a separate legal entity, a company can sue and be sued. Incorporation thus protects the underlying shareholders from being sued. This is part of the long-established principle of the 'veil of incorporation'. This veil can be lifted or pierced, however, and the shareholders may be held to account by the courts. In addition, banks may demand personal guarantees from company officers or shareholders, undermining the concept of the veil of incorporation.

---

[5] Section 281 CA 2014.
[6] Section 282 CA 2014.
[7] Section 175 CA 2014.
[8] Where an LTD opts not to hold an AGM, and where it has more than two members, all the members entitled to attend and vote at the AGM must sign, before the latest date for the holding of that meeting, a written resolution to the effect that they have received the financial statements, resolved all matters ordinarily dealt with at the AGM and confirm that there has been no change to the appointment of the company's statutory auditor (section 175(3) CA 2014).
[9] Section 149 CA 2014.
[10] Section 169 CA 2014.
[11] Section 343 CA 2014.

The veil of incorporation is most likely to be lifted if there is suspicion of fraud or tax evasion, or as a result of activity against the public interest, such as trading with an enemy of the state during a time of war.[12] The following comments from Lord Denning in *Littlewoods Mail Order Stores v. IRC* (1969) are also worth noting in this regard:

> "The doctrine laid down in Salomon v. Salomon has to be watched carefully. It has often been supposed to cast a veil over the personality of a limited company through which the courts cannot see. But that is not true. The courts can and do draw aside the veil. They can, and often do, pull off the mask. They look to see what lies behind."[13]

The Companies Act 2014 specifically allows the veil of incorporation to be pierced in regard to liability for fraudulent or reckless trading.[14]

As a principle, the veil of incorporation refers to all types of companies under the Companies Act. While it does give important protection to the members of a company, members, and more specifically company officers, should be aware that it can be lifted.

Types of Company

The first 14 Parts of CA 2014 address the private limited company, being the most common form of company. Thus, a private company limited by shares (LTD) is the basis for the Companies Act. The remaining parts of the Act refer to different types of company and explain, where appropriate, how they differ from the LTD.

The other main types of company are:
- a designated activity company (DAC), limited by shares or by guarantee;
- a public limited company (PLC), which is a company that can raise capital by selling shares to the public; and
- a company limited by guarantee (CLG).

Template 'constitutions' for each type of company are included in the schedules to the Companies Act.

---

[12] *Daimler Co Ltd v. Continental Tyre And Rubber Co Ltd (Great Britain) Ltd* [1916] 2 A.C. 307.
[13] Lord Denning M.R. in *Littlewoods Mail Order Stores v. IRC* (1969) 1 W.L.R. 1241.
[14] Section 610(2) CA 2014.

Some of the key characteristics of each main company are set out in **Table 2.1** below.

TABLE 2.1: KEY CHARACTERISTICS OF MAIN COMPANY TYPES

Type of Company	Constitution	Max. No. of Members	Min. No. of Directors	AGM	Majority Written Resolutions	Able to Sell Securities?
LTD	Simplified, no objects[15]	149[16]	One[17] but cannot be the Company Secretary[18]	No[19]	By a majority[20]	No[21]
DAC	Includes company's objects[22]	149	2[23]	Yes, unless one member[24]	By a majority, unless company's constitution prohibits[25]	May list qualifying debt securities[26]
PLC	Includes objects[27]	None	2[28]	Yes, unless one member[29]	No	Yes[30]

(Continued)

---

[15] Section 19 CA 2014.
[16] Section 17(4)(5) CA 2014.
[17] Section 128 CA 2014.
[18] Section 129(6) CA 2014.
[19] Section 175(3) CA 2014.
[20] Section 194 CA 2014.
[21] Section 68 CA 2014.
[22] Section 967 CA 2014.
[23] Section 985 CA 2014.
[24] Section 988 CA 2014.
[25] Sections 194 and 990 CA 2014.
[26] Section 68(3) CA 2014.
[27] Section 1011 CA 2014.
[28] Section 1088 CA 2014.
[29] Section 1089 CA 2014.
[30] Section 1020 CA 2014.

Type of Company	Constitution	Max. No. of Members	Min. No. of Directors	AGM	Majority Written Resolutions	Able to Sell Securities?
CLG	Includes objects[31]	None[32]	2[33]	Yes, unless one member[34]	No[35]	Debentures[36]

Private Company Limited by Shares (LTD)[37]

This type of private company was introduced in the Companies Act by simplifying the requirements of the limited company as set out in previous Companies Acts.

The most important feature of an LTD is that it can undertake any activity other than that of a credit institution or insurance undertaking. It has full, unlimited legal capacity. This means that it can engage in business in the same way as an individual can and its constitution cannot contain any restrictions as to what it can do.[38] The concept of *ultra vires* – beyond its power – does not apply. The company has the power to carry on any legal business.

Having unlimited capacity, a bank or other creditor will not need to scan its constitution to check if the company is allowed to undertake a certain activity or not. It cannot do anything *ultra vires*, beyond its power, as it has the power to carry on any legitimate business activity.

The name of the company must end with the word Limited, LTD or Ltd, or Teoranta, TEO or Teo.[39]

The liability of a member of an LTD company is limited to the amount, if any, unpaid on the shares registered in the member's name.[40]

---

[31] Section 1176 CA 2014.
[32] Section 1199 CA 2014.
[33] Section 1194 CA 2014.
[34] Section 1202 CA 2014.
[35] Section 1173 CA 2014.
[36] Section 1191 CA 2014.
[37] Parts 2 to 14 CA 2014.
[38] Section 38 CA 2014.
[39] Section 26 CA 2014.
[40] Section 17(2) CA 2014.

The LTD, as set out in the Companies Act 2014, is much simpler than the LTD that existed under previous Acts. It is easier to operate, requires a minimum of only one director (though it must have a separate Company Secretary). It does not have to have a physical AGM and can pass relevant matters by majority written resolutions.

A small anomaly in CA 2014 as initially enacted, is that there is no clear definition of what a 'credit institution' is. Until this is clarified, a company whose main business is providing credit, for example a treasury company within a group, should register as a DAC.

Designated Activity Company (DAC)[41]

As set out in Part 16 of CA 2014 a designated activity company (DAC) is a new type of company, in name at least (see below), created under the Act. The DAC is similar in one key respect to the limited company under previous Companies Acts in that it has an objects clause, i.e. it has specific objectives. This is a key difference between it and the new simplified LTD under CA 2014 which has no objects clause.

This type of company is suitable for those who wish to outline and define specific objectives for the company in its constitution rather than have the unlimited powers of the new LTD type of company. As a company with specific objectives, a DAC must have at least two directors as it will generally be a company of more substance than a LTD company and therefore require greater oversight.

The types of company that are likely to avail of the DAC format are those:
- that are incorporated to complete a specific purpose and wish to have the company's powers restricted, such as a joint venture or a charity;
- that wish to be limited by guarantee, while having a share capital (a company limited by guarantee is one that does not have a share capital – the company's constitution provides that the liability of its members is limited to such amount as the members may respectively undertake to contribute to the assets of the CLG in the event of it being wound up);
- with shareholders who have a strong preference to be incorporated as a DAC because they want to ensure that the company has certain defined objectives;
- a private company that intends to operate as a credit institution or insurance undertaking (as an LTD cannot operate in these fields).

[41] Part 16 CA 2014.

2. WHAT IS A COMPANY?

The company name must end in 'Designated Activity Company' or 'Cuideachta Ghníomhaíochta Ainmnithe' or, once registered, DAC, D.A.C, d.a.c, dac, CGA, C.G.A, c.g.a. or cga.[42]

The liability of a member of a DAC is limited to the amount, if any, unpaid on the shares registered in the member's name or, if limited by guarantee, the amount undertaken to be contributed by him or her to the assets of the DAC in the event of its being wound up.[43]

A director of a DAC cannot hold more than 25 directorships.[44]

It is worth noting that the DAC is very similar to the old LTD under the previous Companies Acts, with its objects clause and the fact that it must have two directors. Under the 2014 Act, it is the LTD company that is the new company type rather than the DAC, with new features of unlimited capacity and the option to have just one director.

Public Limited Company (PLC)

The law relating to PLCs is set out in Part 17 of CA 2014.
- The authorised minimum nominal share capital of a PLC is €25,000.[45]
- Individual or group acquisitions of certain percentages of shares must be disclosed.[46]
- A PLC can acquire its own shares if it pays for them using profits available for distribution.[47]
- A PLC must prepare statutory audited accounts.[48]

The term 'listed' is used to describe shares, debentures (i.e. debt) or other securities traded on a recognised market or exchange. A company that can trade its shares on such a market and is a PLC is often referred to as a 'listed company'.

Company Limited by Guarantee (CLG)

A company limited by guarantee without a share capital[49] is deemed to be a company limited by guarantee (CLG). Not having a share

---

[42] Section 969 CA 2014.
[43] Section 965 CA 2014.
[44] Section 986 CA 2014.
[45] Section 1000 CA 2014.
[46] Section 1048 CA 2014.
[47] Section 1071 CA 2014.
[48] Section 1117 CA 2014.
[49] Section 1172 CA 2014.

capital means that the company's owners are referred to as 'members' rather than shareholders, as there are no shares. CLGs are commonly used for charities, property management companies and non-profit entities.

The law relating to CLGs is set out in Part 18 of the Companies Act 2014.

The name of a CLG must end with Company Limited by Guarantee or Cuideachta Faoi Theorainn Ráthaíochta, or the abbreviations CLG, C.L.G, CTR or C.T.R.[50] There are certain exemptions from this requirement; for example, a charity does not have to use the description CLG.[51]

The liability of a CLG's members is "limited by its constitution to such amount as the members may respectively thereby undertake to contribute to the assets of the company in the event of its being wound up".[52]

The financial statements of CLGs must be filed with the CRO unless they have availed of certain exemptions.[53] Accounts of all charities must be filed with the Charities Regulator.[54] SORP financial reporting requirements for charities assist in providing greater transparency as to how donor money has been spent. However, SORP reporting is not mandatory for all charities in Ireland.

Conversion and Change of Name

Private limited companies formed under previous Companies Acts must convert to either an LTD or a DAC under CA 2014. During the 18-month transition period, which started with the commencement of the Act (1 June 2015) "old private Ltd companies" were deemed to be DACs. Following the end of the transition period, they will automatically be designated as

---

[50] Section 1178 CA 2014.
[51] Section 1180 CA 2014.
[52] Section 1172 CA 2014.
[53] Section 1219(1) and (2) CA 2014.
[54] The 'SORP' is a Statement of Recommended Accounting Practice for charities. It requires certain information to be presented in the financial statements and the annual reports in a specific manner. This includes that the Statement of Financial Activities is presented in a specific layout that distinguishes between specific categories of income and expenditure, for example, income and expenditure categorised as restricted and unrestricted activities.

an LTD unless the directors take steps to convert the company to a DAC or other type of company.

An existing private company could simply re-register as a DAC within 18 months from 1 June 2015, which would allow it to keep its Memorandum and Articles of Association in place. The Memorandum and Articles of Association are the governing documents of a company. It is essential that these documents correctly reflect the objectives of the company. The Memorandum and Articles are replaced by a simpler, single-document constitution for the new private company limited by shares (LTD) (see above).

Regardless of whether a company is becoming a new LTD or a DAC, a special resolution needs to be passed by the members adopting the new constitution.

Conclusion

This chapter has outlined the origin and benefits of the limited liability company. A company is a legal entity in its own right, separate from its members, though the 'veil of incorporation' may be drawn aside.

The Companies Act 2014 introduced the simplified private company limited by shares, the LTD. This is intended to be easier to set up and run and has the same unlimited ability to make contracts as an individual person. This is an important innovation in Irish company law. The DAC, introduced in the same Act, is in fact similar to the limited company under previous Companies Acts, apart from its name. The other main types of company detailed in the 2014 Act are the PLC and CLG.

Remember: there are other forms of legal entity that should be considered when setting up a business. Acting as a sole trader, a partner in a partnership or in a limited liability partnership (LLP)[55] implies different roles and carries different responsibilities from being a shareholder or director of a company. All such types of legal entities have their pros and cons, which should be considered before deciding on the most appropriate form of legal entity to support a business. Very often tax, rather than limitation of liability, is a deciding factor.

---

[55] An LLP is a partnership where one or more of the partners are registered with the CRO as having limited liability under the Limited Partnership Act 1907. None of these legal entities is separate from its members. This right is bestowed exclusively on companies.

10 Key Points: What is a Company?

1. A company exists in law as a separate legal entity.
2. The 'veil of incorporation' can be pierced by the courts and as a result, shareholders and company officers may be held liable rather than the company.
3. A company must keep adequate accounting records and prescribed registers.
4. The most common type of company is a private company limited by shares (LTD).
5. The constitution of a company is its founding document. In all companies, apart from an LTD, it is made up of two elements: the Memorandum of Association and the Articles of Association.
6. The focus of the Companies Act 2014 is on private companies limited by shares (LTDs) rather than PLCs, as in previous Acts.
7. The Companies Act 2014 has simplified the rules governing a private company limited by shares (LTD). Such a company does not have an objects clause. It has full, unlimited legal capacity.
8. A private company limited by shares (LTD) needs to have only one director, though it must have a separate Company Secretary.
9. The 2014 Act introduced the designated activity company (DAC). A DAC maintains its objects clause, i.e. its objectives or specified purposes.
10. A limited company under previous Companies Acts is treated as a DAC until it chooses to be a DAC or an LTD. If it has not made a choice by the end of the transition phase, i.e. 18 months after 1 June 2015, the Registrar will deem it to have converted into a new, simplified LTD under the Companies Act 2014.

3.
The Company Director

- Introduction
- Why Become a Company Director?
- Who Can be a Company Director?
- What is a Company Director?
- Types of Director
- Due Diligence and the Appointment of Directors
- Removal of Directors
- Conclusion
- Key Points

Introduction

In this chapter we consider the implications of becoming a company director and carrying out that role. The role is an onerous one and any person accepting it must be aware of their duties and responsibilities.

Why Become a Company Director?

Many directors are also the owners of their company. The Companies Act 2014 (CA 2014) pays particular attention to such smaller companies, which may have only one director/shareholder. In larger companies, becoming a director on the board may be part of career progression within the organisation. Other individuals join boards to contribute their skills and experience, for example as a non-executive director.

Whatever the pathway to becoming a director, the role brings with it specific legal responsibilities, regardless of whether or not it is remunerated.

Who Can be a Company Director?

Other than the requirement that a company must have at least one director who is resident in the European Economic Area (EEA),[1] and as we have seen, no qualification is required to be a company director, unless that director is also the Company Secretary. However, there are criteria as to who *cannot* be a director in Ireland:
- A director cannot be less than 18 years of age.[2]
- A director cannot be an undischarged bankrupt.[3]
- A company cannot be a director in Ireland,[4] i.e. a director must be what the law describes as a 'natural' person.
- A director who is disqualified cannot act as one[5]– directors may be disqualified if they break company law.
- A director who is restricted cannot act in this capacity, unless under strict conditions prescribed by law.
- The company's statutory auditor cannot also be a director as they would be conflicted in the respective roles.[6]

---

[1] Sections 137 to 142 CA 2014.
[2] Section 131 CA 2014.
[3] Section 132 CA 2014.
[4] Section 130 CA 2014.
[5] Section 838 CA 2014.
[6] Section 230 CA 2014.

What is a Company Director?

A company director runs a company on behalf of its members.[7] The term 'director' is very loosely defined in the Companies Act: it "includes any person occupying the position of director by whatever name called".[8]

Similarly, the primary function of the director is "to manage the business of the company on behalf of the members."[9] The powers of a director are defined by the company's constitution, the Companies Act 2014 and instructions received in general meeting.

The appointment of a director is a matter of public record and carries with it the responsibility to make sure that it is recorded as prescribed by law. This includes advising the Companies Registration Office (CRO), displaying the director's name on company letterheads and in the annual report and accounts.

Directors' duties are now defined in the Companies Act 2014, and are discussed in **Chapter 4**. (The role of the *board* of directors is set out in **Chapter 9**.)

Types of Director

There are a number of different types of director that can be associated with a company. It is important to have a good understanding of each, as the role and its implications can be different:
- executive directors;
- non-executive directors (sometimes referred to as 'NEDs');
- shadow directors;
- de facto directors;
- alternate directors; and
- nominee directors.

Executive Directors

An executive director is a member of the board and employed by the company, generally in a full-time functional capacity, such as the finance

---

[7] Remember: 'member' is simply a wider term for shareholder as it includes the owners of a company limited by guarantee.
[8] Section 2(1) CA 2014.
[9] See www.odce.ie/Portals/0/Directors.pdf

director, marketing director, etc. This would also include the managing director. Executive directors are involved in the day-to-day running of the company. They are responsible for implementing the strategy of the company and running it in accordance with company law, the constitution of the company and any resolutions of the shareholders/members.

Non-executive Directors

A non-executive director is a member of the board and he or she is generally appointed for their objectivity, independence and specialist expertise relevant to the strategy of the company. (Strategy is discussed in greater detail in **Chapter 9**.)

CA 2014 does not specify what a non-executive director is. Its only reference is in the context of audit committees: "a non-executive director is a director who is not engaged in the daily management of the large company or body concerned, as the case may be".[10]

It should be noted that non-executive directors are not necessarily independent. A non-executive director may, for example, represent a shareholder, or group of shareholders. Independent non-executive directors are important for corporate governance. Non-executive directors' independence is particularly important when selecting members for board committees. For example, executive directors should not be members of the audit or remuneration committees as they would be conflicted (see **Chapter 11**).

The Companies Act defines other types of director, who, though they may not describe themselves as directors, nevertheless carry full responsibility: shadow, de facto, alternate and nominee directors.

Shadow Directors

A 'shadow director' is defined in the 2014 Act as "a person in accordance with whose directions or instructions the directors of a company are accustomed to act".[11] Third parties need to be very aware of the status of the individuals they are dealing with in a company and the power and authority they may or may not have.

It is also important to be aware of the risk of being considered a 'shadow director'. It is a wide definition and shareholder representatives may

---

[10] Section 167(10) CA 2014.
[11] Section 221 CA 2014.

easily find themselves in this position. For example, a 'shadow director' may attend board meetings and direct his colleagues. If the company ends up in financial difficulty, however, this 'shadow director' may be held responsible for decisions taken.

The Act also clarifies that a holding company cannot be a shadow director of its subsidiaries.

De Facto Directors

If the position of company director is occupied, regardless of whether there has been a formal appointment, then that person is considered a de facto director.[12] Similarly, if a director is not registered as such but acts as a director, then they are treated in law as a director 'in fact'. This means that they are liable to the same penalties or disqualification as a registered director. However, the Companies Act clarifies that a professional advisor is not considered a de facto advisor if giving advice in their professional capacity.[13]

Alternate Directors

An alternate director is a person who is appointed by a director of a company to act in their place, as director, when they are unable to do so. It is important to note that alternate directors do not hold office in their own right and they only hold office for such time as the director they represent specifies. The Companies Act 2014 provides that, "Any director of a company may from time to time appoint any other director of it or, with the approval of a majority of its directors, any other person to be an alternate director as respects him or her."[14]

Notice must be given in writing to the board by the 'appointer', i.e. the director who has appointed the alternate director. The appointment can be revoked at any time by the appointer, by a majority of the board, or by the company in general meeting.

Alternate directors tend to be used in smaller companies or joint ventures, particularly where there are two parties that have significant stakes and each has the right to appoint one or more directors. These companies will often appoint alternates to ensure 'the numbers' in any voting situation. If a director is absent, the alternate director stands in.

[12] Section 222 CA 2014.
[13] Section 222(4) CA 2014.
[14] Section 165 CA 2014.

It should be noted that the risks associated with being an alternate director are the same as those of their appointing director. Thus, an alternate director is held equally accountable by the courts for any breach of directors' duties.

The disadvantage of using alternate directors is that one person may not have a full understanding of the business and the context of a decision taken by the board. There is also the risk that directors may not take ownership of decisions that were taken when their alternate was present.

Nominee Directors

There is no formal definition of a nominee, or appointee, director in the 2014 Act. The term is used to denote a director that is an employee or appointee of a shareholder or interested party, e.g. financier, trade union, etc. It can also be used to describe a director whose employment depends on the shareholders of the holding company. He or she can be nominated to sit on the board of a subsidiary to represent the holding company.

The potential conflict for a nominee director between his or her duties as a director of a company and the interests of the appointer was illustrated in the case of *Irish Press plc v. Ingersoll Irish Publications*, in which the court concluded that:

> "there is nothing wrong with the appointing party having a view as to where the interests of the company lie and ensuring that their nominees follow that direction, provided that in so doing they are not seeking to damage anybody else's interest in the company."[15]

The Companies Act recognises that a shareholder representative on the board may have different interests, and states that a director appointed by a member may have regard to the interests of that particular member, on the condition that they are always acting in good faith and in the interests of the company.[16]

Thus, a director appointed by a third party, sometimes described as a 'nominee director', has the same responsibility to act in the interests of the company as the other directors. It can be a difficult role to fulfil because of the potential conflict of interests.

---

[15] *Irish Press plc v. Ingersoll Irish Publications* (1995) 2 I.R. 175.
[16] Section 228(3) and (4) CA 2014.

Due Diligence and the Appointment of Directors

Due Diligence to be Carried out before Deciding to become a Director

On being asked to become a director, it is essential to understand the company and all that the role entails. It may be flattering to be asked to serve on a board, but due diligence should be carried out proportionate to the risks involved to ensure that it is something worth proceeding with.

It is essential to understand the following about the company:
- **Legal Status and Shareholding Structure** Is the company an LTD, DAC, PLC, etc.? It is also important to know who owns the company, the type of shares in issue and where control lies within the shareholding structure.
- **Constitution** This will depend on the type of company. If the company's constitution has an objects clause, it is important to understand these objectives clearly, as they define what the company can do.
- **The Board and the Executive** The prospective director should meet with the chair and some of the existing directors to discuss the current governance structure. It may be useful to research the backgrounds of current directors to assess their integrity and competence and to talk to senior executives to understand the culture and values of the organisation.
- **Structure** It is important to understand how the company is organised at executive level and the responsibilities of the executives and board committees. A review of board papers and committee reports will highlight current issues.
- **Strategy and Current Business Plan** The strategy for the company and how it is performing against it should be examined, while gaining an insight into the industry sector, the key trends and the competition.
- **Regulatory Environment** It is vital to understand the company's regulatory environment and the laws under which it operates.
- **Financing** This covers working capital facilities, bank loans, other credit facilities, leasing, non-bank financing, etc.
- **Financial and Operational Performance** This would involve a detailed review of the company's financial statements and management reports, a discussion with the CEO and the CFO to gain an understanding of the business model, its key performance

indicators (KPIs) and trends, and how the company makes money. Audit reports and management letters from the auditors should be reviewed.
- **Risk Appetite and Key Risks to which the Company is Exposed**
  The prospective director should assess how the company's risks are being addressed and whether there are any contingent liabilities. The company's directors' and officers' insurance policy should also be reviewed to assess the cover available for the personal risks of being one of its directors.

Finally, prospective directors should also consider the following:
- Do they believe in the mission, vision and strategy of the company?
- Are they happy to be associated with the company and the other directors?
- Are they confident as to how they can add value to the board?
- Is board renewal evident and how long have the existing directors served on the board?
- Do they have the time necessary to devote to the role?

The purpose of the due diligence process is to ensure that prospective directors really understand the strengths and weaknesses of the company and, specifically, where they might add value. Every company has certain issues and unique features. Carrying out due diligence identifies these and evaluates them.

Fitness and Probity Requirements of Company Directors

There are no fitness and probity requirements for individuals who wish to become directors of companies in Ireland. The only exception to this is the fitness and probity regime introduced by the Central Bank of Ireland for all regulated financial service providers, which came into effect on 1 December 2011. The introduction of the concept of fitness and probity in Ireland was a reaction to the financial crisis. Its objective is to ensure that there is a formal assessment of prospective directors' suitability and to consider whether they have adequate experience and are of good repute.

While the Central Bank's fitness and probity regime applies directly only to the directors of regulated financial service providers, nevertheless its concept is valid for other company directors. Companies of all sizes should perform due diligence on prospective directors and review their experience and reputation.

Appointing a Director

Apart from formally assessing the candidates for director, the board needs to take into account what the company actually requires. It needs to consider:
- the skills and experience on the current board;
- the strategy of the company and the future skills required;
- the extent to which greater diversity could add to the board's capability;
- gaps in experience and skills that the board is seeking to address to support the strategy;
- independence and objectivity requirements; and
- softer skills, such as communication and the ability to engage.

An appointee must formally consent to becoming a director.[17] A director may be appointed for a fixed term, which is typically three years. After this term has expired, the director retires, but may be re-elected by the shareholders/members provided they are still eligible and seek reappointment. The Companies Act 2014 stipulates that PLCs[18] rotate their boards unless their constitutions require otherwise.

A company must keep a copy of each director's contract of service or a written memorandum setting out the terms of the contract and any amendments.[19]

Directors' Contracts of Service

Once an executive has been appointed to the board as a director, it is important that a contract of service is put in place. This would replace the executive's existing contract of employment with the company. It is in the interests of the company and executive directors to have a new contract that clearly sets out the revised relationship between the director and the company. Legal advice should be sought on this by the board.

The Companies Act 2014 states that a director cannot have a contract for over five years unless it has been approved in general meeting. The information must be available for inspection 15 days before the meeting and on the day of the meeting.[20]

---

[17] Section 144(1) CA 2014.
[18] Section 1090 CA 2014.
[19] Section 154 CA 2014. In addition, where the director is employed under a contract of service, the Terms of Employment (Information) Act 1994 also requires maintenance of statements of particulars for the entire period of employment and for a period of one year thereafter (section 3(5)).
[20] Section 249 CA 2014.

When a non-executive director is appointed, they should be issued with a letter of appointment covering their role, fees and term of office (see **Chapter 9**).

Removal of Directors

It is relatively straightforward to remove a director. All that is required is the passing of an ordinary resolution by the members in general meeting.[21] An ordinary resolution requires a simple majority of the votes cast at a general meeting to be passed.

The company must give 28 days' notice of the resolution to the members. A copy of the notice must be sent to the director concerned, who is entitled to be heard on the resolution at the general meeting concerned. The members must also be given notice not less than 21 days before the meeting. The director may make a written representation of reasonable length to the members, unless it is defamatory. Where this written representation is made in advance of the meeting, the Company Secretary is obliged to circulate it to members with the notice and agenda of the meeting.

It is important to note, however, that the right of a director to claim for wrongful termination is not affected by the company's right to remove a director.[22]

A director must vacate his or her office if[23]:
- he or she is adjudicated bankrupt;
- he or she becomes or is deemed to be the subject of a disqualification order;
- if he or she fails to acquire his or her share qualifications, pursuant to section 136 CA 2014.

and, unless the constitution of the company states otherwise, a director should also vacate the office if:
- if he or she resigns in writing;
- he or she is absent from board meetings for more than six months without the permission of the directors;
- the health of the person is such that he or she cannot be regarded as possessing an adequate decision-making capacity.

---

[21] Section 146 CA 2014.
[22] Section 147 CA 2014.
[23] Section 148 CA 2014.

- a restriction order has been made by the courts on that director due to non-compliance with CA 2014 and, consequently, the other directors resolve that the post should be vacated; or
- the director is sentenced to a term of imprisonment, including a term that is suspended, following conviction for an indictable offence.

Where a director to be removed is also a member of the company which has issued oppression of minorities proceedings,[24] the director may seek to get an injunction to prevent their removal pending the resolution of the issue. Oppression of minority interests occurs when shareholders who own a minority of shares in a company complain that the affairs of the company are being conducted in a manner that is oppressive or that disregards their interests as shareholders (see **Chapter 4**).

Conclusion

This chapter has set out the questions to be considered before becoming a director. Potential directors should think carefully about why they want to be a director and the implications of taking on the role. All potential directors should be careful about accepting invitations to join company boards and ensure that they carry out the appropriate due diligence.

Whether the director of a PLC, a charity or a private company, and whether remunerated or not, every director has the same duties under the law. We will examine these duties in the next chapter.

10 KEY POINTS: THE COMPANY DIRECTOR

1. Being the director of a company carries important legal responsibilities and breaches can lead to personal liability.
2. A minor (less than 18 years of age) cannot be a director of a company.
3. If a person acts like a director, the law treats them as a director. Simply not using the title of director does not mean that you can avoid the responsibilities.
4. Due diligence should always be performed before deciding whether or not to accept a directorship.

---

[24] Section 212 CA 2014.

5. A potential director should consider how they can add value and complement the skills and experience of the other directors on the new board.
6. It is in the interests of the company and each of its executive directors to have a contract in place that clearly sets out their relationship.
7. A director must consent formally to being a director.
8. Other than those prescribed by the Central Bank for directors of regulated financial services providers, there are currently no fitness and probity requirements for individuals who wish to become directors of companies in Ireland.
9. A director can be removed from a company by the passing of an ordinary resolution by the members in general meeting.
10. All directors have the same duties in law, whether they are remunerated for their services or not.

4.
Duties of a Director

- Introduction
- A Director's Duties are Owed to the Company
- Principal Fiduciary Duties of Directors
- Other Directors' Duties
- Directors' Duties to Other Stakeholders
- Breach of Directors' Duties
- Conclusion
- Key Points

Introduction

In the last chapter we saw that the role of a director is onerous and should be carefully considered. The Companies Act 2014 (CA 2014) codifies the fiduciary duties of directors and details the consequences of a breach of those duties. The purpose of this chapter is to look more closely at those duties and responsibilities, noting that directors must act in the interests of the company at all times.

This chapter is intended as a useful aide-mémoire for prospective directors in deciding whether or not they want to be directors.

A Director's Duties are Owed to the Company

The general principle is that directors owe their fiduciary ('of trust') duties to the company as a whole and not to any individual shareholder.

This is a long-standing principle, illustrated in the 1902 case of *Percival v. Wright*,[1] in which a shareholder in a private company, based upon an independent valuation, sold his shares to the directors, who subsequently sold them at a profit. The profit arose as the directors were negotiating the sale of the whole company (which would increase the value of the shares), but they failed to disclose this fact to the shareholders. The shareholder sued the directors for breaching their fiduciary duty, but the judge held that the directors owed their duties to the company and not to individual shareholders. As Lord Cullen said in a case over 80 years later, "Directors have one master, the company."[2]

'Fiduciary' in this context means that the director is in a position of trust to the company. The company, being a separate legal entity from its shareholders, has a separate identity and interests (see **Chapter 2**). The principle was confirmed more recently in the case of *Peskin v. Anderson* (2000)[3]:

> "I am satisfied ... that Percival and Wright is good law in the sense that a director of a company has no general fiduciary duty to the shareholders ... To hold that he/she has some sort of general fiduciary duty to shareholders (a) would involve placing an unfair, unrealistic and uncertain burden on a director and

---

[1] *Percival v. Wright* [1902] 2 Ch. 421.
[2] *Dawson International plc v. Coats Paton plc* [1989] BCLC 233.
[3] Neuberger J. in *Peskin v. Anderson* (2000) EWCA Civ 326 affirmed by Court of Appeal.

(b) would present him frequently with a position where his two competing duties, namely his undoubted fiduciary duty to the company and his alleged fiduciary duty to the shareholders, would be in conflict."

The Companies Act 2014 reinforces this principle that directors owe their duties to the company[4]:

"Without prejudice to the provisions of any enactment (including this Act), a director of a company shall owe the duties set out in section 228 (the 'relevent duties') to the company (and the company alone)."

This is an important general principle for directors to understand, as many erroneously would consider that the directors have a general fiduciary duty to the shareholders.

Principal Fiduciary Duties of Directors

The First Duty of a Director

It is the duty of each director of a company to ensure that the Companies Act is complied with.[5] This must be confirmed by the director(s) and Company Secretary when a company's constitution is delivered to the Registrar of Companies,[6] or when a new director or Company Secretary is being registered.[7]

The statement is clear:

"I acknowledge that, as a director, I have legal duties and obligations imposed by the Companies Act, other statutes and at common law."[8]

Thus, the defence that a director was unaware of their duties and obligations will not stand up in court.

---

[4] Section 227(1) CA 2014.
[5] Section 223(1) CA 2014.
[6] Section 21(1)(a) and 22(2) CA 2014.
[7] Section 149(8) CA 2014.
[8] Section 223(3) CA 2014.

Codifying Directors' Duties

The Companies Act 2014 codifies for the first time the fiduciary duties of company directors, most of which were previously recognised in case law as opposed to statute. Section 228 of the Act sets out the following eight general duties of company directors:[9]

1. to act in good faith in what the director considers to be the interests of the company;
2. to act honestly and responsibly in relation to the conduct of the affairs of the company;
3. to act in accordance with the company's constitution and exercise his or her powers only for the purposes allowed by law;
4. not to use the company's property, information or opportunities for his or her own or anyone else's benefit;
5. not to agree to restrict the director's power to exercise independent judgement;
6. to avoid any conflict between the director's duties to the company and his or her own interests;
7. to exercise the care, skill and diligence that would be exercised in the same circumstances by a reasonable person; and
8. in addition to the duty to have regard to the interests of the company's employees in general,[10] to have regard to the interests of its members.

These are the eight general duties set out in statute. There are certain exceptions and there is a large volume of case law refining the detail. Every director should have a reasonable understanding of each of these duties. They are discussed separately below.

1. Act in Good Faith and in the Interests of the Company

As a result of the financial crisis there has been heightened awareness of the need for greater corporate responsibility. However, CA 2014 does not widen company directors' responsibilities to include other stakeholders. The Act is clear that the responsibilities of the directors are to the company and the company alone.

Directors must demonstrate that they are acting in good faith and that they believe their actions to be in the best interests of the company. In this context, 'good faith' is interpreted to mean that they are acting without malice, ulterior motive or personal interest. An example of this

---

[9] Section 228(1) CA 2014.
[10] Section 224 CA 2014.

would be a director entering in to a contract, which then goes wrong. If this decision is later challenged, the director should be able to demonstrate why they thought that the contract was in the best interests of the company, even though it turned out not to be.

Directors can find it difficult to act in the interests of the company when they are a director of a parent and a subsidiary at the same time. Decisions taken by the board of the parent company may not be in the interests of the subsidiary, for example relocating manufacturing capacity to another subsidiary in Asia when it was previously carried out by the subsidiary of which they are also directors. A director can 'only wear one hat' in the boardroom, and that is of the company whose boardroom they are in.

Even if their actions cause harm to the company, the director's *intention* is an important consideration in company law. A director will generally always want to carry out actions that are for the benefit of the company; occasionally, however, adverse events may cause a loss when a profit was anticipated. For example, deciding to fix the interest rate for a bank loan, believing that interest rates will go up over the fixed period but they go down instead, which results in the company paying more for the loan than if it had not fixed the interest rate.

As stated by Mr Justice Jonathan Parker in *Regentcrest plc v. Cohen*:

> "The question is not whether, viewed objectively by the court, the particular act or omission which is challenged was in fact in the interests of the company, still less is the question whether the court, had it been in the position of the director at the relevant time, might have acted differently. Rather the question is whether the director honestly believed that his act or omission was in the interests of the company. The issue is as to the state of the director's mind."[11]

The law does not define what is in the interests of the company; that is for the directors to decide:

> "The law does not say that there are to be no cakes and ale, but there are to be no cakes and ale except such as is required for the benefit of the company."[12]

---

[11] *Regentcrest plc v. Cohen* [2001] 2 BCLC 80 at 105b.
[12] Bowen L.J. in *Hutton v. West Cork Railway Co* (1883) 23 Ch. D. 654.

A good case example, however, as to the meaning of best interests of the company can be seen in *Re Lee, Behrens and Co. Ltd*.[13] In this case the company entered into an agreement with the widow of a former director to pay her a pension for life. Three years later the company was placed in liquidation and the widow made a claim for the capitalised value of the pension. This claim was rejected by the liquidator and the applicant asked the court to review the validity of this decision. The court upheld the decision of the liquidator, on the basis that the granting of this pension was not in the best interests of the company. According to Justice Eve:

> "[T]here are no grounds for impugning the *bona fides* of the Board or the applicant, [but] no one of them has given evidence to suggest that the course adopted was taken for the benefit or to promote the prosperity of the company ... [or] the assumption of so burdensome a liability was reasonably incidental to the carrying on of the company's business."[14]

Finally, it is important to note that unless the board agrees otherwise, a director must maintain the confidentiality of the boardroom, as dissemination of such information is unlikely to be in the interests of the company.

2. Act Honestly and Responsibly in Relation to the Conduct of the Affairs of the Company

A good indicator of honesty is to ensure that one's words or deeds would stand up to public scrutiny. It is not enough just to be honest; a director must also be responsible in his or her decision-making. This has always been the test when assessing if a director should be restricted in acting as a director (see **Chapter 18**). For example, a director of an insolvent company may be restricted by the court unless the court is satisfied that the director concerned acted honestly and responsibly in relation to the conduct of the affairs of the company, both before and after it became insolvent.[15]

In *La Moselle Clothing Limited v. Soualhi* (1998), Shanley J. stated that in ascertaining whether a company officer has acted responsibly one should take the following into consideration:
"(a) The extent to which the director has or has not complied with any obligation imposed on him by the Companies [Act 2014].
(b) The extent to which his conduct could be regarded as so incompetent as to amount to irresponsibility.

---

[13] [1932] 2 Ch. 46.
[14] *Ibid*. at 52.
[15] Section 819(2) CA 2014.

(c) The extent of the director's responsibility for the insolvency of the company.
(d) The extent of the director's responsibility for the net deficiency in the assets of the company disclosed at the date of the winding up or thereafter.
(e) The extent to which the director, in his conduct of the affairs of the company, has displayed a lack of commercial probity or want of proper standards."[16]

3. Act in Accordance with the Company's Constitution and Exercise Powers Only for the Purposes Allowed by law

The extent of directors' powers and authority are restricted by law and the company's constitution. A director should be familiar with the company's constitution and make an effort to understand the law and to take legal advice when in doubt. In *Cockburn v. Newbridge Sanitary Steam Laundry Company Limited and Llewellyn* an agreement between the managing director and his co-directors that he would retain a portion of profits arising from contracts he had entered into in his own name on behalf of the company with a customer, was set aside on the basis that this action was not permitted by law.[17]

For example, if a director of a DAC or CLG is uncertain as to whether the company can undertake a specific activity, such as borrowing funds from a third party, the director should check the constitution and if they are still in doubt, seek legal advice. Furthermore, any restrictions imposed upon a director in the exercise of their powers and duties stated in the company's constitution must be complied with. This could include a limit on borrowing (without authorisation) or a maximum cap on directors' remuneration.

4. Not use the Company's Property, Information or Opportunities for own or Anyone Else's Benefit

Directors work in the interests of the company. They must not use information or opportunities for the benefit of themselves, a particular shareholder or a third party, **unless** it is expressly permitted in the company's constitution or has been approved by resolution in general meeting.

[16] [1998] 2 I.L.R.M. 345.
[17] [1915] 1 I.R. 237.

They must not make an undisclosed profit and must account for any profit that they receive as a result of their position as director. In *Boston Deep Sea Fishing Co v. Ansell* (1888),[18] the defendant was a former managing director of the company who received secret bonuses and commissions from company suppliers. When this was discovered he was dismissed and the court ordered him to account for the monies he had received based on his gross breach of duties.

5. Not to Agree to Restrict the Director's Power to Exercise Independent Judgement

A director must not fetter their discretion by giving away their powers to another person or restricting their ability to change their mind.[19] This applies even if the director has nothing to gain personally. However, the 2014 Act does allow a director to restrict their power to execute an independent judgement if it is in the interests of the company[20] or is expressly permitted in the company's constitution.

In *Fulham Football Club Ltd v. Cabra Estates plc*,[21] the club obtained substantial sums of money in return for undertakings by its directors to their landlord, Cabra Estates, to support its planning application for the future development of the club's ground and, in return, not to object to, support or refuse to provide evidence in support of an application by Hammersmith and Fulham Borough Council for the compulsory acquisition of these grounds. The issue arose as to whether this action had resulted in the directors not exercising independent judgement. The court concluded that, as this agreement conferred significant benefits on the company, the directors, in giving their undertaking to Cabra, had not improperly fettered the future exercise of their discretion.

6. Avoid any Conflict Between the Director's Duties to the Company and his or her Own Interests

Company directors have a duty to avoid any conflict between their director's duties to the company and their other interests, unless it is specifically

---

[18] [1886–90] All E.R. Rep 65.
[19] *Clark v. Workman* [1920] 1 Ir. R. 107. In this case, the managing director of the company entered into a collusive agreement with another company, which was trying to effect a takeover of his company, that its bid would be recommended.
[20] Section 228(2) CA 2014.
[21] [1994] 1 BCLC 363.

stated in the company's constitution and agreed in a general meeting. Where a conflict does arise, the director has a duty to disclose it.

A director must not compete with the company or divert business from the company.[22] The law is framed so that directors should not benefit from a conflict, even if they are acting in good faith. No director should:

> "Enter into engagements in which he has, or can have, a personal interest conflicting or which possibly may conflict, with the interests of those whom he is bound to protect ... So strictly is this principle adhered to that no question is allowed to be raised as to the fairness or unfairness of the contract entered into."[23]

The duty not to profit from inside information continues after a director leaves a company. A director must ignore their personal interests and put the interests of the company first, disclosing any conflicts to which they are exposed.

In *Industrial Development Consultants Ltd v. Cooley*,[24] the defendant, while the managing director of the plaintiff company, was approached by the Eastern Gas Board regarding taking on a contract for the construction of four depots in his personal capacity. The plaintiffs (IDC) had attempted to secure this contract, but their attempts failed as the Eastern Gas Board disliked the set-up of their organisation and was not prepared to deal with them in any capacity. Cooley did not disclose to the IDC that he had been approached to personally take on this contract, but instead resigned his position, citing ill health. Upon discovering that Cooley had contracted personally with the Eastern Gas Board, the IDC sued him for breach of duties. In concluding that Cooley had in fact breached his duties, Roskill J. stated that:

> "... [i]t was his duty once he got this information to pass it to his employers and not to guard it for his own personal purposes and profit. He put himself into the position when his duty and his interests conflicted."[25]

7. Exercise Care, Skill and Diligence

This duty – to exercise the care, skill and diligence that may reasonably be expected of a person in the same position as the director in the same circumstances – requires a director to act to the standard of

---

[22] As seen in *Spring Grove (Ireland) Ltd v. O'Callaghan*, unreported, High Court, 31 July 2000.
[23] Per Lord Cranford in *Aberdeen Ry v. Blaikie* (1854) UKHL 1.
[24] [1972] 2 All ER 162.
[25] *Ibid.* at 175.

a reasonable person. A director may be liable for losses resulting from negligence, but not for mere errors of judgement.

If a director has specific skills or experience, then that can set the standard of what would be expected of them:

> "A director need not exhibit in the performance of his duties a greater degree of skill than may reasonably be expected from a person of his knowledge and experience."[26]

A director is not required to be an expert in all areas. However, when delegating, the director must assume responsibility for the competence of the person chosen to carry out the task at hand:

> "The amount of care which a director must show in executing his duties is the care that may reasonably be expected from a person carrying out those obligations."[27]

Diligence, as well as skill, is important and a director should pay "such care as an ordinary man might be expected to take on his own behalf".[28]

A director may be held liable if they choose not to act on information of which they are aware.[29]

When appointed, directors assume responsibilities and duties that must be carried out diligently. If they are not prepared to assume these responsibilities, then they should not become a director.[30]

Though non-executive directors may not have much day-to-day knowledge of the operations of the company, they are expected to use reasonable care to be alert and diligent in their inquiries. Recent case law, however, has acknowledged a distinction between executive and non-executive directors and the work that would be expected of each of them.[31]

For example, the High Court in *Re Tralee Beef and Lamb Limited (In Liquidation)* held that:

> "In considering whether a person has acted responsibly whilst a director of the company, it appears to me that this court must recognise the distinction between executive and non-executive

---

[26] *Re City Equitable Fire Insurance Co.* [1924] Ch. D.
[27] *Norman v. Theodore Goddard* [1992] BCLC 1028.
[28] *Dorchester Finance Co Ltd v. Stebbing* [1989] BCLC 498.
[29] *Jackson v. Munster Bank* [1884] 13 LR, Ir 118.
[30] *Re Hunting Lodges* [1985] I.L.R.M. 75.
[31] *Re Tralee Beef and Lamb Limited (In Liquidation)* [2008] 3 I.R. 347.

directors. A person may, from time to time, be appointed as a non-executive director to bring a particular expertise to a board of directors. Where this is done it appears appropriate to consider such person's conduct as a director inter alia in relation to any such particular ... purpose."[32]

The real challenge for non-executive directors is to ensure that they seek and are provided with the information they require to carry out their role. They are at a distinct disadvantage to executive directors on the board, who will have a much better insight into company performance and any underlying issues. Nevertheless, non-executive directors should ensure that they exercise reasonable care, skill and diligence while performing their role as they have the same responsibilities as executive directors. This is discussed in greater detail in **Chapter 9**.

8. To have Regard to the Interests of the Members of the Company as well as those of the Company's Employees

The Companies Act emphasises the principle that directors must act in the best interests of the company. Despite this core position,[33] it has been judged that the directors may put themselves in a fiduciary relationship with shareholders/members in circumstances such as in private family-owned companies where the shareholders heavily rely on the directors for information.[34]

Regarding the interests of the shareholders/members of the company, directors need to be aware of minorities, particularly as directors may be held to account by minority shareholders. The Companies Act allows for a member of a company to apply to the courts if they consider that the company or the directors are acting in an oppressive manner or are disregarding their interests as members.[35]

The court can make an order for the following remedies for a company member seeking relief for breach of minority rights[36]:
- to stop or change a transaction;
- to change how the company is run, including changing its constitution;
- for the company or other members to buy the member's shares;
- for the payment of compensation.

[32] *Re Tralee Beef and Lamb Limited (In Liquidation)* [2008] 3 I.R. 347.
[33] *Percival v. Wright* [1902] 2 Ch. 401.
[34] *Allen v. Hyatt* (1914) 30 T.L.R. 444; also *Coleman v. Myers* [1977] 2 NZLR 225.
[35] Section 212 CA 2014.
[36] Section 212(3) CA 2014.

Thus, directors only have a duty to shareholders in very specific circumstances.

It should also be noted that while the law includes a reference to the 'interests of employees', employees appear to have no means of enforcing this duty under company law.

Other Duties of a Director

In addition to the fiduciary duties codified in section 228 discussed above, the Act specifically refers to other directors' duties. These include the duty to disclose to the company any interest they may have in contracts entered into by the company[37] and to disclose payments that are made to them in connection with the transfer of shares in the company by way of compensation for loss of office, or as a consideration for, or in connection with, their retirement from office.[38]

Directors also have an obligation to:
- ensure that the person appointed as Company Secretary has the skills necessary to discharge their statutory and other legal duties, and such other duties as may be delegated to the Secretary by the directors (see **Chapter 9**)[39];
- prepare entity financial statements for the company under the relevant financial reporting framework (see also **Chapter 13**)[40];
- not to approve financial statements unless they are satisfied that they give a 'true and fair view' of the company's financial position and performance (see **Chapter 14**)[41];
- prepare a 'directors' report' for every financial year (see **Chapter 13**);[42]
- arrange for an audit of the statutory financial statements, unless the company is eligible for an exemption of which the directors wish to avail (see **Chapter 14**);[43]
- lay before the company in general meeting copies of the financial statements, the directors' report and the statutory auditors' report (see **Chapter 13**);[44] and

---

[37] Section 231 CA 2014.
[38] Section 253 CA 2014.
[39] Section 129(4) CA 2014.
[40] Section 290 CA 2014.
[41] Section 289 CA 2014.
[42] Section 325 CA 2014.
[43] Section 333 CA 2014.
[44] Section 341 CA 2014.

- convene an extraordinary general meeting of the company "on the requisition of one or more members holding, or together holding, at the date of the deposit of the requisition, not less than 10% of the paid up share capital of the company" (see **Chapter 12**)[45];
- comply with the rules regarding directors' loans (see **Chapter 5**)[46];
- comply with the provisions of section 238 CA 2014 regarding substantial transactions in respect of a non-cash asset (see **Chapter 5**);
- comply with the rules regarding political donations[47];
- disclose details of directorships in other companies (see also **Chapter 5**)[48]; or
- maintain proper books of account (see **Chapter 13**).

Directors' Duties to Other Stakeholders

Directors may owe a duty to other 'stakeholders', particularly creditors, in certain circumstances. For example, a nominee director representing the interests of a debenture holder also owes a duty to that creditor. Companies, by law, do not have a duty of social responsibility, although it is generally accepted that they should act as good citizens.

Directors' Duties to Creditors

The Companies Act 2014 provides for a director's duties to the company. However, when the company becomes insolvent, a director's duties are owed to its creditors.

A company has a responsibility to pay all creditor debts as they fall due. If the company does not, creditors can go to the courts to recover the debt due. In the case where a company becomes insolvent, the assets of the company no longer belong to the members but to the creditors:

> "When a company is insolvent the interests of the creditors intrude."[49]

Creditors fall into two categories:
- secured; and
- unsecured.

---

[45] Section 178(3) CA 2014.
[46] Section 239 CA 2014.
[47] Section 26 of the Electoral Act 1997 as amended by the Electoral (Amendment) Act 2012.
[48] Section 149(2)(f) CA 2014.
[49] Street C.J. in *Kinsella v. Russell Kinsella Pty Ltd* (1986) 10 ACLC 395.

If a financial institution lends money against a property, then the institution will require security over the property and will usually take the deeds as security. Unsecured creditors are typically trade creditors (or suppliers).

If a director of a company pays off a specific debt when the company is insolvent, they are breaching their duty as director by disregarding the interests of other creditors[50]:

> "As soon as a winding up order has been made, the company ceases to be the beneficial owner of the assets, with the clear result that the directors no longer have power to dispose of them."[51]

A director has an obligation to ensure that the assets of a company facing insolvency are dealt with in a manner designed to ensure the distribution of those assets in accordance with insolvency law.

The Companies Act 2014 has defined the term 'insolvency' for the purpose of an application to liquidate the company. In accordance with section 570, a company is deemed unable to pay its debts if:
1. a creditor has served on the company a demand for a sum owed exceeding €10,000 and this demand has not been satisfied within three weeks, or two or more creditors have served on the company a demand for a sum owed exceeding €20,000 and this demand has not been satisfied within three weeks; or
2. a creditor has attempted to execute a decree, judgment or order of the court and this has been returned unsatisfied by the county sheriff; or
3. it is proved to the satisfaction of the court that the company is unable to pay its debts.

However, it can be difficult to judge at what moment a company becomes insolvent and, therefore, when the director's duty is no longer to the company but to its creditors. An attempt to define this timing was made in the case of *Re Creation Printing Company*, where the test of solvency was reckoned to be whether the company could pay its debts as they fall due immediately after making any payment,[52] i.e. it can continue to make payments as and when they fall due without undue stress. If a company cannot pay its debts as they fall due, then it is questionable as to whether the company is a 'going concern' or not. At this stage, directors should take professional advice.

---

[50] *West Mercia Safetywear Ltd v. Dodd* [1988] BCLC 250.
[51] *Re Frederick Inns* [1994] 1 I.L.R.M. 387.
[52] *Re Creation Printing Company Ltd: Crowley v. Northern Bank Finance* [1981] I.R. 353.

When there are financial difficulties in a company, it is an extremely difficult time for directors. The stress of a failing business and the desire to protect one's own family or third parties may lead to the most honourable of directors acting in ways that are not in keeping with the law. For example, a company is insolvent and a former director's widow is in extreme difficulties. A director who is still in control of the cheque book may choose to provide the widow with material assistance. While this may be considered a worthy instinct, it is unlikely to impress the liquidator, creditors or shareholders. In fact, it is also acting against the interests of the company in favour of the widow.[53] These decisions are difficult, and taking external advice is strongly advised.

A receiver or liquidator, when called in, reviews each transaction for the previous year. Directors must be aware that on a receivership or liquidation there is always an inspection of all payments made.

We will be exploring directors' duties to creditors in greater detail in **Chapter 17**.

Duty to Promote the Success of the Company

Clearly, the success of the shareholders is linked to the success of the company and it is worth mentioning here an interesting innovation in the UK's Companies Act of 2006 requiring directors "to promote the success of the company".[54] There are six stated factors that UK directors must take into consideration:
- the likely long-term consequences of any decision;
- the interests of employees;
- the need to foster business relationships with suppliers, customers and others;
- the impact of the company's operations on the community and the environment;
- the desirability of maintaining a reputation for high standards of business conduct; and
- the need to act fairly between members.

This reflects the idea of 'enlightened shareholder value', meaning that shareholders should seek sustainable growth and profits based on responsible consideration of relevant stakeholder interests.

---

[53] See *Re (W&M) Roith Ltd* [1967] 1 W.L.R. 432.
[54] Section 172 CA 2006 (UK).

Corporate Social Responsibility

While there is no wider duty in Irish company law to have regard to the success of the company or embrace enlightened shareholder value, public opinion tends to expect companies to be good corporate citizens, be socially responsible and to take into account the interests of all stakeholders.

'Stakeholders' include anyone or anything that has influence over or is influenced by the company, for example:
- employees;
- lenders;
- customers;
- suppliers;
- the State;
- local communities; and
- the environment.

So, although companies may be conscious of their perceived duty to stakeholders, even this is not written in law. They may demonstrate their concern in the form of voluntary participation in local projects and philanthropy. In law, however, and as seen above, directors must be aware that their duty is to the company.

Breach of Directors' Duties

The previous section focused on directors' duties under the Companies Act 2014, which has been informed by case law precedent. This section outlines the various remedies for a breach of such directors' duties.

It is important to note at this point that section 235 CA 2014 prohibits the use of an exclusion clause to exempt company officers from liability arising from a breach of their duties. Any such clause is automatically void.

Remedies for a Breach

Breaches for obligations in company law can have serious implications for a director. Court proceedings may be brought against those who are considered to have been responsible for breaches. Such an action will normally be brought by a receiver or liquidator who is protecting the rights of creditors.

The remedies for a breach of a director's duties under company law are set out in the Companies Act 2014. If there is a breach by a director, then that director must:[55]
- account to the company for any gain made directly or indirectly from the breach of duty; and
- indemnify or compensate the company for any loss or damage that the company may have incurred as a result of that breach of duty.

The company also has a right to claim damages from the director for breach of duty or to make an application seeking the grant of equitable relief.[56] 'Equitable relief' is what is considered fair and just in the circumstances, and may include:
- specific performance, i.e. an order made by a court requiring a party to perform a specific act, usually that stated in a contract (an alternative mechanism to awarding damages);
- injunction; and
- rescission, i.e. the contract is declared void as if it never existed.

Considerations on Breach of Duty by Directors

In proceedings for negligence, default, breach of duty or breach of trust against an officer of a company, there is a defence if it appears that the director has acted honestly, responsibly and reasonably in the circumstances. In this case, the director may be relieved wholly or partly of liability.[57] If a director is judged to have acted honestly and reasonably, then that director can apply to court for relief from an anticipated claim made against them.[58]

The director's duties are owed to the company, so a shareholder cannot claim for damages or other relief against a director for breach of duty. The exception to this is if a company is insolvent, a liquidator will pursue a director if there is a breach of duty in order to maximise the assets of the company available to the creditors.

Penalties for a Breach of Duty

Criminal Penalties The Companies Act 2014 rationalises offences into four categories, which are outlined in **Table 4.1** below.[59] These penalties

---
[55] Section 232 CA 2014.
[56] Section 232(5) CA 2014.
[57] Section 233 CA 2014.
[58] Section 234 CA 2014.
[59] Section 871(1–4) CA 2014.

are applied to persons who are guilty of offences under the Act, not only for those guilty of breaching directors' duties.

Summary proceedings against directors may be brought by the Director of Public Prosecutions, the Director of Corporate Enforcement or, in some cases, the Registrar of Companies. A summary proceeding is tried in front of a judge in the District Court. An indictable offence is usually a more serious offence and is tried in front of a judge and jury at the Circuit Court.

TABLE 4.1: OFFENCE TYPES AND RELATED CONVICTIONS

	Summary Conviction	Conviction on Indictment
Category 1 Offence	Class A fine* and/or imprisonment for a term not exceeding 12 months	Fine not exceeding €500,000 and/or imprisonment for a term not exceeding 10 years
Category 2 Offence	Class A fine and/or imprisonment for a term not exceeding 12 months	Fine not exceeding €50,000 or imprisonment for a term not exceeding five years
Category 3 Offence	Class A fine and/or imprisonment for a term not exceeding six months	Not applicable
Category 4 Offence	Class A fine	Not applicable

* 'Class A fine' is a fine not exceeding €5,000.[60]

Typical offences under Categories 1 to 4 are shown in **Table 4.2** below.

TABLE 4.2: OFFENCE TYPES AND EXAMPLES

Offence	Example
Category 1	• Knowingly being a party to the carrying on of the business with intent to defraud creditors.[61] • Inadequate accounting records for company that is subsequently wound up and that company is unable to pay its debts.[62]

(*Continued*)

---

[60] Fines Act 2010.
[61] Section 722 CA 2014.
[62] Section 286(3) CA 2014.

Offence	Example
Category 2	• Failure to make full disclosure to a liquidator in a winding up.[63] • Failure to keep accounting records for at least six years.[64]
Category 3	• Failure to notify the Registrar of an alteration in share capital.[65] • Failure to have at least one director for over 28 days.[66]
Category 4	• Contravention of the provisions on allotment of shares, as set out in section 70 CA 2014.[67] • Failure to register charges existing on property acquired.[68]

Civil Penalties Possible civil penalties against a director for breach of duty include:
- **Disqualification** A person is automatically disqualified from being a director if they are convicted on indictment of any offence under CA 2014 or of any offence involving fraud or dishonesty.
- **Restriction** A person who has been a director of an insolvent company is likely to be restricted from acting as a director or company secretary for five years.
- **Strike Off** This is a penalty on the company rather than the director. When 'struck off', the assets of the company revert to the state, but the directors continue to be liable until the company is dissolved.

This is dealt with in more detail in **Chapter 18**.

Officers in Default

The 'officers' of a company are usually considered to be its directors and the Company Secretary. An officer is guilty of an offence if they are in breach of their duty or permit or authorise the provisions of the Companies Act to be broken, i.e. the company is in default.[69] For example,

---

[63] Section 716 CA 2014.
[64] Section 286 CA 2014.
[65] Section 92 CA 2014.
[66] Section 128 CA 2014.
[67] This relates to an obligation on the company to deliver particulars of the allotment of shares in the prescribed form to the Registrar of Companies within 30 days. Failure to comply imposes liability on the company and its officers.
[68] Section 411 CA 2014.
[69] Section 270 CA 2014.

if a director allowed the company to grant a substantial loan to a director without due process.

It is presumed that an officer permitted a default if no reasonable steps were taken by the officer to prevent that default. However, it is considered a defence if it can be proved that, due to circumstances beyond the control of the officer, all reasonable steps were taken.[70]

Enforcement of Orders and Judgments

In the previous sections we focused on the implications of breaches by officers of the company, the nature and type of offences, and the penalties associated with them. This section examines how such orders and judgments are enforced.

The Companies Act 2014 provides that:

> "Any judgment or order against a company wilfully disobeyed may, by leave of the court, be enforced by sequestration against the property of the company …"[71]

A court judgment may also allow an 'attachment' against the directors or other officers of the company, or 'sequestration against' the property of such directors or other officers. 'Attachment' is a legal process by which a court, at the request of a creditor, designates specific property owned by the debtor to be transferred directly to the creditor or sold for the benefit of the creditor.

'Sequestration' is the act of removing, separating, or seizing any assets in the possession of the debtor for the benefit of creditors.

Compliance and Protection Orders

The court may order an officer to comply with a provision of the Companies Act 2014 and to remedy any default within a certain period of time.[72] Such a compliance order can be made on the application of one of the following:
- any member of the company;
- any creditor of the company;

---

[70] Section 271(2) CA 2014.
[71] Section 53 CA 2014.
[72] Section 797 CA 2014.

- the Director of Corporate Enforcement (see **Chapter 7**); or
- the Registrar of Companies (see **Chapter 7**).

The court may also make a protective order restraining directors and others from removing assets from the State or from reducing the assets of the company.[73]

Disclosure Orders

It may not be obvious who is the owner of certain shares from the share register or indeed who is the beneficiary of a debenture from the statutory accounts. Consequently, a disclosure order as to the beneficial ownership of shares or debentures can be made by anyone who has a financial interest in the company or by the Director of Corporate Enforcement.

A financial interest is defined quite widely and includes any interest held as a member, contributor, creditor, employee, co-adventurer, examiner, lessor, lessee, licensor, licensee, liquidator or receiver, either in relation to the company in respect of whose shares or debentures the disclosure order is sought or a related company.

A disclosure order will only be made if the court considers that:

"(a) It is just and equitable to do so; and

(b) In the case of an application made other than by the Director, the financial interest of the applicant is or will be prejudiced by the non-disclosure of any interest in the shares in or debentures of the company."[74]

Conclusion

The focus of this chapter has been on the duties of the director, which are codified in the Companies Act 2014 for the first time. The 2014 Act brings much greater clarity to where a breach may occur and the consequences of a breach by the officers of the company.

Though there are huge differences in the size and complexity of companies, from small start-ups to multinational corporations, there are, however, no material differences in the obligations of a director. A director has

[73] Section 798(1) CA 2014.
[74] Section 800(3) CA 2014.

certain duties in law and these are identical, regardless of whether they are a volunteer or a highly paid executive of a publicly quoted company.[75]

A director, even one with no involvement in the daily running of the business, cannot abdicate responsibility in relation to the management of a company.[76]

All directors have a responsibility to ensure that they know what the role entails and the duties and obligations that go with it. Becoming a director is not for the ill-informed.

In the next chapter, we will look at potential conflicts of interest that a director may have with the company.

10 Key Points: About Directors' Duties

1. Directors owe their fiduciary ('of trust') duty to the company and not to any individual shareholder.
2. A director has legal duties and obligations imposed by the Companies Act 2014, in addition to other statutes and case law.
3. The Companies Act 2014 codifies the eight principal duties of directors, which are to:
   - act in good faith;
   - act honestly and responsibly;
   - act within the company's constitution and law;
   - not use the company's property, information or opportunities for one's own or other's benefit;
   - not to restrict the power to exercise independent judgement;
   - avoid conflicts of interest;
   - exercise care, skill and diligence; and
   - have regard to the interests of the members.
4. The Companies Act allows for a member of a company to apply to the courts if they consider that the company or the directors are acting in an oppressive manner or are disregarding their interests as members.
5. While directors have a duty to employees, employees cannot enforce that duty and the duty is always linked with the director's duty to have regard to the interests of the members.

---

[75] *Re Walfab Engineering Ltd* (2016) IECA 2.
[76] *Kirk v. Kershaw* (2016) IEHC 122.

6. Where a company becomes insolvent, the directors owe a duty to its creditors. "When a company is insolvent, the interests of the creditors intrude."
7. From the moment the company is unable to pay its debts as they fall due, the director's duty is no longer to the company, but to its creditors.
8. Corporate social responsibility is seen by the public, if not in law, as a duty of a company. Society expects companies to be good corporate citizens.
9. The Companies Act 2014 rationalises criminal offences under the Act into four categories.
10. Civil penalties include restriction and disqualification of directors or strike-off of the company.

5.
Conflicts of Interest and Restricted Activities

- Introduction
- Areas of Conflict of Interest
- Connected Persons and Loans
- Summary Approval Procedure
- Conclusion
- Key Points

Introduction

Chapter 4 highlighted the fiduciary duties of a director as set out in the Companies Act 2014. Among these was the duty to avoid any conflict between the director's duties to the company and his or her own interests and the duty to act in the best interests of the company.

This chapter covers conflicts of interest and the procedures in the Companies Act to deal with such conflicts. The chapter also looks at 'restricted activities', i.e. actions that may be taken by the company that might prejudice the interests of shareholders/members or creditors.

Areas of Conflict of Interest

One of the key principles of company law is that individuals in a fiduciary position should not put themselves in a position where self-interest and duty conflict. This is demonstrated by the ruling in *Bray v. Ford* (1896), where Lord Herschell stated that:

> "It is an inflexible rule of a Court of Equity that a person in a fiduciary position ... is not ... entitled to make a profit; he is not allowed to put himself in a position where his interest and duty conflict."[1]

However, there are many areas where conflicts may arise. The Companies Act 2014 and case law do much to address these areas.

Directors' Interests in Company Contracts

If a director perceives that they may have a conflict of interest in a transaction with the company, then they should declare that interest to the board at the earliest possible opportunity.

The board and the director with the conflict of interest should note any steps taken to avoid the conflict, e.g. by not voting on relevant contracts and/or indeed leaving the room at the time of the vote. If the director only finds out about the conflict after the event, then the director who has an interest in the contract must ensure that it is declared at the first meeting that occurs after he or she becomes aware of the conflict.

For example, the director could also be a shareholder in a company that cleans the company's office. When the contract is up for renewal the director in question should declare his interest in this contract, abstain

---

[1] Lord Herschell in *Bray v. Ford* [1896] A.C. 44.

from voting and leave the room before any discussion takes place to avoid being in a position where self-interest and duty conflict.

However, it should be noted that according to the Companies Act, in a LTD or DAC:

> "a director may vote in respect of any contract, appointment or arrangement in which he or she is interested and he or she shall be counted in the quorum present at the meeting."[2]

Consequently, this highlights that the emphasis is placed on the disclosure of the interest, and not the interest *per se*.

Such an interest must be included in a register kept by the company for this purpose. The director's interest in the contract is to be recorded within three days of the declaration being made. It must be available for inspection at every general meeting and at board meetings, if requested. Default in relation to making such a disclosure is classed as a Category 2 offence.

This duty does not apply to an interest that cannot reasonably be regarded as likely to give rise to a conflict of interest.[3]

Substantial Non-cash Asset Transactions involving Directors

The Companies Act specifically deals with non-cash transactions involving a director. A 'non-cash asset' is defined as "any property or interest in property other than cash."[4] In effect, these are transactions where a company officer purchases a non-cash asset from the company (such as a property) or sells his non-cash assets to the company.

There are strict rules to protect against a conflict of interest in the transfer to a director of substantial non-cash assets. A substantial 'non-cash asset' is one that is not less than €5,000, but subject to that, where the value of the asset is €5,000 or over and exceeds:
- €65,000; or
- 10% of the company's 'relevant assets', which means the net assets as determined by reference to the accounts prepared and laid before the company's AGM in respect of the last preceding financial year in

---

[2] Section 161(7) CA 2014.
[3] Section 231(2) CA 2014.
[4] Section 238(8) CA 2014.

respect of which accounts were so laid (or the called-up share capital where no accounts have been prepared and laid).[5]

Such a transaction must be approved at a general meeting or else the transaction is voidable.

For the purpose of ascertaining whether transactions fall within the financial thresholds pertaining to substantial transactions in respect of a non-cash asset, cognisance must be taken of the fact that financial statements do not usually show fixed assets at market value but at historical cost. Therefore, net assets may be relatively low in comparison to actual value.[6] Consequently, directors are obliged to ascertain that the transaction does not fall foul of the provisions of section 238 by ensuring reference is made to the correct and current value of the company's assets.

The key here is to ensure that all the parties involved in the transaction are aware of their responsibilities, that the interest is notified to the board and that approval of the members is obtained in general meeting.

Where a company enters into a transaction in contravention of this provision, the arrangement is voidable at the instance of the company unless the company has been indemnified for any loss resulting and the director accounts to the company for any gain made directly or indirectly.[7]

The prohibition in relation to any arrangement for the acquisition of non-cash assets does not apply:
- if it is acquired by a holding company from any of its wholly owned subsidiaries; or
- if it is acquired from a holding company by any of its wholly owned subsidiaries; or
- if it is acquired from one wholly owned subsidiary to another wholly owned subsidiary;
- if it is acquired by a person who is a member of the company and the arrangement is made in the character of such a member; or
- if the arrangement is entered into by a company which is being wound up (this excludes a members' voluntary winding-up (see **Chapter 18**); or
- if the arrangement involves the disposal of a company's assets by a receiver.[8]

---

[5] Section 238(2) CA 2014.
[6] Section 241(5) CA 2014. Furthermore, if the value of net assets falls, it is the duty of the company, its directors and any person involved in the transaction to amend the terms within two months so that the transaction falls within legal limits.
[7] Section 238(3) CA 2014.
[8] Section 238(4) CA 2014.

Use of Company Property or Information

Apart from transactions with the company, there is a potential conflict in the use of company property or information for profit. The principle here is that the director should not be entitled to any profit and that this is rigorously and severely enforced. In the case of *Regal (Hastings) Ltd v. Gulliver*, the judge recognised that though the directors had acted in good faith, the fact was that they had made a profit:

> "... what the directors did was so related to the affairs of the company that it can properly be said to have been done in the course of their management and in the utilisation of their opportunities and special knowledge as directors; and that what they did resulted in profit to them."[9]

As a result of the directors' actions in this case, they had to account for their profits to the company. Thus, it is important to note that if a director makes a personal profit simply by using company information, that profit belongs to the company. It is not a question of misuse of information here, just that the directors were able to acquire this information while working at the company.

Competing with the Company

It may seem obvious to state that there is a conflict if a director competes with the company of which he or she is a director; however, it should be noted that this also includes the use of information.

A director should not compete with the company or be a director of a competing company. For example, the court in *Spring Grove Services (Ireland) Ltd v. O'Callaghan* held that a director's fiduciary duties "include a duty not to compete with the company" in the context where a director had used confidential information obtained as a director otherwise than for the benefit of the company.[10]

There may be an exception where a board has rejected a proposal for true business reasons and a director acting in a private capacity may subsequently take up the proposal, provided that confidential information derived from their role as a director is not used or they have obtained

---

[9] Lord MacMillan in *Regal (Hastings) Ltd v. Gulliver* [1942] All E.R. 378.
[10] *Spring Grove Services (Ireland) Ltd v. O'Callaghan* (unreported High Court, 31 July 2000) quoted by I. Lynch-Fannon *et al.*, *Corporations and Partnerships in Ireland* (Kluwer Law International, 2010) p. 103.

approval to take up this proposal by a resolution of the members. (This is a complicated area and directors should seek professional advice.)

When a director leaves a company, they may use confidential information or 'know how' acquired during their employment, provided they are not using trade secrets to undermine and compete with that company, for example databases, customer lists, business and sales strategies.[11]

Disclosure of an Interest in Shares or Debentures

If directors hold shares or debentures in the company, this may conflict with their duties as directors of the company. For example, a director who is a shareholder and has a requirement for cash in the short term might support the sale of a substantial property in the company and a subsequent special dividend being paid to shareholders, but this might not be in the interests of the company in the long term.

Directors or company secretaries must disclose in writing to the company any interest that they, their spouse, civil partner or child may have in the shares or debentures of a company within 30 days.[12] Furthermore, it is illegal for an officer to authorise another person to purchase or sell interests in shares or debentures on their behalf.[13]

The disclosure notice should include:
- the name of the director/Company Secretary;
- the relevant details of the shares or debentures in question, so that they can be uniquely identified; and
- the purchase or sale price thereof.

Disclosure notices must be entered into the company's disclosable interests register, which is a register of interests in the company's shares or debentures[14] and is distinct from the register discussed above that records a director's interest in a contract.[15] Breach is classed as a Category 3 offence.

A welcome change in the Companies Act 2014 is that small shareholdings of less than 1% need not be disclosed,[16] which reduces the amount of administration for the Company Secretary and the onus on the shareholder of declaring small holdings.

---

[11] Alan Dignam and John Lowry in *Company Law* (8th edition, Oxford University Press).
[12] Sections 261 and 265 CA 2014.
[13] Section 266 CA 2014.
[14] Section 267 CA 2014.
[15] Section 231 CA 2014.
[16] Section 260(f) CA 2014.

Connected Persons and Loans

Another important area of potential conflict is directors' loans. CA 2014 recognises that the area of potential conflict is wider than just the director and therefore refers to 'connected persons'. A 'connected person' is a group or person who is in some way associated with the company and could potentially have an interest that is considered conflicting.

Who is a Connected Person?

In respect of the duties of directors and other officers, and as set out in Part 5 of the Companies Act 2014, a 'connected person' includes:[17]

- a director's spouse;
- a director's civil partner;
- a director's parent or sibling;
- a director's child, including that of the director's civil partner who is ordinarily resident with the director and civil partner;
- a person acting in his or her capacity as the trustee of any trust, the principal beneficiaries of which are that director, the spouse (or civil partner) or any children of that director or any company which that director controls;
- a company that is controlled by the director, 'control' meaning that the director owns more than 50% of the shares or the voting rights; and
- a subsidiary of a company controlled by the director.

In the context of company loans, connected persons are treated as if they were the person that they are connected with. For instance, if the company gives a loan to a person connected with a director, that person would be subject to the rules for directors' loans (see below). Thus, a director must be careful to declare not only their own interests but also those of connected persons.

Loans to Directors and Connected Persons

A company is generally prohibited from:
- making a loan or quasi-loan (where one party settles a liability on behalf of another party) to a director of the company or its holding company or a connected person with such a director;
- entering into a credit transaction as creditor for such a director or a person so connected;

---

[17] Section 220 CA 2014.

- entering into a guarantee or providing any security in connection with a loan, quasi-loan or credit transaction made by any other person for such a director or a person so connected;
- arranging for the assignment to it of any rights, obligations or liabilities under a transaction which, if entered into by the company, would be a breach of any of the above.[18]

This general rule is subject to a number of exceptions, as follows:
- the value of the arrangement and the total amount outstanding under all arrangements is less than 10% of the company's relevant assets ('relevant assets' is explained above in the section, 'Substantial Non-cash Transactions involving Directors')[19]; or
- the arrangement was entered into by the company in accordance with the 'Summary Approval Procedure' for the transaction (see below)[20];
- the arrangement is an inter-group transaction (i.e. a transaction with a holding company, a subsidiary, or a subsidiary of its holding company)[21]; or
- the arrangement involves the provision of funds to a director to meet vouched expenses properly incurred:
  ○ for the purposes of the company; or
  ○ for the purpose of enabling the director to perform his or her duties.[22]

Where a company enters into an arrangement in contravention of this general prohibition the arrangement is voidable at the instance of the company, unless the company is compensated or the arrangement is affirmed by a resolution of the company in general meeting or the rights acquired become bona fide (meaning that the company acquired fair value for the arrangement).[23]

Suspected breaches of these requirements are reportable to the Director of Corporate Enforcement by the company auditors – this is dealt with in **Chapter 14**.

This can be a vulnerable area for directors and, if there is any doubt, professional advice should be sought. As noted above, it is an area that liquidators will always thoroughly investigate. Therefore, proper documentation is essential.

---

[18] Section 239 CA 2014.
[19] Section 240 CA 2014.
[20] Section 202 CA 2014. Summary Approval Procedure means the procedure whereby the authority for the carrying on of the restricted activity has been conferred by a special resolution of the company accompanied by a statutory declaration by the directors.
[21] Section 243 CA 2014.
[22] Section 244 CA 2014.
[23] Section 246 CA 2014.

Loans from a Director

In the way that loans to directors are subject to detailed scrutiny, so are loans from directors. All loans from directors should be agreed by the board and terms and conditions properly documented.

It is presumed in law that, unless documented clearly, a loan or a quasi-loan made by a director or connected party to a company[24]:
- does not bear interest;
- is not secured; and
- if secured but the security is ambiguous, then the security is subordinated to all other loans that have already been given as security. (Being subordinated means that all other loans must be paid back before that loan can be repaid.)

Loans may be made to companies by directors for many good reasons; for example, provision of short-term working capital. However, a key personal issue for the director should be to ensure that the money is repaid. Directors should be wary of propping up a company that is already failing and should take clear professional advice.

The Summary Approval Procedure

So far in this chapter we have examined how both the Companies Act 2014 and case law work to deal with conflicts of interest between directors and the company. There are also certain actions that a company and its directors can take that might conflict with the interests of, or prejudice, shareholders or creditors. These actions are called 'restricted activities' and companies are only allowed to perform them if certain conditions are fulfilled. Previously, this involved, depending upon the nature of the transaction, a court procedure, in other words, going before the court. However, the Companies Act 2014 has introduced a simplified procedure to enable companies to engage in such restricted activities. This is called the Summary Approval Procedure (SAP).

Restricted Activities

The Companies Act lists seven restricted activities that can be addressed by the Summary Approval Procedure. These are[25]:

---

[24] Section 237 CA 2014.
[25] Section 200 CA 2014.

- financial assistance for acquisition of shares in a company or its holding company[26];
- reduction in company capital[27];
- variation on reorganisation of a company's capital (i.e. where a company disposes of an asset or part of a business in exchange for shares being issued to its members)[28];
- treatment of pre-acquisition profits or losses (i.e. being treated in holding company's financial statements as profits available for distribution)[29];
- loans or quasi-loans to directors and connected persons[30];
- mergers[31]; and
- members' voluntary winding-up (see **Chapter 18**).[32]

The Procedure

The SAP varies, depending on the type of restricted activity, but in each case there needs to be:
- a special resolution allowing the restricted activity, except in the case of a merger; and
- a declaration of solvency covering the nature of its transaction and its financial effect passed by a majority of the directors 30 days before the general meeting required to effect the passing of a special resolution. It must then be filed with the Registrar of Companies within 21 days after the meeting.[33]

For example, if financial assistance for the purchase of the company's own shares is proposed, a declaration needs to be made, setting out:
- the circumstances in which the transaction is to be entered into;
- the nature of the transaction or arrangement;
- the person or persons to or for whom the transaction or arrangement is to be made;
- the purpose for which the company is entering into the transaction or arrangement;

---

[26] Section 82 CA 2014.
[27] Section 84 CA 2014.
[28] Section 91 CA 2014.
[29] Section 118 CA 2014.
[30] Section 239 CA 2014.
[31] Section 464 CA 2014.
[32] Section 579 CA 2014.
[33] Section 202 CA 2014.

- the nature of the benefit which accrues to the company directly or indirectly from entering into the transaction or arrangement; and
- that the declarants have made a full inquiry into the affairs of the company and that, having done so, have formed the opinion that the company, having entered into the transaction or arrangement, is able to pay or discharge its debts and other liabilities in full as they become due.[34]

The volume of information and statements that are required from the directors is substantial. They are asked to confirm that there is no conflict between their proposed action and the interests of the creditors or shareholders. It is *their* responsibility. In particular, it should be noted that if a director makes a declaration as to solvency without reasonable grounds, then they may be held personally liable.

The information requirements are particularly stringent in the case of mergers. A merger availing of the SAP may be between a private company limited by shares,[35] i.e. an LTD, and any other type of company, but not a PLC. In the merger, the assets and liabilities are transferred into one company and then the transferor company is dissolved. Where a merger is effected by the SAP, a unanimous resolution, rather than a special resolution, of each of the merging companies is required.

Conclusion

Directors must at all times be aware of the danger of a conflict of interests between them and the company or in prejudicing the interests of other shareholders or creditors. This is part of their fiduciary and statutory duties.

In this chapter we have seen how conflicts can arise as a result of:
- directors' transactions with the company, including transfers of non-cash assets;
- directors' use of company property or information;
- directors competing with the company; and
- loans to or from directors.

Conflict with shareholders or creditors may result from what are described as 'restricted activities'. The Companies Act 2014 introduced an important innovation, the Summary Approval Procedure, to

---

[34] Section 203 CA 2014.
[35] Section 462 CA 2014.

simplify the procedures when a company is dealing with a restricted activity. Though it is no longer necessary to go to the court for permission to carry out a restricted activity, directors now have to provide substantial information and assurances to justify the procedure.

10 Key Points: Conflicts of Interest and Restricted Activities

1. A person in a fiduciary position must not be in a position where their interests and duties conflict.
2. A director must not use company property, information or opportunities for personal profit.
3. Substantial non-cash asset transfers to a director must be approved by the company in a general meeting, otherwise they are voidable.
4. Any profit derived by a director belongs to the company, even if it is acquired when acting in good faith.
5. A director can sit on the boards of competing companies. However, any potential conflict should be declared upfront and monitored on an ongoing basis.
6. The definition of a 'connected person' is wide and extends beyond a director's immediate family.
7. If a loan is made by the company to a director without the appropriate documentation, it is assumed repayable on demand and at an interest rate prescribed by the Revenue Commissioners.
8. If a loan is made by a director to the company without the appropriate supporting documentation, it is assumed there is no interest payable and the loan is not secured.
9. Restricted activities can only be undertaken where an action might prejudice creditors or shareholders if they have been approved by the Summary Approval Procedure.
10. In general, the Summary Approval Procedure requires as a minimum a special resolution and a declaration covering the nature of the transaction, including its financial effect.

6.
Directors' Responsibilities: What Directors Need to Know

- Introduction
- Strategy
- Finance
- Risk Management
- Internal Control
- Information Communication Technology
- Insurance
- Conclusion
- Key Points

Introduction

Although no qualifications are required to be a company director, to be an effective director requires knowledge of key areas that are the remit of any board. One of these areas is strategy development, which is a key role of a director. However, in developing and implementing strategy, the effective director needs a strong understanding of company financing and risk management. This chapter considers the contents of a strategic plan and the financing options available. It also discusses some of the typical terms and conditions of financing.

Given the number of failures of companies in recent years, directors also need to ensure that risk is regularly reviewed and that steps are taken to mitigate it where appropriate. Good internal controls will help to manage and mitigate risk, and facilitate accurate and timely financial reporting.

A significant risk for almost all companies today is information and communications technology (ICT). ICT plays a vital role in the strategy of most companies. On the other hand, reliance on ICT brings added risks.

Insurance is a useful tool in mitigating risk. In this chapter, therefore, we will consider the area of specific insurance to protect directors and officers.

Strategy

Strategic Planning

A key responsibility of directors is to make sure that there is a strategic plan for the company, typically covering a period of three to five years, and that this plan is implemented and its progress monitored on a regular basis. Without a coherent strategic plan, it is difficult for the directors to hold the executive management team to account for their performance. This plan could also be called the 'corporate plan'.

The strategic planning process should take into account the views of the members and other stakeholders, such as employees, the government, suppliers, etc.

Developing Strategy

The process used in developing the corporate plan should be carefully designed and appropriate to the size of the company and its stage of development. While the board is ultimately responsible for strategy, the process is typically led by the CEO, assisted by the executive management team.

Strategy development takes into account the following components:
- vision and mission;
- culture, ethics and values;
- objectives and ambition;
- market opportunities;
- competitive environment;
- distribution channels;
- information and communications technology (ICT);
- quality of leadership and management;
- internal strengths and weaknesses;
- regulatory environment;
- risk appetite of the company; and
- availability of finance and people.

The strategy should help determine where best to allocate scarce resources, such as capital, in order to achieve the optimal return.

The typical contents of a strategic plan are as follows:
- executive summary;
- market and environmental context;
- vision and mission statements;
- strategic objectives;
- key actions to achieve the objectives;
- balance sheet, profit and loss (P&L) and cash-flow forecasts, key performance indicators (KPIs) and sensitivity analysis (see **Chapter 13**);
- risks to be managed and mitigation strategies
- financing; and
- high-level implementation plan.

Vision and Mission

It is important to note that 'vision' and 'mission' should not be empty words at the front of a strategy presentation. These statements should be memorable and understandable. In practice, they must be promoted by the board and senior management, and communicated to all stakeholders on a regular basis. The vision statement should be a clear, motivating message about what the organisation wants the future to look like. An example of an effective vision statement is that of Greencore plc:

> "Our vision is to be a fast-growing, international convenience food leader."[1]

The mission statement should be a clear and succinct representation of the organisation's reason for existence, indicating what the organisation is, what it does, and who it serves. Another good example of a mission statement is that of the Gaelic Players Association:

> "Investing in a better and more sustainable future for county players."[2]

Strategic Objectives and Supporting Actions

The company should also develop a set of strategic objectives to help achieve its vision. Ideally, there should be no more than five or six objectives. Each strategic objective should be underpinned by the specific actions that will need to be carried out to achieve that objective.

Financial Forecasts

The forecasts included in the strategy should be based on documented assumptions. A strategic plan will usually include sensitivity analysis, i.e. analysing the effect of changes in assumptions, e.g. foreign exchange rates. Performance is often measured by key ratios and figures called 'key performance indicators' (KPIs), e.g. the number of 'widgets' produced per head of staff.

The strategy should also be reflected in the company's annual business plans and budgets.

Financing and analysis of risks are fundamental to any strategy and are discussed in more detail below.

---

[1] www.greencore.ie
[2] www.gaelicplayers.com

Implementing Strategy

The critical task of translating strategy into action is achieved through an implementation plan. This plan is key to setting future direction, assessing progress and measuring performance. The typical contents of a strategy implementation plan are as follows:
- key actions and tasks;
- responsibilities (who will do what?);
- resource requirements in terms of finance, people, technology;
- risks to be managed and mitigating actions;
- timescales; and
- interdependencies (key actions that need to be carried out before others can commence, e.g. agreeing on branding before entering a new market).

Reports on progress with the implementation plan should be given by the executive management team to the board on a regular basis.

Finance

A key responsibility of the directors is to ensure that the business is appropriately and adequately financed to support its strategy. The company may be constrained by a lack of resources on the part of shareholders to invest further capital. Therefore, it may be in the interests of the company for the directors to consider other sources and types of external finance.

Sources of Finance

There are two main ways to finance a business:
- **debt** – the business borrows from a third party to meet its growing business needs; or
- **equity** – cash is injected by its owners or shareholders.

Directors should look at the funding requirements of the company in the short and long term.

Short Term
- **Overdraft** Most businesses use an overdraft facility provided by their bank to fund short-term working capital requirements. It should not be used as a long-term financing option as it is expensive, repayable on demand and therefore may at any time be withdrawn.
- **Invoice Discounting** This is a form of working capital finance whereby the lender repays a portion of the value of the debtors at

each month end. This is usually 70% to 85% of the debtors' accounts billed at month end. The company pays interest on the funds drawn down along with an initial or annual fee. The bank providing the facility will generally take a charge on accounts receivable.
- **Short-term Loans from Shareholders** It is essential that these are properly documented (see **Chapter 5**).
- **Management of Working Capital** One of the simplest ways of financing is by actively managing the company's working capital, which means holding a reasonably low level of stock, collecting debtors as they fall due, extending payment periods for creditors and reducing that for debtors.

Long Term
- **Term Loan** This is a loan that is made by a bank or finance house to a customer, which requires the loan to be repaid in regular instalments over a set period of time or, less frequently, in one final bullet repayment. A term loan has a variable or fixed interest rate, and usually a monthly or quarterly repayment schedule.

  The loan may be secured or unsecured. A secured loan is where the lender takes security or collateral on an asset. For instance, collateral may be on the premises of the business, stock or cash to be received from debtors.
- **Equity** Equity is where investors buy shares in a company at an agreed price. Equity can be raised from investors, venture capital firms, Enterprise Ireland, family and friends, etc.

  The type and nature of the equity required depends on the stage of development of the company. For example, the directors might consider a form of equity such as 'redeemable shares'. In this case, the redeemable shares are issued on condition that the company repays the amount of share capital to the holders of this category of shares after the fixed period or even earlier, at the discretion of the company. It is important to note that a share (ordinary or preference) may pay a dividend (variable or fixed), but a debenture pays interest. The distinction is important as interest must be paid irrespective of whether the company is making a profit, whereas dividends may only be paid where declared and where the company has profits available for distribution.

  Raising equity takes time and needs careful consideration and professional advice. It can be an expensive source of funding. On the other hand, it is worth noting that greater equity funding may help to raise debt financing from other sources with less onerous conditions. The more equity there is in a business, the lower the risk for the lender.

- **Crowdfunding** This is the practice of funding a project or venture by raising many relatively small amounts of money, typically up to €50,000, from a large number of people, often via online crowdfunding platforms or services.
- **Asset Finance** This type of long-term finance is used to fund a wide range of moveable business plant and equipment, from machinery to transport vehicles. An asset is leased to the company in return for regular payments. At the end of the lease period, the business can either extend the lease by paying a small annual rental to the lender, it can trade the asset in, or the asset may be bought outright. One of the advantages of leasing is that it spreads payments over the life of the asset.

There are many technical terms and concepts involved when raising financing. Some of the more common terms are discussed below.

Common Lending Ratios

In assessing a company's application for an overdraft or a term loan, lenders commonly examine the following ratios:
- **Debt Ratio** This is debt divided by total assets, a ratio that shows to what extent the company relies on debt to finance its assets. A challenge here for the lender is to obtain comfort on the actual realisable value of the assets (stock, intellectual property, etc.) in comparison to the amount of debt.
- **Debt Service Coverage Ratio** This is the business's net operating income divided by its total debt. It measures the company's ability to generate income to meet its debt servicing costs. For example, if net operating income is €100,000 and debt servicing costs are €50,000, then the debt service coverage ratio is 2.00.
- **Loan to Value Ratio** This is the market value of the property expressed as a percentage of the loan. The lower the percentage the loan required is of the market value of the asset, the less risk there is for the lender. For example, if the value of the loan is €400,000 and the property is worth €600,000, then the loan to value ratio is 66%.

Representations and Warranties

A loan document usually contains representations and warranties, which the borrower is asked to reconfirm quarterly or annually.
- A **'representation'** is a statement that a certain fact is true on the date the statement is made, e.g. that the company has no outstanding tax liabilities. The borrower is asked to reconfirm these representations

periodically (e.g. every quarter). If a representation is no longer true, a lender may enforce its remedies against the borrower, for example call in the loan.
- A **'warranty'** is a guarantee or promise which provides assurance by one party to the other party that specific facts or conditions are true or will happen.

Conditions Precedent

Conditions precedent are conditions that must be satisfied before a loan can be drawn down. A borrower must provide certain information or take certain actions before funds are made available. This allows the lender to check that the assumptions on which they based their lending decision are correct. These conditions are called '**conditions precedent**', and without them there is no contract with the lender.

Typical conditions precedent include:
- a copy of the borrower's company constitution;
- financial information – historic and projected;
- relevant insurance policies;
- relevant reports prepared by third parties, e.g. property valuations by independent third parties; and
- executed transaction documents, including security and intercreditor documents (which establish how various banks's competing interests with the borrowing company will be handled in the event of a dispute).

The borrower must ensure that the conditions requested can be met. If information is required from a third party, the content and format should be defined and the third party notified as early as possible. The third-party report, such as a property valuation, is usually addressed to the lender.

The conditions to be met before the loan facility is considered are usually required, in both form and substance, to be satisfactory to the lender, i.e. the lender may agree to defer certain of these conditions. If the condition is not met by a specified date, it is in default and the lender will probably have the right to call in the loan.

As well as conditions precedent there may be 'conditions subsequent' that must be **continuously** satisfied. A condition subsequent may invalidate the loan contract if it is not met. For example, there may be a requirement to restrict directors' salaries to a certain agreed level over the period of the loan.

Personal Guarantees

Lenders want to minimise their risk when approving an overdraft or a loan to a company. They will usually do this by requesting collateral to cover the risks. Collateral may be a charge (see below) or a personal guarantee.

If a director is asked for a personal guarantee, the conditions need to be carefully examined with the advice of a solicitor. It is essential that each director thinks through the 'what if' scenario: what if the business fails? Much of the hardship caused during the financial crisis was as a result of banks enforcing personal guarantees. If at all possible, directors should try to avoid providing personal guarantees.

If personal guarantees are taken, they should be very specific as to what is provided and over what time period. The borrower should seek to review these with the bank on a regular basis and to reduce them as a loan is being repaid.

Charges

Collateral demands may be in the form of a charge. A charge is when a company gives security over an asset to a third party. According to the Companies Act 2014, a 'charge' is defined as a mortgage, or a charge, in a written or oral agreement, that is created over an interest in any property of the company and which must be registered.[3] However, a charge over cash or a bank account does not need to be registered.

The lender may demand a charge over the personal property of a shareholder/director, for example their home. Borrowers need to be very careful, because if the business fails, their home may be at risk. Legal advice is essential and the borrower must seriously consider the consequences before allowing a charge over their personal property.

Charges can either be **fixed** or **floating** charges:
- a fixed charge is secured on a particular asset, e.g. land or buildings, machinery; and
- a floating charge is a security, such as a mortgage or a lien, that has an underlying asset or group of assets which are subject to change in quantity and value. An example of an asset often subject to a floating charge would be stock. It has a variable quantity and value over time and can be used as a type of collateral in a loan. The stock itself is the asset providing collateral for the loan in the form of a floating charge.

---

[3] Sections 408 and 409 CA 2014.

For example, if Dunnes Stores Ltd wanted to borrow money it could use the stock in its stores as collateral for the loan. In this situation the security must be registered as a floating charge, as the asset changes during the day-to-day operation of the business.

With a floating charge, the company can continue to trade and sell the assets in the ordinary course of business; thus, it is less restrictive than a fixed charge. But when a certain event happens, e.g. failure to meet the terms of the loan, the floating charge 'crystallises' and the assets in existence at that moment may become fixed under the floating charge.

A floating charge was described in the case of *Illingworth v. Houldsworth* as:

> "ambulatory and shifting in nature, hovering over and so to speak floating with the property which it is intended to affect until some event occurs or some act is done which causes it to settle and fasten on the subject of the charge within its reach and grasp."[4]

However, it is the description of a floating charge given in a subsequent case, *Re Yorkshire Woolcombers Association Limited*, that is generally considered definitive:

> "… it is a floating charge (1) if it is a charge on a class of assets of a company present and future; (2) if that class is one which, in the ordinary course of the business of the company, would be changing from time to time; and (3) if you find that by the charge it is contemplated that, until some future step is taken by or on behalf of those interested in the charge, the company may carry on its business in the ordinary way as far as concerns the particular class of assets".[5]

A floating charge ranks behind a fixed charge in a winding up or insolvency because a fixed charge is against a specific and identifiable asset. A floating charge may be considered invalid where a company is being wound up and the floating charge was created within the 12 months preceding the date of commencement of the winding up, unless it is proved that the company immediately after the creation of the charge was solvent.[6]

---

[4] *Illingworth v. Houldsworth* [1904] A.C. 355.
[5] Re *Yorkshire Woolcombers Association Limited* [1903] 2 Ch. 284.
[6] Section 597 CA 2014. Where this charge is in favour of a connected person, then the timeframe extends from 12 months to two years.

In general, lenders will seek to lend 60–70% of the value of an asset so that in the event of depreciation in the value of the asset they are well covered. Lenders also prefer to take a charge on assets that are easily realisable.

Procedure for Registering a Charge

For a charge to be valid it must be registered with the Registrar of Companies. If it is not registered, the charge is not enforceable, although the underlying loan remains in place.

A charge can be registered with either a one-step or a two-step procedure.
- **One-step procedure** The details of the charge created (Form C1) must be delivered to the Registrar within 21 days of its creation.[7]
- **Two-step procedure** This allows a company to state its intention of creating a charge (Form C1A), which is then followed up with a further notification (Form C1B) within 21 days of the creation of the charge.[8]

This second procedure was introduced in the Companies Act 2014 and it makes it simpler for a company to complete its financing as it allows a lender to improve the priority of its security.

Priority runs from the date the Form C1A has been filed, which allows a company to state its intention of creating a charge. Therefore, even if a Form C1, filed as part of the one-step procedure, is filed after a Form C1A but before a Form C1B, the submission made by way of the two-step procedure will have priority, provided that the C1B is filed within 21 days from its corresponding Form C1A.

The priority of charges created by a company is determined by reference to the date of receipt by the Registrar of the prescribed details.[9]

Retention of Title

A retention of title is a particular form of charge. If a company sells goods on credit terms, there is a credit risk. To minimise this, a company can sell with retention of title, which gives the seller collateral or some protection against non-payment.

---

[7] Section 409(3) CA 2014.
[8] Section 409(4) CA 2014.
[9] Section 412(1) CA 2014.

A retention of title clause in a contract means that ownership of the goods remains with the seller until the goods have been paid for. This means that the goods can be repossessed if the buyer gets into financial difficulty.

A simple retention of title clause purports to reserve title until the goods are paid for. If the goods are processed or mixed, it is unlikely that a simple retention clause will succeed. For example, in *Borden (UK) Ltd v. Scottish Timber Products*, resin was supplied on retention of title terms to a chipboard manufacturer to be processed into chipboard. However, the identity of the goods supplied, the resin, was lost with the manufacture of the new product, the chipboard. Thus, the retention of title claim failed.[10]

In *Aluminium Industrie Vaassen BV v. Romalpa Aluminium Ltd*, a Dutch aluminium foil producer managed to claim retention of title successfully. It was judged that the producer was still the owner of the aluminium foil and that they could trace the price due to them into the proceeds of sale of the finished goods, ahead of Romalpa's unsecured and secured creditors.[11] As a result of this case, a retention of title clause is sometimes referred to as a '*Romalpa* clause'.

Risk Management

All financing and credit involves risks for the borrowers and the lenders, and these risks must be managed. However, the risk is not only financial.

Historically, capitalism flourished and trade grew partly because of the evolution of the company as a separate legal entity with limited liability, which allowed entrepreneurs to take risks. Nevertheless, the level of risk that can be tolerated by a company and its shareholders must be carefully considered, as no board will want to expose the company to unacceptable levels of risk. Directors should consider the particular risks to which the company is exposed in pursuing its strategic objectives, bearing in mind the nature of the company, its resources and its capabilities. They should take into account what is described as their 'risk appetite', which may be defined as:

> "the aggregate level and types of risk an organisation is willing to assume within its risk capacity to achieve its strategic objectives and business plan."[12]

---

[10] *Borden (UK) Ltd v. Scottish Timber Products* [1981] Ch 25.
[11] *Aluminium Industrie Vaassen BV v. Romalpa Aluminium Ltd* [1976] 1 W.L.R. 676.
[12] Financial Stability Board definition, quoted in Central Bank of Ireland, *Risk Appetite–A Discussion Paper* (2014).

The company's strategy should reflect the risk tolerance of the organisation, and the board should recognise the principal risks inherent in the strategy. The allocation of capital to a company is made with a certain strategy and level of risk and return in mind. Greater strategic ambition is generally related to greater risk. Risk, and its mitigation, necessitates risk management and internal control. Risk management is not about the avoidance of risk, but being clear about the risks to which the company is exposed and how the company will address each specific risk.

It is a principal objective of any board to manage risk. The *UK Corporate Governance Code* states the following principle in relation to risk:

> "The board is responsible for determining the nature and extent of the principal risks it is willing to take in achieving its strategic objectives. The board should maintain sound risk management and internal control systems."[13]

Consequently, the role of the directors is to ensure that the company:
- carries out a robust assessment of the principal risks[14];
- describes those risks and explains how they are being managed or mitigated[15];
- the directors should assess the prospects of the company in the annual report, the period covered and why they consider that period to be appropriate[16];
- monitors the company's risk management and internal control systems.[17]

The board may delegate the work, but not the overall responsibility, to a risk committee. (The roles and responsibility for the risk committee are discussed in **Chapter 11**.)

As a result of their work on risk, the directors must report to shareholders, explaining that:

> "They have carried out a robust assessment of the principal risks facing the company, including those that would threaten its business model, future performance, solvency or liquidity. The directors should describe those risks and explain how they are being managed or mitigated."[18]

---

[13] *UK Corporate Governance Code* (FRC, April 2016) C.2.
[14] *Ibid.*, C.2.1.
[15] *Ibid.*, C.2.1.
[16] *Ibid.*, C.2.2.
[17] *Ibid.*, C.2.3.
[18] *Ibid.*, C.2.1.

Risk can be a complex topic and it needs to be approached in a robust and structured manner. Examples of the types of risk to which a company can be exposed are detailed below.

Types of Risk

There are many different types of risk to which a business can be exposed. These include:
- **Financial risks** For example, interest-rate or foreign-exchange-rate risk, credit risk, liquidity risk, price risk, cash-flow risk.
- **Operational risks** For example, accidents, theft, fire.
- **Information and technological risks** For example, breach of firewalls, cybersecurity, identity and access, as well as data protection breaches.
- **Brand and reputational risks** For example, a software product accidentally includes a virus that could damage the purchaser's systems. What will be the impact on the company's brand and its reputation?
- **Joint-venture risks** For example, where the joint-venture partner goes out of business.
- **Human resource risks** For example, over-reliance on certain key individuals with no succession plan in place.
- **Tax** For example, exposure to new tax regulations and to potential tax liabilities in other jurisdictions.
- **Sovereign risk** For example, when exporting a significant volume to a country that becomes politically unstable.

The directors' report (see also **Chapter 13**) should, where material for an assessment of the company's financial position and profit or loss, describe the use of financial instruments by the company and discuss:
- the financial risk management objectives and policies of the company, including the policy for hedging each major type of forecasted transaction for which hedge accounting is used; and
- the exposure of the company to price risk, credit risk, liquidity risk and cash-flow risk.[19]

A useful tool when assessing risk is the matrix in **Figure 6.1** below, which assesses the consequences of each risk from an impact and likelihood point of view.

---

[19] Section 326(3) CA 2014.

Figure 6.1: Risk Impact and Likelihood Matrix

		Minimal	Minor	Moderate	Major	Catastrophic
Likelihood	Certain	R1				
	Likely		R2	R3		
	Possible		R4		R5	
	Unlikely				R6	
	Rare					R7

(Impact across the top)

The idea is for the company to go through a process to identify all the risks to which it is exposed and then plot the risks on the matrix above. A typical process is shown below.

The likelihood and impact of each key risk is determined using the risk likelihood–impact assessment matrix shown in **Figure 6.1**.
- Each issue identified is rated on its probability (certain; likely; possible; unlikely; rare).
- Each issue identified is then rated on its potential impact should the issue remain unaddressed (minimal; minor; moderate; major; catastrophic).
- The impact matrix uses the combination of urgency and impact scores to prioritise the issues identified according to their relative importance.

Assume the company is an airline flying into Dublin Airport. These are some of the risks it may have to manage, with the risk number and the description of the risk as plotted on the matrix above:

R1 – Baggage Delays
R2 – Delayed take-off time due to delayed appearance of a passenger
R3 – Weather delay
R4 – Plane runs out of food

R5 – Overbooking
R6 – Bomb scare
R7 – Ashcloud in British/Irish airspace.

The matrix could also show the change in the status of each risk. These should be numbered so they can be identified since the last board meeting, by way of an arrow, for example.

Mitigating Risk

Once a company has identified the risks, the next step is to identify what measures can be taken to reduce or mitigate the risk. Examples of responses to risk mitigation can include:
- avoiding the risk by redesigning business processes;
- mitigating the risk through in-house training and refinement of policies;
- transferring the risk using insurance or financial instruments, e.g. hedging; or
- accepting a risk where, if it were to occur, the company believes its downside is acceptable.

High-impact/high-likelihood risks need to be mitigated or transferred while the company may choose to self-insure from, or just monitor, low-impact risks. 'Self-insurance' means that the company takes the loss if the risk transpires, as it will not have a major impact, or the cost of insurance is excessive in relation to the value that it is covering.

Good risk management includes:
- clear identification of the risks and their relative priority;
- a risk register that is kept up to date;
- risk-management strategies and mitigation measures;
- key risk responsibilities for the executive management team;
- regular risk reporting; and
- ongoing training.

It is essential that risk is kept alive on the board's agenda, including the vitally important area of the health & safety of staff, and any possible related risks.

Internal Control

Risk management includes checking that the appropriate internal controls are in place in the company. This may involve using internal auditors (see **Chapter 14**).

The *UK Corporate Governance Code* states that "the board should establish formal and transparent arrangements for considering how they should apply the corporate reporting and risk management and internal control principles".[20]

'Internal control' means putting in place controls over processes to ensure that they function correctly. Common internal controls include:
- **Segregation of Duties** This is a control to ensure that one person is not responsible for an entire process and it is desirable even in the smallest company. For example, a person who can approve an invoice should not be able to approve and make the payment as well. If this were the case, there would be a risk that the unscrupulous individual could approve invoices from a friend or relative and make payments for a substantial amount. The probability of this happening would be less if two people were involved. The lack of segregation of duties is a common cause of fraud.
- **Counter-signature for Payments** Regardless of whether the company is large or small, to reduce the risk of fraud it should always have a counter-signature on bank payment instructions. With electronic payments, this is relatively straightforward.
- **Approval of Invoices** Creditors' invoices should always be checked against the purchase order or contract. Furthermore, it should be confirmed that the goods or services were received or performed, and that the invoice is arithmetically correct. This ensures payments are only made when due and reduces the risk of incorrect payments.
- **Bank Reconciliations** Bank reconciliations are an important mechanism for internal control, ensuring that all payments and expected receipts are recorded correctly. They allow any discrepancies on the bank statement to be investigated. Bank reconciliations should be performed by someone other than the person who makes payments. Bank reconciliations should be reviewed monthly by a director or the financial controller. The review should show the items that have not cleared through the bank and ensure that bank reconciliations are being performed accurately on a timely basis.

Designing, implementing and monitoring internal controls can be expensive, so it is vital to ensure that they are proportionate to the risk involved and reviewed on a regular basis. On the other hand, ensuring that internal controls are functioning properly reduces risk. Good internal controls are fundamental to risk management.

---

[20] *UK Corporate Governance Code* (April 2016) C.3.

Information Communications Technology (ICT)

Information communications technology (ICT) is now an essential part of most businesses. Issues such as cybersecurity, data protection and social-media use are a concern for all companies, large or small. However, many directors do not have the background or skills and knowledge to deal with ICT issues.

An ICT strategy should be developed to support the overall strategy of the company. The ICT strategy will guide the decisions as to which systems to invest in and which to maintain. There is a danger of updating old systems incrementally rather than replacing them. The real cost of maintenance versus replacement can be complex and needs to be regularly assessed.

The board must clearly understand the position relating to the company's licences and use (or abuse) of intellectual property. The legal and public-relations risks can be considerable. Legal advice should be taken if necessary.

If there is not a separate information technology committee, the audit or risk committee should have or avail of an expert on ICT, who needs to have sufficient knowledge to challenge the in-house ICT team. An assessment of ICT risk is not only about assessing the risk of being 'hacked'; it is a much broader issue, as data may be corrupted accidentally, or even intentionally, from internal sources.

The board needs regular information on:
- ICT strategy in line with the overall strategy;
- ICT projects;
- ICT hardware, software and outsourcing;
- ICT licences;
- a tested disaster-recovery plan;
- internal controls relating to ICT;
- updates as to new technology and security;
- external reviews; and
- security.

The board or ICT committee should:
- approve the ICT strategic plan and monitor its completion;
- approve third-party suppliers of systems;
- approve and monitor major projects, budgets and procedures;
- ensure liaison between ICT and the remainder of the company;
- survey and listen to user feedback; and
- approve resources available to ICT.

The directors, in exercising their fiduciary duty of care, skill and diligence (see **Chapter 4**), need to ensure that there are proper internal controls in place. This includes:
- ensuring there is a good understanding of ICT risks;
- retaining experts to evaluate the company's ICT risks;
- ensuring that there is an expert qualified to report to the board on ICT issues;
- training employees to understand and be aware of ICT risks; and
- protecting data.

The effective director must set the tone in being meticulous about ICT security. Every director has a duty to gain a reasonable understanding of cyber risk. Even the smallest company should ensure that systems are regularly backed up, anti-virus software is up to date and that there is a reliable ICT expert on hand.

Data Protection

An important area of ICT is data protection. Compliance with data protection obligations should be a priority of directors once the General Data Protection Regulation (GDPR) (Regulation (EU) 2016/679) comes into effect in May 2018, as a breach can result in fines of up to €20 million or 4% of the total worldwide annual turnover of the company in preceding financial year.

Companies that handle individuals' data must ensure that this is protected in line with good practice and any statutory requirements. The Data Protection Commissioner publishes guidance for data controllers. A data controller is the individual or the legal person who controls and is responsible for the keeping and use of personal information on digtal computer files or in structured manual files.[21] Based on the Data Protection Acts, the guidance sets out the eight rules of data protection:
- obtain and process information fairly;
- keep it only for one or more specified, explicit and lawful purpose(s);
- use and disclose it only in ways compatible with these purposes;
- keep it safe and secure;
- keep it accurate, complete and up to date;
- ensure that it is adequate, relevant and not excessive;
- retain it for no longer than is necessary for the purpose or purposes; and
- give a copy of his or her personal data to an individual, on request.[22]

---

[21] Data Protection Acts 1988 and 2003.
[22] See https://www.dataprotection.ie/docs/A-Guide-for-Data-Controllers/696.htm

Directors and officers of the company can be found guilty under the Data Protection Acts:

> "Where an offence under this Act has been committed by a body corporate and is proved to have been committed with the consent or connivance of or to be attributable to any neglect on the part of a person, being a director, manager, secretary or other officer of that body corporate, or a person who was purporting to act in any such capacity, that person, as well as the body corporate, shall be guilty of that offence and be liable to be proceeded against and punished accordingly."[23]

Directors need to be aware of data protection law. In particular, care needs to be taken in the company's use of e-mail addresses – for example, in sending out marketing literature – and how these e-mail addresses were sourced, as an individual's email address is likely to be considered personal data.

Another problematic area is in accessing employees' email accounts, for example where there is a charge of harassment or accessing online pornography. Directors should take specialist legal advice if they have any doubts.

Insurance

As discussed above, it is the responsibility of the directors to ensure that all risks to which the company is exposed are considered and mitigated where necessary. Insurance cover is one of the tools available to reduce business risk as part of a risk-management strategy. There are a range of risks that need to be covered, such as:
- employers' liability;
- public liability;
- product liability;
- insurance against legal costs; and
- professional indemnity.

Claims are usually made against the company, for example by injured employees. However, claims may also be made against the directors personally. A company can indemnify its officers in certain circumstances and it can choose to buy insurance to protect them.

---

[23] Section 29(1) of the Data Protection Act 1988.

Indemnities

The Companies Act 2014 provides that a company can indemnify an officer in defending legal proceedings[24] or in a claim where the officer seeks judgment that they have acted honestly and reasonably, or judgment is given in the officer's favour.[25] This means that, regardless of insurance, a company can give an indemnity to a director and the company can cover the officer's costs of defence, but only if the director is found innocent or to have acted honestly and reasonably.

A company cannot indemnify a director against negligence, default, breach of duty or breach of trust when the director is guilty.[26]

Directors' and Officers' Insurance

The Companies Act specifically states that a company may purchase insurance for its officers.[27] In this context an 'officer' means current or former directors, company secretaries and statutory auditors.[28]

Directors' and Officers' (D&O) insurance is designed to protect officers of a company against personal claims made against them. Before becoming a director of a company, it is advisable that one is satisfied that adequate D&O insurance is in place. In fact, the *UK Corporate Governance Code* encourages this, stating that "the company should arrange appropriate insurance cover in respect of legal action against its directors".[29]

On being elected or appointed, new directors should review the terms of the company's D&O insurance policy and ensure that they have been added to it. They should also check the provisions regarding termination of their role as director, and their liability for any subsequent claims.

Some key issues to be considered regarding D&O insurance include:
- Are all directors and officers of the company/group covered?
- Are past and present directors covered?

---

[24] Section 235(3) CA 2014.
[25] Sections 233, 234 and 235(3) CA 2014.
[26] Section 235(1) CA 2014.
[27] Section 235(4) CA 2014.
[28] Section 235(8) CA 2014.
[29] *UK Corporate Governance Code* (April 2016) A.1.3.

- What are the key exclusions (e.g. fraud, etc.)? (A list of typical exclusions is set out below.)
- What costs are actually covered, and how and when can an officer claim?
- Is there cover for claims made by the company against an officer?
- What are the limits and what excesses are there, if any?

Depending on the policy, D&O insurance usually covers claims against officers arising out of a wrongful act, such as:
- breach of duty;
- actual or alleged breach of trust;
- neglect, error, omission, misstatement;
- defamation;
- breach of warranty of authority; and
- reckless trading.

D&O insurance does not usually cover directors' liability for:
- fraud and dishonesty;
- direct claims for bodily injury and property damage;
- environmental damage;
- prior and pending litigation;
- a legal action taken by a director or officer, or the company, against another director or officer;
- impact of war and terrorism; and
- failure of company computer systems.

Conclusion

In this chapter we have looked at important areas that a director is likely to have to deal with: strategy formulation; risk management; finance; information communications technology; and insurance. We also covered D&O insurance in protecting directors from certain types of claims.

Directors should continuously aim to improve and expand their knowledge by obtaining up-to-date information and attending training or conferences.

This part of the book has discussed the 'hard' and 'soft' law aspects of the compliance environment for company directors. The next chapter will look at other elements of the regulatory framework for companies, the regulatory bodies with which directors need to be familiar and the broader regulatory environment within which they need to formulate the strategy of the company.

10 Key Points: Directors' Responsibilities

1. Reviewing and approving the strategic plan and overseeing its implementation is a key responsibility of the board of directors. Without a coherent strategic plan, it is difficult for the board to hold the executive management team to account for their performance.
2. An overdraft should not be used as a long-term financing option as it is repayable on demand and therefore may at any time be withdrawn.
3. Directors should ensure that they understand any representations, warranties or conditions in loan agreements when seeking funding for the company.
4. It is vital that directors consider the implications of a personal guarantee or a charge on their home should the company fail.
5. A fixed charge is secured on a particular asset, e.g. land or buildings, machinery. A floating charge 'floats over' a class of assets, such as stock or debtors, which can continue to be traded until an event occurs which causes it to crystallise.
6. The board of directors is responsible for assessing a company's risk appetite and for ensuring ongoing risk management. The strategy should reflect the risk tolerance of the organisation.
7. Once a company has identified the risks, the next process is to identify what measures can be used to reduce or mitigate those risks.
8. Strong internal controls are fundamental to risk management.
9. Information communications technology (ICT) is an essential part of operating any business. Cybersecurity, data protection and social-media use are a concern for all businesses, small and large. An ICT strategy should be developed to support the overall strategy of the company.
10. An indemnity, given by the company, is void against negligence, default, breach of duty or breach of trust, unless judgment is given in the officer's favour. However, D&O (directors' and officers') insurance can be purchased to fund defence costs, awards and damages.

7.
Regulatory Environment

- Introduction
- The Registrar of Companies
- Office of the Director of Corporate Enforcement
- Anti-Competition
- Money Laundering
- Bribery and Corruption
- Environmental Protection
- Relevant Foreign Legislation
- Key Points

Introduction

The previous chapter discussed some of the key skills and knowledge essential to the effective director. The purpose of this chapter is to consider the environment in which Irish companies operate, provide an overview of the roles of the various regulatory bodies that provide the legal framework for overseeing and regulating the affairs of companies and their officers. Directors need to be aware of both the current and emerging regulatory environment so they can understand the implications for their company and plan accordingly.

Of all the regulatory authorities referred to in the Companies Act 2014, directors will have most contact with the Registrar of Companies (the Registrar). In particular, every director should make sure that deadlines are complied with and accurate returns are made. Timely and accurate interaction with the Registrar at the Companies Registration Office (CRO) is a source of evidence as to directors' diligence and care in running the company.

Every director should also be aware of the existence and potential power of the Office of the Director of Corporate Enforcement (ODCE) and its authority to initiate investigations.

There are other regulators that may affect a company, many specific to particular sectors. In this regard, this chapter also deals with competition, anti-money laundering and environmental legislation. It also touches on the impact of relevant foreign legislation.

The Registrar of Companies

Role of the Registrar of Companies

As set out in the Companies Act 2014, the objective of the Registrar, at the CRO, is to register all companies, giving them the right to exist as a separate legal entity and to strike them off when that legal entity is no longer required.

When the constitution of a company is registered, the Registrar certifies that the company is incorporated and issues a certificate of incorporation, i.e. its 'birth certificate'. Similarly, when a company is wound up, the Registrar is notified of its 'death' and in due course will strike it off the register.

The main returns a company has to make to the Registrar are as follows:
- A1 – Company Incorporation.
- B1 – Annual Return.[1] The first annual return date shall be six months after the date of incorporation and subsequently on the anniversary of the first annual return date.[2] The annual return is a key public document to which is annexed, unless an exemption is claimed, the statutory financial statements, the directors' report and the statutory auditors' report (see **Chapters 13** and **14**).
- B2 – Change of Registered Office.
- B4 – Notice of increase in authorised share capital.[3]
- B10 – Change of a Director or Company Secretary.
- B69 – Notification by individual that they have ceased to be a director or Company Secretary.

A complete list of forms for making the above returns can be accessed on the CRO website.[4]

Other key events that must be notified to the Registrar at the CRO include:
- alterations of share capital[5];
- appointment of a receiver[6];
- making of a winding-up order[7];
- notice of appointment of a voluntary liquidator[8]; and
- delivery of the accounts of a receiver.[9]

The Registrar holds documents for 20 years after the dissolution of a company before passing them to the National Archives.[10]

Office of the Director of Corporate Enforcement

Role of the Director of Corporate Enforcement

The role of the Director of Corporate Enforcement includes[11]:
- encouraging compliance with the Companies Act;

---

[1] Section 342 CA 2014.
[2] Section 345 CA 2014.
[3] Section 93 CA 2014.
[4] www.cro.ie/Publications/Company-Forms
[5] Sections 83 and 92 CA 2014.
[6] Section 436 CA 2014.
[7] Section 591 CA 2014.
[8] Section 592 CA 2014.
[9] Section 441 CA 2014.
[10] Section 709 CA 2014.
[11] Section 949 CA 2014.

- investigating suspected offences and non-compliance with the Companies Act or with the duties and obligations to which companies and their officers are subject;
- enforcing the Act, including by the prosecution of summary proceedings; and
- exercising a supervisory role over liquidators and receivers.

In encouraging compliance, the Office of the Director of Corporate Enforcement (ODCE) publishes a variety of useful publications online on:[12]
- companies;
- company directors;
- company secretaries;
- members and shareholders;
- auditors and creditors; and
- liquidators, receivers and examiners.

The ODCE has substantial powers to compel the collection of evidence. Furthermore, the ODCE can petition to wind up a company on the grounds that it is in the public interest.[13] Every director should be aware of the existence and potential power of the ODCE and its authority to initiate investigations.

Investigations Initiated by the Office of the Director of Corporate Enforcement

The ODCE is responsible for receiving and responding to allegations of company law breaches. Such allegations and reports are mandatory in certain cases, e.g. from statutory auditors, but can also be made by the public. For example, an auditor must report to the ODCE if they have reasonable grounds to suspect that a Category 1 or Category 2 offence (see **Chapter 4**) has been committed[14] or that adequate accounting records are not being kept.[15]

In addition, the ODCE may initiate investigations into:
- share dealing[16];
- company ownership[17]; and
- interests in shares or debentures.[18]

---

[12] www.odce.ie/en-gb/publications/companylawguidance/informationbooks.aspx
[13] Section 569(1)(g) CA 2014.
[14] Section 393 CA 2014.
[15] Section 392 CA 2014.
[16] Section 763 CA 2014.
[17] Section 764 CA 2014.
[18] Section 767 CA 2014.

The ODCE has the right to impose restrictions on shares in connection with an investigation or an inquiry.[19] The restriction could involve a share issue or share transfer being declared void or ruling that no voting rights are exercisable.

The ODCE has the power to:
- require a company to produce books or documents[20];
- require a third party to produce books or documents[21]; and
- enter and search a premises with a search warrant.[22]

It should be noted that it is an offence to:
- fail to produce the books or documents requested[23];
- obstruct the exercise of a right of entry or search conferred by a search warrant[24];
- obstruct the exercise of a right conferred by a search warrant to seize and retain material information[25]; and
- falsify, conceal, destroy or otherwise dispose of documents or records.[26]

It is a defence in law if, when a person cannot produce the books or documents referred to above, it can be proven that they were not in that person's possession or under that person's control, and it was not reasonably practicable for that person to comply with the requirement.[27]

Finally, it is worth noting that the ODCE may assist the authorities of a foreign jurisdiction if satisfied that such assistance is for the purpose of assisting that foreign regulatory body to discharge its supervisory or regulatory functions.[28]

Competition Law

The purpose of the Competition and Consumer Protection Commission (CCPC) is "to make markets work better for consumers and businesses". To enable this, it works to ensure that markets are as competitive as

---

[19] Section 768 CA 2014.
[20] Section 778 CA 2014.
[21] Section 780 CA 2014.
[22] Section 787 CA 2014.
[23] Section 785 CA 2014.
[24] Section 789(1)(a) CA 2014.
[25] Section 789(1)(b) CA 2014.
[26] Section 793 CA 2014.
[27] Section 785 CA 2014.
[28] Section 796 CA 2014.

possible, consumers are protected and empowered, and that businesses actively compete.[29]

As well as enforcing consumer protection law, the CCPC is responsible for enforcing Irish and EU competition law. Directors need to be aware of the main features of the Competition Act 2002 and its subsequent amendments, including Parts 3 and 4 of the Competition and Consumer Protection Act 2014. Anti-competitive practices can include:
- price-fixing;
- abusing a dominant market position;
- limiting production;
- market sharing; and
- setting up a cartel with a view to market manipulation.

The Competition (Amendment) Act 2012 increased penalties, strengthening competition law. These penalties include:
- imprisonment up to 10 years where the offence is committed by an individual;
- fines for competition offences up to €5 million[30] or 10% of the turnover of the undertaking in the financial year ending in the 12 months prior to the conviction, whichever is the greater; and
- disqualification as a director.[31]

It is vitally important that all directors and staff in the company, but particularly those in management, sales or production, are aware of competition law and the potential penalties, and are aware that any contact with competitors must be carefully managed and recorded. Many companies and trade associations work together on issues that are common to their industry, such as contributing to government policy on regulation, consumer protection, health & safety, etc. Care should be taken at such meetings to ensure that conversations do not stray into illegal topics, for example pricing. Trade associations typically have policies in place to help avoid the risk of members being involved in or accused of collusion and anti-competitive behaviour. Individual companies should have similar policies.

---

[29] www.ccpc.ie
[30] Section 2 of the Competition (Amendment) Act 2012.
[31] Section 9 of the Competition (Amendment) Act 2012.

Money Laundering

"Money laundering is the processing of criminal proceeds (cash and assets obtained from criminal activities) to disguise their original origin."[32] It is a worldwide problem and governments have taken major steps in recent years to combat it.

Directors should identify areas in the business that could be at risk from money laundering. In Ireland, the Criminal Justice (Money Laundering and Terrorist Financing) Act 2010 is quite explicit as to the responsibilities of the directors. The Act refers to 'designated persons'; any person or business trading that accepts cash payments for goods in the normal course of business may be considered to be a 'designated person'.[33] Designated persons also include credit and financial institutions, lawyers, accountants, estate agents, trust and company service providers, and tax advisors. Designated persons must[34]:

- identify customers and undertake customer due diligence in business dealings, adopting a risk-based approach;
- report suspicious transactions to An Garda Síochána and the Revenue Commissioners;
- have specific procedures in place to provide for the prevention of money laundering and terrorist financing. These procedures relate to record-keeping, staff training and the maintenance of appropriate procedures and controls.

Directors need to be aware of the possibility of money laundering and, in particular, ensure that they perform due diligence on their counterparties in any transaction. There is a particularly high risk in companies dealing with high-value goods, especially property. Cash-intensive businesses are also vulnerable to money laundering, for example banks, casinos, etc.

Finally, it is important to note that the Fourth Anti-Money Laundering Directive (2015/849/EU) is due to be implemented in Ireland in 2017.

Its aim is to further strengthen the EU's defences against money laundering and terrorist financing, and ensure greater confidence in the financial system as a whole.

---

[32] www.antimoneylaundering.gov.ie

[33] Section 25 of the Criminal Justice (Money Laundering and Terrorist Financing) Act 2010 specifies the types of cash transactions involved.

[34] Anti-Money Laundering Compliance Unit. Available at www.amlcu.gov.ie

Bribery and Corruption

The Prevention of Corruption Act originally dates from 1889. A new statute is planned to consolidate and update the law in this area. It will include company and officer liability for employee actions as follows:

> "Where an offence under this Act has been committed by a director, manager, secretary, officer, employee, subsidiary or agent of a body corporate with the intention of obtaining or retaining business for the body corporate or obtain or retain an advantage in the conduct of business for the body corporate, that body corporate shall also be guilty of an offence."[35]

A defence by the company and its directors under the new Act will be to show that all reasonable steps were exerted to avoid prosecution. However, directors who consent to, approve of or wilfully neglect the commission of an offence under the Act will be criminally liable.

Environmental Protection

The Environmental Protection Agency (EPA) is the statutory body responsible for protecting the environment in Ireland. The basic principle is that where an individual or a company harms the environment, the polluter pays.

In its published guidance,[36] the EPA explains that the aim of the relevant EU Directives[37] is to prevent and remedy environmental damage, encouraging operators to:
- assess proactively their environmental risks and manage them to prevent environmental damage occurring in the first place; and
- initiate preventive measures where there is an imminent threat of environmental damage.

Proactive risk management involves the systematic review of business, operational and development activities that could pose a hazard,

---

[35] Heads of the General Scheme of the Criminal Justice (Corruption) Bill (20 June 2012), Head 13. It is noteworthy that (as of July 2017) this Bill has not been presented to the Oireachtas.

[36] *Environmental Liability Regulations: Guidance Document* (EPA, 2011). Available at http://www.epa.ie/pubs/advice/general/Liability_Regulations%20Final%20August%202011.pdf

[37] For example, the Environmental Liability Directive 2004/35/EC.

coupled with an assessment of the sensitivities of the environment that could be affected.

Environmental liability is the cost to which a company could be exposed in repairing the damage caused by environmental accidents, such as pollution of land, water and air, and in rectifying biodiversity damage.

While specific insurance may be purchased by the company to mitigate environmental risks, directors should note that they may be held personally liable for breaches under environmental law. In the case of *Wicklow County Council v. Clifford, Fenton*, an action was taken under the Waste Management Act 1996. Although judgment was found against the company, the judge made it clear that the directors would be personally liable for carrying out any remedial works in the event that the defendant company was unable or failed to carry out its share of such works.[38]

Directors should be aware that not all insurance policies cover environmental remedial costs, particularly if the insurance company has not been kept fully informed. Exposure to environmental risks should, of course, feature as part of risk assessment and management (see **Chapter 6**).

Relevant Foreign Legislation

The Sarbanes–Oxley Act ('SOX'), introduced in the US in 2002, is far-reaching legislation with clear demands made on the directors of Irish-based directors of US companies. Additionally, there are increasing obligations to ensure that information on individuals is exchanged with other jurisdictions, where appropriate. Directors of affected Irish companies should be familiar with the US Foreign Account Tax Compliance Act (FATCA) and the Common Reporting Standard (CRS).

Sarbanes–Oxley

The Sarbanes–Oxley Act (SOX) was introduced in the US in response to corporate scandals, particularly the Enron and WorldCom scandals, where huge companies had failed dramatically without warning. SOX increased criminal penalties for white-collar crime.

In general, SOX applies to all US companies, their foreign subsidiaries, as well as non-US companies who are obliged to file reports with the US Securities and Exchange Commission (SEC). The importance for the Irish director of such a foreign subsidiary or non-US company

---

[38] *Wicklow County Council v. Clifford, Fenton (No 2)* [2002] 4 I.R. 44.

is that the directors are mandated to take individual responsibility for the accuracy and completeness of reports filed. Under SOX, the CEO and CFO of these companies must certify that:
- the information in the periodic financial statement ("the report") fairly represents the financial condition and results of operations of the reporting company;
- they have reviewed the report; and
- the report does not contain any untrue statements of material facts or omissions of material facts.

The key provisions of SOX are usually referred to by their section numbers and include:
- section 302: for example, the CEO and CFO must certify that they are responsible for internal controls[39];
- section 404: management must produce an internal control report in which they must affirm "the responsibility of management for establishing and maintaining an adequate internal control structure and procedures for financial reporting"[40];
- section 906: which sets out criminal penalties for failure to certify the reports.[41]

These penalties would also apply to Irish-based directors of US subsidiaries and non-US companies in Ireland with a listing in the US.

US Foreign Account Tax Compliance Act

The demand for greater transparency and the automatic exchange of information led the US to introduce the Foreign Account Tax Compliance Act (FATCA) in 2010, which requires foreign financial institutions, including Irish entities, to collect account information and report to the US Internal Revenue Service about their US clients.

Irish financial entities must determine whether or not they are classified as a reporting Irish financial institution under Ireland's Intergovernmental Agreement with the US.[42] If they are, then they must comply with the terms of FATCA.

---

[39] Section 302, Sarbanes–Oxley Act 2002.
[40] Section 404, Sarbanes–Oxley Act 2002.
[41] Section 906, Sarbanes–Oxley Act 2002. These penalties can be upwards of $5 million in fines and 20 years in prison.
[42] *Agreement Between the Government of Ireland and the Government of the United States of America to Improve International Tax Compliance and to Implement FATCA.* Available at www.revenue.ie/en/business/international/agreement-ireland-usa-compliance-fatca.pdf

Ireland's Intergovernmental Agreement, signed in December 2012, allowed the implementation of FATCA in Ireland and "provides for a bilateral and reciprocal exchange of information with the US in relation to accounts held in Irish financial institutions by US persons, and accounts held in US financial institutions by Irish tax residents".[43]

The first information was exchanged in 2015.

Any Irish company dealing with a financial institution in Ireland or abroad will most likely be asked to fill out a FATCA form in which they have to give their tax number and declare who controls the company. This applies even though they may have no links with the US at all.

This automatic collection of information is targeted at US tax evasion, and FATCA law has been criticised for forcing foreign financial institutions and governments to collect information for the US at their expense while enabling the US to impose costs and penalties on foreign financial institutions.

The Common Reporting Standard

The growing international trend of collecting information and exchanging it across jurisdictions became more systematised with the publication in 2014 of the Common Reporting Standard (CRS) by the OECD.

The Common Reporting Standard (CRS) was developed in response to a request by the G20 countries and approved by the OECD Council on 15 July 2014.[44] Under the CRS, participating jurisdictions are required to exchange certain information held by financial institutions regarding their non-resident customers. The CRS is a step towards a global approach to the disclosure of income and of ownership of assets.

The general interest in tax avoidance and tax evasion received further impetus in 2016 with the leak of the 'Panama Papers'. Over 11.5 million documents, detailing confidential client information and usage of offshore companies, was made publicly available. While much of this use is not illegal, it has again turned the spotlight onto what is acceptable and if even more information should be exchanged between countries.

Information exchange and common reporting standards mean that directors need to be aware not only of the laws of Ireland, but also of the

---

[43] See www.revenue.ie/en/business/aeoi/
[44] See www.oecd.org/tax/automatic-exchange/common-reporting-standard/

laws of countries with which their company is dealing. A transaction that may be legal in one country, for example receiving of interest from a foreign entity, may be prohibited in the other country, i.e. the paying of interest on a loan to a foreign entity without Central Bank permission. The exchange of information and public scrutiny of information is not only a tax issue but can bring personal security concerns, particularly to high net worth individuals. Public opinion is increasingly questioning the taxation practices of multinationals and Irish directors need to take tax and legal advice to ensure that they understand the issues, reputational risk and any personal risks.

Conclusion

Having reviewed company law compliance context in previous chapters, this chapter considered other key elements of the regulatory environment in which an Irish company operates. Every company has a specific range of regulations applicable to it and directors need to be aware of both current and emerging regulations, and their effect on the company.

The role of the Registrar of Companies is fundamental to the existence of a company as a separate legal entity. Directors need to ensure that all company returns are submitted to the CRO on a timely basis.

The Office of the Director of Corporate Enforcement has considerable powers to enforce company legislation. These powers should not be underestimated.

Foreign legislation is increasingly relevant. A director of a US subsidiary in Ireland needs to be aware of SOX and ensure that appropriate advice is taken, as there are severe penalties for non-compliance.

Finally, the exchange of information between countries is rapidly becoming the 'norm' and directors need to consider if the Foreign Account Tax Compliance Act (FATCA) and the Common Reporting Standards might affect their business.

10 KEY POINTS: REGULATION AND COMPLIANCE

1. The objective of the Registrar of Companies is to register all companies, giving them their right to exist as a separate legal entity and to strike them off when that legal entity is no longer required.

2. A company's annual return is information, including the financial statements, that must be sent to the Registrar every year showing the current directors, Company Secretary and shareholders. The Company Secretary should ensure that this is performed on a timely basis.
3. Directors should be aware of the existence and potential power of the Office of the Director of Corporate Enforcement (ODCE) and its authority to initiate investigations.
4. The ODCE has considerable powers to compel the collection of evidence. It can require a company or a third party to produce accounting records or certain documents.
5. The Competition and Consumer Protection Commission (CCPC) can impose severe penalties for anti-competitive practices.
6. Money laundering is the processing of criminal proceeds (cash and assets obtained from criminal activities) to disguise their original origin. Directors should identify areas in the business that could be at risk from money laundering.
7. The key principle in environmental legislation is that 'the polluter pays'. Directors can be held personally liable for carrying out any remedial works in the event that the defendant company is unable or fails to carry out its share of such works.
8. Under the US Sarbanes–Oxley Act (SOX), directors are mandated to take individual responsibility for the accuracy and completeness of reports. SOX includes strong sentencing and criminal penalties for white-collar crime.
9. The US Foreign Account Tax Compliance Act (FATCA) requires foreign financial institutions, including Irish entities, to report to the US Inland Revenue about their US clients.
10. The Common Reporting Standard (CRS) calls on countries to obtain information from their financial institutions on their non-resident customers and automatically exchange that information with other jurisdictions on an annual basis.

Part II

THE BOARD

The board of directors is appointed by the company's members to govern the company and oversee executive. All directors have collective responsibility. Whether there is one director or 10, they have the same responsibilities under the law. Importantly, there is no differentiation in law between the responsibilities of an executive director and a non-executive director. Directors can be held *personally* liable for decisions taken, such as reckless trading.

The Companies Act 2014 allows the board of directors considerable flexibility; there is no set structure for a board. While the roles of the chair of the board, board committees, the Company Secretary and the managing director are referred to in the Companies Act, no great detail is given.

Although the Companies Act codifies procedures relating to meetings, voting and resolutions, in many cases a company can choose to change these procedures. However, the Act insists that a record be kept of all present at the meetings and that the proceedings and resolutions are minuted.

An effective board is not so much dependent on its structure as on the values, skills, experience, behaviours and interpersonal relationships of individuals on the board and how well these are managed by the chair. A strong chair is crucial to an effective board, and not just as a chair but as a leader.

Companies should not only be ethical but should demonstrate that they live up to their ethical values. The chairman and the directors should set the 'tone from the top'.

While boards may delegate work to board committees, e.g. an audit committee, ultimately the board remains responsible. The board cannot delegate responsibility, though it can delegate limited decision-making if it makes sense to do so to free up board time.

The directors implement resolutions passed by members in general meetings. The Companies Act 2014 simplifies procedures for general meetings; in particular, a private company limited by shares (LTD) need not hold an annual general meeting in any year where all the members who are entitled to attend and vote at such a general meeting sign a written resolution to that effect.

Thus, Part II addresses the practicalities of being on a board, the role of a director on the board and board committees, in the following chapters:

8. Ethics
9. Roles and Responsibilities of the Board
10. How the Board Works
11. Board Committees
12. General Meetings, Resolutions and Registers

8.
Ethics

- Introduction
- Ethics and the Role of the Board
- Ethics in Practice
- Ethical Challenges
- Good Faith Reporting
- Conclusion
- Key Points

Introduction

"Ethics is knowing the difference between what you have the right to do and what is right to do."

Potter Stewart, US Supreme Court Judge

This chapter sets out to ensure that the importance of ethics is understood by every director, as well clarifying the role that directors have in developing and communicating this to their organisation. Ethics and values cannot be painted onto an organisation. They need to originate with and be reflected by the board of directors, part of whose role is to ensure that they are embedded in the organisation.

In a business context, ethics involves the exercise of values, such as trust and integrity, that influence and determine the day-to-day behaviours and actions of a company. Embedded values and ethical behaviours are hard-won company assets that can easily be destroyed by actions that are, or are perceived to be, unethical. Ethical behaviour instils trust and empathy, and it enhances reputation, which can in turn improve income by attracting more customers and greater financial sustainability. Finally, while good behaviour engenders more good behaviour, the opposite is also true.

Company directors are responsible for setting the ethical standards and values for their organisation. This is the most valuable asset that directors can bring to an organisation. If these standards are embedded in the organisation, they will form the bedrock for the future sustainability of the company.

Ethics and the Role of the Board

Ethical standards and the appropriate behaviours must be led, developed and disseminated by the board. The board sets the tone from the top of the company. Ethics and values are the key platform for the mission of the company and should underpin its strategy.

Directors play a crucial role in establishing the ethical framework and practices throughout a company. The board's responsibilities include:
- developing, agreeing and documenting the values and ethical framework of the company;
- living these values as the leaders of the company;
- supporting ethics programmes for staff; and

- ensuring that the company lives up to its stated ethical values, e.g. through appropriate monitoring mechanisms.

Board members should be given ethics training, which should in turn be provided to the whole company. During the recruitment process, board members should evaluate closely the ethics and values of any potential director against those of the company. The induction process for all board members, as well as staff, presents a good opportunity to introduce ethics and discuss the company's values, i.e. what it feels strongly about.

Boards often face tough ethical decisions. For example, a retailer selling clothing in Ireland might have questions over the type of labour and the employment conditions used in developing countries to produce their goods. Similarly, if a company is seen to exploit tax planning to the limit, even though it may be permissible within the tax codes, it may impact on the values and the reputation of the company.

Ethics in Practice

The larger the company, the more difficult it is to maintain consistency in the application of values and ethical behaviour. It is unlikely that all staff can be relied upon to react in the same way, particularly where there is significant cultural diversity in different countries in which a company operates. This is why a **code of ethics** is essential. A well-written code, consistently applied, will minimise uncertainty and raise awareness of ethical issues in the company. Ultimately, good ethical practice in a company should improve transparency, decrease the risk of fraud, for example, and reduce the likelihood of reputational damage.

A good example of this is the demise of Arthur Andersen in the wake of the Enron scandal. The damage to Andersen's reputation destroyed the viability of the firm's US and international practices and it went out of business. A number of partners were convicted of obstruction of justice for shredding documents related to the audit of Enron.

A company's ethics programme should include:
- **A code of ethics:**
  - A code of ethics is a written set of guidelines issued by a company to its management and staff to help them conduct their behaviour and actions in accordance with its values and ethical standards.
  - Communication of the code of ethics is important. It should be included in the induction process for new staff and in staff handbooks. It should also be available online as a staff resource.

- **Training:**
    - Training in ethical behaviour ensures that all directors and employees know what is expected of them. It helps instil ethics in the culture of the company.
    - Companies should have a person responsible for ethics. For instance, Coca-Cola's code of ethics is administered by an Ethics & Compliance Committee composed of a cross-functional senior management team. It oversees all ethics and compliance programmes and determines code violations and discipline. The Ethics & Compliance Office has operational responsibility for education, consultation, monitoring and assessment related to the code of conduct.
- **A means to report breaches of the code of ethics:**
    - Companies should provide the means for staff and others to raise ethical concerns.
    - Companies should encourage good faith reporting ('whistleblowing') and foster a culture whereby whistleblowers are protected.
- **Rewarding those who 'live the ethical culture':**
    - Ethical behaviour should be recognised and rewarded. Adherence to the company's code of ethics should be part of the performance review process for all staff, including the directors.
    - Those who breach the code of ethics should face disciplinary action.
    - The requirement to follow and conform to the code of ethics should be included in employees' contracts and directors' service agreements.
- **Monitoring and reporting:**
    - Companies should monitor the impact of their ethics programme and report the findings internally with an improvement plan to address areas of concern.
    - Many companies issue corporate social responsibility (CSR) reports annually, which cover ethics and values.

Contents of a Code of Ethics

A written code of ethics should clearly set out the values and principles that are important to that company. Relevant values might include:
- integrity;
- objectivity;
- confidentiality;
- loyalty;
- fairness;
- consideration for the environment;

- personal safety;
- zero tolerance for bribery or corruption;
- security of data; and
- diversity.

A code of ethics should include a conceptual framework as to how to deal with ethical problems, such as the *Code of Ethics* provided by the Chartered Accountants Ireland Professional Standards. While aimed at chartered accountants, the general principles and approach of this code are also relevant to company directors. The conceptual framework outlined involves:
- identifying threats to compliance with fundamental principles;
- evaluating the significance of the threat identified; and
- applying safeguards, when necessary, to eliminate the threats or reduce them to an acceptable level.[1]

Where safeguards are not available to address the threats to values or principles, the circumstance or relationship creating the threats should be avoided.[2]

Resolution of Ethical Dilemmas

Importantly, the Chartered Accountants Ireland *Code of Ethics* deals with how to resolve ethical dilemmas, or the resolution of ethical conflict. It recommends that one should consider the following factors in the resolution process:

"(a) Relevant facts;
(b) Relevant parties;
(c) Ethical issues involved;
(d) Fundamental principles related to the matter in question;
(e) Established internal procedures;
(f) Alternative courses of action".[3]

The benefit of this is that it provides a process that is codified and can be followed in resolving ethical conflict. It is a framework that is open and transparent.

Determining what is ethical behaviour can be difficult. Often, there is no clear right or wrong answer. What may seem right to one person

---

[1] Chartered Accountants Regulatory Board, *Code of Ethics* (2014) Section 100.2. Available at www.carb.ie/en/Bye-Laws-and-Regulations/Ethics/
[2] *Ibid.*, Section 100.3.
[3] *Ibid.*, Section 100.18.

may seem wrong to another. Directors must make judgements based on the information available to them, and having a written code of ethics, including recommended information-gathering amd decision-making processes, helps a company have a uniform, consistent approach to this.

Ethical Challenges

Ethical challenges can arise from the very first day a business is created. Therefore, a code of ethics should be developed as soon as it is practical to do so. The following table provides examples of ethical challenges that a company may have to address.

Area of Ethical Challenge	Examples
Gifts/Hospitality	• Giving gifts to customers or staff • Receiving gifts over a certain value from customers • Attending conferences and/or golf outings overseas funded by a supplier
Executive Director Remuneration	• Interest in contracts • Expenses/payments in kind
Employee Matters	• Paying bribes in less developed countries • Claims of bullying or harassment • Not protecting a whistleblower • Asking an employee to do something illegal • Exploiting vulnerable staff • Being an illegal beneficiary of a successful procurement process
Financial Reporting	• Creative accounting • Poor internal controls • Misleading auditors • Being 'economical with the truth'

(*Continued*)

Area of Ethical Challenge	Examples
Tax	• 'Under-the-counter' cash payments to employees or suppliers • Use of tax loopholes which, while legal, may be perceived as sharp practice • Use of offshore or special-purpose vehicles
Safety	• Illegal/irresponsible disposal of waste • Overweight lorries • Use of machinery without adequate safety equipment
IT	• Unlicensed software • Poor data protection
Insolvency	• Warning or tipping off favoured suppliers or customers not to supply goods as they may not get paid • Paying off only certain creditors

These are examples of just some of the ethical dilemmas that a company can face. At best, it is an incomplete checklist. Each company is likely to have its own unique set of ethical issues. A code of ethics and guidelines for its application in an ethics programme of induction and training will assist staff in dealing with these issues.

Good Faith Reporting

Directors are responsible for making sure that the company has appropriate good faith reporting procedures and channels. The Protected Disclosures Act 2014 (PDA 2014) aims to give wide-ranging protection for good faith reporting, or what is commonly described as 'whistleblowing'. Underlying this Act is the concept of 'protected disclosure', i.e. disclosure of relevant information made by a 'worker'.[4] In this regard, the definition of a worker is quite broad and includes: employees, independent contractors, an individual who is contracted to do some work for the other party to the contract outside that party's premises, agency workers, persons on work experience/Job Bridge programmes, as well

---

[4] Section 5(1) PDA 2014.

as members of An Garda Síochána, army personnel and civil servants (section 3 PDA 2014).

Where an employee makes a protected disclosure and is penalised or dismissed as a consequence, under PDA 2014 they can sue the employer. Under the Act, penalisation can result in an award of compensation not exceeding 260 weeks' (five years') salary. Similarly, a dismissal is actionable under the Unfair Dismissals Acts 1977–2015 and can also result in compensation not exceeding 260 weeks' salary. In the context of dismissals, there is no minimum service requirement to invoke protection against a dismissal arising from a protected disclosure. The employee's tenure of employment is irrelevant and protection applies from the first day of their employment.

Regarding non-employees penalised or dismissed as a consequence of making a protected disclosure, they are entitled to sue in tort for *causing detriment*. To succeed, the non-employee must prove that arising from the disclosure they were exposed to:
- coercion, intimidation or harassment;
- discrimination, disadvantage or adverse treatment in relation to employment (or prospective employment);
- injury, damage or loss; and/or
- the threat of reprisal.

Information is 'relevant information' if, in the reasonable belief of the worker, it tends to show one or more relevant wrongdoings, and it came to his or her attention in connection with his or her employment.[5] (For example, in 2009 four former employees of Eli Lilly & Co. in the US brought an individual suit against the pharmaceutical company for marketing its anti-psychotic drug Zyprexa for uses not approved by the US Food and Drug Administration.[6])

The PDA 2014 identifies the key areas of wrongdoings under relevant headings, including the following:
- where an offence has been or is likely to be committed;
- where a person has failed to comply with the law;
- that a miscarriage of justice has occurred, is occurring or is likely to occur;
- that the health or safety of any individual has been, is being or is likely to be endangered;
- that the environment has been, is being or is likely to be damaged;
- the improper use of public funds.[7]

---

[5] Section 5(2) PDA 2014.
[6] See https://www.justice.gov/archive/opa/pr/2009/January/09-civ-038.html
[7] Section 5(3) PDA 2014.

While the PDA 2014 encourages protected disclosures to be made to the employer, it also allows for a stepped approach. Disclosures may be made to the employer, a 'prescribed person' or, if it is a public body, to the relevant Minister. A 'prescribed person' is the recommended point of contact within the organisation to which someone may report a protected disclosure. This is likely to be a non-executive director or a member of the audit committee.

Disclosure may be made by employees to a person external to the company, such as a barrister, solicitor or a trade union official, if:
- the worker reasonably believes that the information disclosed, and any allegation contained in it, are substantially true;
- the disclosure is not made for personal gain; or
- in all the circumstances of the case, it is reasonable for the worker to make the disclosure.[8]

Similarly, employees may make a protected disclosure if:
- they reasonably believe that they will be victimised by the employer if a disclosure is made;
- no relevant person has been prescribed and the employee reasonably believes that the evidence will be concealed or destroyed if the employee makes a disclosure to the employer;
- the employee has previously made a disclosure of substantially the same information to the employer or prescribed person; or
- the relevant wrongdoing is of an exceptionally serious nature.[9]

A protected disclosure differs from a grievance in that the whistleblower is not directly affected and has no personal interest. Companies should have a clear good faith reporting policy as well as a grievance policy. (A grievance policy sets out the procedures for when employees have a problem with their employer, and could include issues with fellow employees.)

A company's good faith reporting policy for protected disclosures should ensure:
- alternative reporting lines;
- support and protection for the reporter; and
- a commitment to investigate concerns and issues raised.

The reporting worker should be kept updated on the investigation and their identity should be protected as much as possible.

---

[8] Section 10(1) PDA 2014.
[9] Section 10(2) PDA 2014.

Although the PDA 2014 protects a reporting employee acting in good faith, the disclosure is only protected if it is reasonable. Before taking the matter to someone other than a prescribed person, the employee should seek legal advice.

Conclusion

Ethics should underpin the values, decision-making processes and actions of a company, from the board down. High-profile corporate scandals have highlighted the dangers and risks of not adhering to a code of ethics that is lived and applied daily by a company's directors and staff.

Each director must uphold the integrity and accountability of the company. Ethical behaviour is crucial to ensuring the maintenance and development of long-term trusting relationships with shareholders and stakeholders.

10 KEY POINTS: ETHICS

1. Ethical behaviour is about doing the right thing, rather than what one has the right to do.
2. A written code of ethics will help guide the behaviours of a company's directors and employees.
3. Ethical standards and appropriate behaviours must be led, developed and disseminated by the board. The board sets the 'tone from the top'.
4. The board should ensure that the company has a code of ethics.
5. Implementation of the code of ethics should be supported by an induction process for new directors and staff, ongoing training and a monitoring process to identify compliance issues.
6. The Protected Disclosures Act 2014 encourages disclosures to be made to the employer, but allows a stepped approach. Disclosure may be made externally to other parties, such as a barrister, solicitor or trade union official, if the worker reasonably believes that the information disclosed, and any allegation contained in it, is substantially true and that the disclosure is not made for personal gain.
7. Relevant information that might be disclosed must show one or more wrongdoings and have come to the attention of the worker in connection with his or her employment.

8. A protected disclosure differs from a grievance in that the whistleblower is not directly affected and has no personal interest.
9. Although the Protected Disclosures Act 2014 gives protection to a reporting worker acting in good faith, the disclosure is only protected if it is *reasonable*.
10. A company's good faith reporting policy should ensure that there are alternative reporting lines, support and protection for those reporting issues and their concerns, and a commitment to investigate these.

9.
The Role of the Board and of Individual Directors

- Introduction
- The Board of Directors
- The Chairman
- The Chief Executive Officer (CEO)
- Non-executive Director
- The Company Secretary
- Conclusion
- Key Points

9. THE ROLE OF THE BOARD AND OF INDIVIDUAL DIRECTORS

Introduction

In this chapter we look at the board and the roles of individuals on the board. The board is made up of a chairman, a Company Secretary and the directors. The chairman and the Company Secretary are usually directors, though they do not have to be. Directors may be executive, i.e. participating in the management of the company, or non-executive, i.e. they have no day-to-day management responsibilities. Similarly, the chief executive or chief executive officer (CEO), whose role it is to lead the executive management of the company, may not always be a director. If the CEO is a director, he or she could also be known as the 'managing director'.

The Board of Directors

The Overall Role of the Board

The basic functions of a board of directors include:
- leadership;
- setting strategy;
- approving policies;
- managing risk;
- monitoring performance;
- accounting to shareholders and stakeholders; and
- ensuring the appropriate governance is in place.

Bob Tricker, a well-known commentator on corporate governance, neatly summarises the board's functions in a diagram as shown in **Figure 9.1** below.

FIGURE 9.1: FUNCTIONS OF THE BOARD[1]

	Past and present focused	Future focused
Outwardlooking	Accountability	Strategy formulation
Inwardlooking	Supervising executive activities	Policy making

[1] Bob Tricker, *Corporate Governance: Principles, Policies and Practices* (2nd Edition, Oxford University Press, 2012) p. 174.

The role of the board involves performance and conformance. The directors should drive performance, thinking about future direction, strategy and the achievement of goals. At the same time, they must ensure that the company conforms with the law, shareholder expectations and compliance requirements.

Theoretical Perspectives on the Board

There are a number of theoretical perspectives as to how a board should work. Two of the principal theories are stewardship theory and agency theory. The stewardship theory assumes that the directors are acting as responsible stewards of the assets of the company and that their objectives are aligned with those of the members.

Agency theory, conceptualised by Jensen and Meckling (1976),[2] is an alternative theory of how a board works. This theory assumes directors are agents of the shareholders, but that they act in their own self-interest at the expense of the shareholders. While it is a rather cynical view of directors' behaviour, many corporate governance frameworks are designed on the basis of the assumptions of agency theory; for example, that there should be non-executive directors to monitor and control the executive.

The Authority of the Board

As provided by the Companies Act 2014, the powers of a company's board are set out in the company's constitution. Amendments to the constitution are made by way of ordinary or special resolutions in general meetings. These amendments could include:
- changes to authorised capital;
- changes in the designation of the company, e.g. from a LTD to a DAC;
- increase in the number of directors allowed.

The shareholders delegate the running of the company to the board. Therefore, they should not then usurp its powers. A single shareholder or group of shareholders may not be acting in the best long-term interests of the company if they do so.

It is the responsibility of the board to govern the company, regardless of whether some of the directors own shares in the company or not. While shareholders may seek to get involved in day-to-day decision-making, that is the role of the executive management guided by the board.

---

[2] M. Jensen and W. Meckling, "Theory of the Firm: Managerial Behavior, Agency Cost, and Capital Structure" (1976) *Journal of Financial Economics*, 3: 305–360.

Occasionally, the directors may have to make decisions that are against the wishes of the majority of the shareholders of the company, and the shareholders cannot restrain them.³ Of course, shareholders, if they are not happy with the directors, may decide not to vote for them at the AGM when they come up for re-election to the board. A recourse for smaller shareholders is to take a court action claiming that as minority shareholders they are being oppressed (see **Chapter 4**). They can also bring a derivative action on behalf of the company under common law, where a wrong is committed by the directors against the company (as per the exceptions to *Foss v. Harbottle* (1843)).⁴

Thus, the board exerts considerable power over the company and has more day-to-day authority than the shareholders of the company. This was neatly set out by Lord Justice Greer in the case of *Shaw & Sons (Salford) Ltd v. Shaw*:

> "A company is an entity distinct alike from its shareholders and its directors. Some of its powers may, according to its constitution, be exercised by directors; certain other powers may be reserved for the shareholders in general meeting. If powers of management are vested in the directors, they and they alone can exercise these powers. The only way in which the general body of shareholders can control the exercise of powers by the constitution in the directors is by altering the constitution, or, if opportunity arises under the constitution, by refusing to re-elect the directors of whose actions they disapprove. They cannot themselves usurp the powers which by the constitution are vested in the directors any more than the directors can usurp the powers vested by the constitution in the general body of shareholders."⁵

The Board vs Executive Management

The larger the company, the more likely there will be a need for greater formality in the roles of the board and that of executive management. There should be a clear line in the sand between the respective roles and the responsibilities of each.

Whereas in smaller and growing companies, the board and executive management could well be the same people. As a company grows, the governance of it will be improved by separating the two entities and by bringing non-executive directors onto the board. This needs to be

---

³ *Howard Smith Ltd. v. Ampol Petroleum Ltd* [1974] A.C. 821.
⁴ [1843] 67 ER 189.
⁵ *Shaw & Sons (Salford) Ltd v. Shaw* [1935] 2 K.B. 113.

very carefully thought through as many of the founding board could well be substantial shareholders who may not want to see their authority constrained by outsiders. However, they may well see the merit of the value of external experience and the necessity of demonstrating to future investors that they are serious about governance.

As a company grows and needs to brings greater formality to its governance, it also needs to give careful thought to the usage of the term 'director'. The term may be used in a broader sense, such as directing a function in a business, e.g. a sales director or operations director, when in fact the individual is not actually a registered company director. It is advisable to avoid this practice and titles such as 'Head of Sales' or 'Head of Operations' may be more appropriate. Otherwise, there is a danger that they may be perceived as shadow directors, as discussed in **Chapter 3**.

The role of the board of directors is different from that of the executive management team. In this regard, the following points are worth noting.
- The board is there to govern and not to manage.
- The board reviews and approves strategy and monitors performance.
- The board is responsible for establishing the company's risk appetite, and assessing and monitoring this on an ongoing basis.
- The board, not the executive management, is accountable to the shareholders in general meeting.
- In an insolvency situation, it is the board that is accountable, not executive management.
- The board can delegate tasks, but not responsibility. For example, though the board may give the CEO authority to enter into contracts of a certain size to facilitate quicker decision-making, the board will always be responsible for the consequences of any such transaction. Another example of this would be a merger and acquisitions committee, which, under delegation from the board, can authorise transactions up to an agreed value; above that value, the transaction must be authorised directly by the board.

Executive management must provide information in a structured and concise manner that enables the directors to do their job. The board should rigorously assess, at least annually, if they are getting the appropriate information in an appropriate format (see **Chapter 13**).

A key challenge for a board is to encourage executive management to share their concerns with the board. It is up to the chairman, in particular, to create the boardroom environment where executive management can raise difficult issues, such as poor performance, for discussion and resolution. Unfortunately, it is human nature to boast of good results and bury problems.

In summary, the board is responsible for the oversight of the company, supporting and guiding executive management in implementing the company's strategy.

The UK Corporate Governance Code on the Board of Directors

The Role of the Board

Though the Companies Act 2014 does not elaborate on the role of the board, it is addressed comprehensively in the *UK Corporate Governance Code*. As we saw in **Chapter 2**, the Code is made up of important general principles supported by more detailed provisions. The very first principle in the Code is that "every company should be headed by an **effective** board which is **collectively responsible** for the **long-term success of the company**".[6]

The key words and phrases here are:
- **'effective':** the board should be active and take decisions;
- **'collectively responsible':** even if a director disagrees with a decision in the boardroom, he or she is still responsible for the decisions of the board as a whole (independent, non-executive directors are as responsible in law as executive directors);
- **'long-term success of the company':** the duty of the director is to the company, not to the shareholders. A shareholder may be more focused on short-term profit, whereas a director should be focused on the long-term success of the company.

The *UK Corporate Governance Code* also provides a wonderfully succinct description of the role of the board of directors:

> "The board's role is to provide **entrepreneurial leadership** of the company within a framework of **prudent and effective controls** which enables risk to be assessed and managed. The board should set the company's **strategic aims, ensure that the necessary financial and human resources are in place** for the company to meet its objectives and **review management performance**. The board should **set the company's values and standards** and **ensure that its obligations to its shareholders and others are understood and met**."[7]

---

[6] *UK Corporate Governance Code* (FRC, April 2016) A.1 (emphasis added).
[7] *Ibid.*, A.1 (emphasis added).

Again, it is useful to look at what is behind these words to gain a greater understanding of what they mean for directors:

- **'entrepreneurial leadership'**: the original reason to create the company, a separate legal entity, was to allow individuals to take risks (particularly relevant for commercial entities) but with limited liability;
- **'prudent and effective controls'**: entrepreneurism is to be encouraged, but risk must be tempered and controlled. The emphasis on risk management has increased, particularly since the financial crisis. Controls should be effective, but should not stifle endeavour. The aim is to have practical, sensible controls that work, but not to burden the company with governance bureaucracy;
- **'strategic aims'**: a key role of the board is to approve and monitor the strategy of the company;
- **'ensure that the necessary financial and human resources are in place'**: adequate funding, as well as people with the appropriate skills and experience, must be available to fulfil the strategy or the strategy should be revised;
- **'review management performance'**: having set the strategic goals, the board must monitor how the executive management team performs against goals (a key role of the board);
- **'set the company's values and standards'**: directors have the responsibility to set the ethical standards and values for the company. As corporate behaviour and ethical standards are increasingly coming under the spotlight, it is vital that the 'tone from the top' is visibly set by the chairman and the board (see **Chapter 8**);
- **'ensure that its obligations to its shareholders and others are understood and met'**: the focus is not only on shareholders but also 'stakeholders', such as staff, suppliers, government, etc.

Accountability of the Board

As we have seen, the directors are accountable for the running of the company. The key instrument used to demonstrate the accountability of the directors is the annual report of the company, which contains the audited (where required) financial statements.

> "The board should present a fair, balanced and understandable assessment of the company's position and prospects."[8]

---

[8] *UK Corporate Governance Code* (April 2016) C.1.

Also included in the annual report is the directors' report, which contains a business review and other mandated disclosures required by the Companies Act 2014.[9] The annual general meeting (AGM) is the forum for shareholder questions about and discussion of this information (see **Chapter 12**).

It is important to note, however, that accountability is not a one-off exercise at year end. The statements made in the annual report by the directors should be valid every day of the year.

Induction and Development

The *UK Corporate Governance Code* also provides guidance on the induction of new directors. An induction programme for new directors ensures that new directors understand the company, the market in which it operates and the role of director, i.e. what is required and expected of them. It also allows new directors to get up to speed as quickly as possible and to start to build relationships with fellow directors, professional advisors and the executive management team.

The *UK Corporate Governance Code* emphasises the importance of induction:

> *"Main principle*
>
> All directors should receive induction on joining the board and should regularly update and refresh their skills and knowledge.
>
> *Supporting Principles*
>
> The chairman should ensure that the directors continually update their skills and the knowledge and familiarity with the company required to fulfil their role both on the board and on board committees. The company should provide the necessary resources for developing and updating its directors' knowledge and capabilities.
>
> To function effectively, all directors need appropriate knowledge of the company and access to its operations and staff."[10]

---

[9] Section 325 CA 2014.
[10] *UK Corporate Governance Code* (April 2016) B.4 (Development).

To be effective, a director needs to keep his or her knowledge and skills up to date. The role and responsibilities of directors are constantly evolving as a company develops and regulatory environment changes. The emphasis should not just be on proper induction but also on continued, relevant training. This would include updates on company law and latest developments in governance, such as the introduction of the compliance statement by the Companies Act 2014 (see **Chapter 13**).

We will now look at the specific roles on a board that a director may take on, starting with that of the chair.

The Chairman

The 'chairman' (the term used by the *UK Corporate Governance Code* to denote a chair of either gender) is the leader of the board. It is up to the chairman to ensure that every director plays an effective role. In being appointed, the chairman should be independent of the company, i.e. he or she should not be an existing executive director and should not be linked to a particular shareholder or group of shareholders. However, the chairman should be someone with relevant industry knowledge and with the authority to lead the board.

As to the responsibilities of a chairman, the *UK Corporate Governance Code* states that "the chairman is responsible for leadership of the board and ensuring its effectiveness on all aspects of its role".[11] In leading the board, the chairman must:
- set the board's agenda;
- ensure that adequate time is available for discussion of all agenda items;
- promote a culture of openness and debate by facilitating the effective contribution of all directors and ensuring constructive relations between executive and non-executive directors;
- ensure that the directors receive accurate, timely and clear information; and
- ensure effective communication with shareholders.[12]

It is arguable that the *UK Corporate Governance Code* does not sufficiently emphasise the role of the chairman in managing the personalities and controlling board discussions. In practice, ensuring that directors express their opinions in a constructive manner and bringing the board

---

[11] *UK Corporate Governance Code* (April 2016) A.3.
[12] *Ibid.*

to a decision is a substantial and important skill in itself. (We will be exploring this in greater detail in **Chapter 10**.)

The 2003 'Higgs Report' (*Review of the Role and Effectiveness of Non-executive Directors*[13]) notes that: "the chairman is pivotal in creating the conditions for overall board and individual non-executive director effectiveness, both inside and outside the boardroom." The report also summarises the attributes of an effective chairman as follows:

"• upholds the highest standards of integrity and probity;
- sets the agenda, style and tone of board discussions to promote effective decision-making and constructive debate;
- promotes effective relationships and open communication, both inside and outside the boardroom, between non-executive directors and the executive team;
- builds an effective and complementary board, initiating change and planning succession in board appointments, subject to board and shareholders' approval;
- promotes the highest standards of corporate governance and seeks compliance with the provisions of the Code wherever possible;
- ensures a clear structure for and the effective running of board committees;
- ensures effective implementation of board decisions;
- establishes a close relationship of trust with the chief executive, providing support and advice while respecting executive responsibility; and
- provides coherent leadership of the company, including representing the company and understanding the views of shareholders."[14]

Crucially, it is the chairman who sets the tone for the company and he or she should at all times demonstrate high ethical standards, valuing and applying honesty and integrity (see **Chapter 8**).

The Chairman and the CEO

The chairman's role is to manage the board, while the CEO's role is to manage the company through the executive management team. The chairman should not encroach on the role of the CEO, and if there is some overlap, it is important to find a balance. Such a balance will vary,

---

[13] Derek Higgs, *Review of the role and effectiveness of non-executive directors* (January 2003), para 5.1. Available at www.ecgi.org/codes/documents/higgsreport.pdf
[14] *Ibid.*, Annex D.

depending on the skills and personalities of the chairman and the CEO. For example, deciding who should deal with the media is often a delicate matter. Normally, it would be the chairman, but if he or she is uncomfortable dealing with the media, then the CEO would be the default position or, failing that, a senior staff member with the appropriate skills.

Ideally, the chairman should have an excellent working relationship with the CEO, one that allows them to challenge each other without falling out.

In some countries, notably the US, it is common for the chairman and CEO to be the same person. However, this is frowned upon by the global investment community as it may jeopardise impartial leadership. In the context of listed companies, the *UK Corporate Governance Code* provides as follows:

> "There should be a clear division of responsibilities at the head of the company between the running of the board and the executive responsibility for the running of the company's business. No one individual should have unfettered powers of decision."[15]

The Code bases the following key provision on this principle:

> "The roles of chairman and chief executive should not be exercised by the same individual. The division of responsibilities between the chairman and chief executive should be clearly established, set out in writing and agreed by the board."[16]

For smaller companies, it may make sense for the chairman and the chief executive to be one person initially. As a company grows, however, these roles should be divided to ensure independent and impartial leadership (though company founders are often reluctant to relinquish the role of chairman, feeling it may constrain their entrepreneurial behaviours). The timing of when this separation should take place can be difficult to judge and implement, particularly where founding shareholders are concerned about losing control. The introduction of third-party investment will often require that the roles are divided and that the chair is non-executive and independent.

---

[15] *UK Corporate Governance Code* (April 2016) A.2.
[16] *Ibid.*, A.2.1.

In order to manage these roles effectively, the actual division of responsibilities between the chair and the CEO should be set out in writing in the terms of reference and agreed by the board.

The Chairman and a Majority or Significant Shareholder

Similarly, where there is a majority or significant shareholder, the chairman needs to ensure that there are written terms of reference for the role of the chair and that he or she can focus on the best interests of the company.

A majority/significant shareholder may seek to influence the chair. In practice, this influence needs to be recognised. The chairman should keep close to the majority/significant shareholder and ensure they understand their motivations and where they see the company going. The chairman must make sure that he or she is not placed in an untenable position. For example, this could occur where a venture capital company becomes a significant shareholder. The venture capital company may have its own approach as to how and when value can be extracted from the company, which may conflict with the rest of the board, who are acting in the interests of the company and taking a longer-term view. The chairman's position in such a scenario can be very difficult, as the investor may have the real power as major funder. Having agreed terms of reference in place for the chairman, as well as a shareholder agreement, may alleviate such situations. A shareholders' agreement is a contract between some or all of the shareholders in a company and frequently the company itself. The prime objective of a shareholders' agreement is to provide for how the company is to be managed and, as far as possible, to proactively address issues that might otherwise become divisive in the future, if not agreed in advance.

The Chief Executive Officer (CEO)

The CEO is responsible for the day-to-day running of the company, leads the executive management team and reports to the board on its behalf. In turn, the CEO communicates the decisions of the board to the company and ensures that they are implemented.

The CEO may also be referred to as the 'managing director' if he or she is a director. The Companies Act 2014 refers to the term 'managing director', stating that the directors of the company may appoint one or more of themselves to the office of managing director, adding that the directors may grant him or her whatever powers they think fit.[17]

Non-Executive Directors

Non-executive directors (NEDs) on the board are expected to operate as a check and balance on the executive directors in the interests of the shareholders. As the NEDs are not involved in the day-to-day issues of the company, they bring a fresh perspective based on their objectivity, independence and experience.

NEDs may or may not be 'independent'. Those that are *not* independent are usually representatives of a certain shareholder or stakeholder, e.g. a financier, the government, the employees, etc. An independent director is a director who does not have a material or pecuniary relationship with company or related persons, except in receiving fees for their role.

Whether strictly 'independent' or not, the NED's role is to challenge the thinking of the chairman and the CEO. Absolute independence will facilitate this.

The *UK Corporate Governance Code* defines the role by stating that "non-executive directors should constructively challenge and help develop proposals on strategy".[18] In so doing, they should:
- scrutinise the performance of management in meeting objectives and agreed goals;
- monitor the reporting of performance;
- satisfy themselves on the integrity of financial information and that financial controls and systems of risk management are robust and defensible;
- determine the appropriate levels of remuneration of executive directors; and
- have a prime role in appointing and, where necessary, removing executive directors, and in succession planning.

The timing of the introduction of one or more NEDs depends on the particular situation of the company, its scale, its rate of growth and its ambitions, as NEDs with different experience and skills may be required at different stages. The input of a skilled NED will facilitate the board in focusing on the longer-term strategic and monitoring functions of the board rather than the day-to-day management issues.

[17] Section 159(1) CA 2014.
[18] *UK Corporate Governance Code* (April 2016) A.4.

In a small company, it is a real risk that a NED will get drawn into an executive role, e.g. promoting the company, and therefore lose their independence.

A good chairman and Company Secretary will have a key role in ensuring the board get the information they need to carry out their role at the appropriate level of detail. In brief, they will need the information that helps them to assess if executive management is delivering on the strategic/business plan. (Board reporting is covered in **Chapter 10**.)

Traditionally, NEDs are seen as bringing new skills and strategic thinking to the board, for example experience of the capital markets, specific industry experience, experience of mergers and acquisitions, risk management and governance skills. The importance of NEDs exercising independent judgement has developed with the evolution of corporate governance.

Essential Characteristics for Non-executive Directors

In a 2005 article titled "Beyond agency conceptions of the work of the non-executive director: Creating accountability in the boardroom", John Roberts, Terry McNulty and Philip Stiles argue that the role of the non-executive is to:
- support executives in their leadership; and
- monitor and control their conduct.[19]

The authors provide a set of three characteristics that are critical for a non-executive director. They should be:
- engaged but non-executive;
- challenging but supportive; and
- independent but involved.

Engaged but non-executive While it is useful for a non-executive director to visit the company and its operations in order to better understand the business, he or she should avoid involvement in the day-to-day management of the company, as this is not their role.

Challenging but supportive Any criticism of the company or its executive management should be constructive and solutions-focused. Non-executive directors should study the information they are provided with

---

[19] J. Roberts, T. McNulty and P. Stiles, "Beyond agency conceptions of the work of the non-executive director: Creating accountability in the boardroom" (2005) *British Journal of Management* 16, 5–26.

and prepare well for board meetings. It can be frustrating for executive directors, who will have spent many hours developing board information, if the non-executives are unprepared. To enable this, NEDs should insist on well-prepared board papers so that they can make informed contributions.

Independent but Involved Shareholders expect NEDs to ask the difficult questions in open debate. NEDs should aim to be supportive and not undermine the executive directors, while providing independent advice as to what is best for the company.

As cited above, the Higg's Report sums up the desired behaviour of a non-executive director:

> "The effective non-executive director:
> - upholds the highest ethical standards of integrity and probity;
> - supports executives in their leadership of the business while monitoring their conduct;
> - questions intelligently, debates constructively, challenges rigorously and decides dispassionately;
> - listens sensitively to the views of others, inside and outside the board;
> - gains the trust and respect of other board members;
> - promotes the highest standards of corporate governance and seeks compliance with the provisions of the [UK Corporate Governance] Code wherever possible."[20]

However, arguably the most important characteristic of a non-executive director is their independence.

The Independence of Non-executive Directors

If NEDs are not independent, their ability to play an objective role in the company is diminished. In this section, we examine the criteria for considering a director to be independent.

The Companies Act 2014 states as one of the eight codified duties of directors (see **Chapter 2**) that all directors have a duty to "not agree to restrict the director's power to exercise an independent judgment".[21] While the Act only refers to non-executive directors once, and this is in

---

[20] Derek Higgs, *Review of the role and effectiveness of non-executive directors* (January 2003) Annex C.
[21] Section 228(1)(e) CA 2014.

the context of audit committees, it defines independence as not having, or for at least three years preceding his or her appointment not having had, a material relationship with the company directly, or as a partner, shareholder, director or employee of the company.[22] (*Note:* while in law, this applies to larger companies only, the principle would also apply generally and would be considered best practice.)

However, the *UK Corporate Governance Code* goes further:

> "The board should determine whether the director is independent in character and judgement and whether there are relationships or circumstances which are likely to affect, or could appear to affect, the director's judgement."[23]

The Code further elaborates on the kind of relationships or circumstances relevant to determining if the director is independent, including if the director:
- has been an employee of the company or group within the last five years;
- has, or has had within the last three years, a material business relationship with the company;
- receives additional remuneration from the company apart from a director's fee;
- has close family ties with any of the company's advisors, directors or senior employees;
- holds cross-directorships with other directors;
- represents a significant shareholder; or
- has served on the board for more than nine years.[24]

Of particular note is the Code's reference to a period of service on a board of nine years or more as being a circumstance that would possibly affect a director's independence. When people have been working together on a board as a team for such a long time, it is unlikely that they would remain independent in judgement.

However, it can be hard to stand down from the role, particularly when working with colleagues on the board of a successful company. Furthermore, and realistically, the director may be reluctant to sacrifice his or her director's fee as, even if perhaps not significant, it is a useful source of income. Nevertheless, succession should be planned as no one is irreplaceable and new directors bring fresh ideas and energy. Board renewal is the

---

[22] Section 167(5) CA 2014.
[23] *UK Corporate Governance Code* (April 2016) B.1.1.
[24] *Ibid.*

oxygen that fuels board effectiveness and efficiency regardless of whether the company is a PLC, an SME or indeed a non-profit organisation.

Finally, being independent in character and judgement is important, but more critically the director must be able to *think* independently.

Appointment of a Non-executive Director

When a non-executive director is appointed, a letter of appointment should be issued to him or her setting out the terms and expectations of the role. The letter should cover:

Term of Office The appointment of a NED is typically for an initial term of three years and they are usually expected to serve two such three-year terms, although this will vary from company to company.

Time Commitment Required This might include attendance at board meetings, committee meetings, the AGM, an annual 'board away day' and visits to key locations to understand how the business works. In addition, there is the need to devote appropriate preparation time ahead of each meeting.

Role The role of the NED should be outlined, and should include
- Strategy – NEDs should constructively challenge and help develop proposals on strategy.
- Performance – NEDs should monitor the performance of executive management in meeting agreed goals and objectives, and the reporting of performance.
- Risk – NEDs should satisfy themselves on the integrity of financial information and that financial controls and systems of risk management are robust and defensible.
- People – NEDs are responsible for determining appropriate levels of remuneration for executive directors, and have a key role in appointing and, where necessary, removing executive directors, and in succession planning.

Board Committees The letter of appointment should cover the director's expected participation and role on board committees (see **Chapter 11**).

Fees and Expenses The letter of appointment should state the fees to be paid per annum and that the company will reimburse the director for all reasonable and properly documented expenses incurred in performing the duties of the office.

Third-party Advice Each director is entitled to avail of third-party advice to carry out their role paid for by the company. This could include, for instance, legal, actuarial or financial advice.

Outside Interests The letter of appointment acknowledges that the director may have business interests other than those of the company. It also should state that any existing or potential conflicts of interest should be disclosed to the chairman and the Company Secretary on appointment or as soon as they become apparent.

Confidentiality Clause All information acquired during a director's appointment is confidential to the company and should not be released, either during a director's term of office or following its termination (by whatever means), to third parties without prior clearance from the chairman.

Non-executive Directors' Duties under Company Law

Irish law does not explicitly distinguish between non-executive and executive directors. As stated in the 2008 case of *Re Tralee Beef & Lamb Limited (In Liquidation)*:

> "There is a yet unmet need to make authoritative findings, after full debate, as to the respective duties of an executive and a non-executive director and, perhaps, a non-executive director appointed (as the appellant was) for a particular and specific purpose. But this has yet to occur."[25]

At the same time, however, a distinction does appear to be emerging (see **Chapter 4**).

It is recognised, at least by the courts, that a non-executive director is very much dependent on executive management for information, though this does not remove their responsibility to inform themselves and be informed. "Directors must inform themselves about the business and affairs of companies, and their own duties, in order to discharge their responsibilities ... Even non-executive directors of companies must be increasingly conscious in the times we live in that they cannot be mere ciphers or purveyors of votes at the whim of management."[26]

---

[25] *Re Tralee Beef & Lamb Limited (In Liquidation)* [2008] 3 I.R. 347.
[26] Mary Carolan, "Restriction order on two directors upheld", *Irish Times*, 14 May 2010 (regarding the case of *Re Mitek Pharmaceuticals & The Companies Acts* [2010] IESC 31).

There will usually be a real difference between the duties of executive and non-executive directors. The NEDs will usually be dependent on the executive for information about the affairs and finances of the company, a fact that will impose correspondingly larger duties on the executive. However, a NED would be unwise to rely on such a distinction and should be very aware of their duties under the Companies Act 2014 (as explored in **Chapter 4**), particularly the duty to "exercise the care, skill and diligence which would be exercised in the same circumstances by a reasonable person".[27]

Senior Independent Directors

In larger companies and in fully listed companies a senior independent director may be appointed[28] from among the independent non-executive directors. Even if an entity is not listed, this role is useful where there is a large board. The senior independent director can be a sounding board for the chairman and individual directors, and also be available to shareholders. The *UK Corporate Governance Code* also recommends that the senior independent director is responsible for the appraisal of the chairman's performance, with input from the other non-executive directors.[29] Having a senior independent director can be particularly useful when members of the board want to provide feedback on a confidential basis to the chairman. The senior independent director can act as the channel for this.

However, there is also a risk that the role may be considered as divisive and perhaps unnecessary as shareholders and individual directors should always be able to contact the chairman or other directors directly. It is therefore a role that needs to be handled with great sensitivity so as not to undermine the chairman or the board.

The Company Secretary

Under the Companies Act 2014, all companies must have a Company Secretary.[30] This is a statutory position established by section 129 CA 2014. Some of the duties of the Secretary are statutory, others are legal duties, and there are also those duties delegated to the Secretary, from time to time, by the board of directors of the company. Some of these duties are exercisable in conjunction with directors, whereas others are not. The statutory duties of a Company Secretary include:

[27] Section 228(g) CA 2014.
[28] *UK Corporate Governance Code* (April 2016), A 4.1.
[29] *Ibid.*, A4.2.
[30] Section 129(1) CA 2014.

- signing the annual return together with a director[31];
- certifying that the financial statements annexed to the annual return are true copies[32];
- preparing a statement of affairs in a winding up or receivership (see **Chapters 17** and **18**).[33]

The Act also refers to "such duties as are delegated to the secretary, from time to time, by the board of directors of the company".[34] Though these are not defined by the Act, see further below when discussing the duties and tasks normally delegated by the board to the Company Secretary.

The 2014 Act stresses the necessity of the Company Secretary having the appropriate skills to carry out the role (which contrasts with its silence on the skills required of directors). This is a new requirement and it points out that a Company Secretary's skills must be such that they can discharge their statutory and other duties[35] as well as maintain the records required by the Act.[36]

The Company Secretary is appointed by and can be removed by the directors.[37] Whether or not he or she is also a director, the Company Secretary is required, on registration of the company or on taking the position as Secretary, to state in writing on the appropriate CRO form:

> "I/we acknowledge that, as a secretary, I/we have legal duties and obligations imposed by the Companies Act, other statutes and at common law."[38]

As an officer of the company, the Secretary may be held personally liable for not performing their role in accordance with the Companies Act 2014. Many offences in the Act refer to "the company and any officer of it", i.e. it includes the Company Secretary whether or not they are also a director. For instance, if the company's financial statements do not give a true and fair view, the Secretary, along with the company and other officers, is guilty of a Category 2 offence, as discussed in **Chapter 4**.

The *UK Corporate Governance Code* sees the Company Secretary as a resource for advice on governance matters and for ensuring that

---

[31] Section 343 CA 2014.
[32] Section 347 CA 2014.
[33] Section 593 CA 2014.
[34] Section 226(1) CA 2014.
[35] Section 129(4) CA 2014.
[36] Section 226(2) CA 2014.
[37] Section 129(3) CA 2014.
[38] Section 226(5) CA 2014.

"good information flows within the board and its committees and between senior management and non-executive directors, as well as facilitating induction and assisting with professional development as required".[39]

Duties and Tasks of the Company Secretary The Company Secretary typically ensures that the company files with the Companies Registration Office (CRO) all the appropriate returns and forms, in addition to the annual return, accurately and on time. Other tasks that may be delegated to the Company Secretary include supporting the board and its committees and preparing for general meetings. It should be noted that these are not statutory duties and may be delegated to another person, e.g. the Secretary to the board.

- **Supporting Meetings of the Board and its Committees** The Secretary liaises with the chairman in preparing the board's agenda, convenes and attends board meetings, and records the board minutes. The Secretary must make sure that procedures are properly followed during the meeting, including disclosure of any director interests. The role may entail supporting director induction and development, and ensuring adequate information is passed between executive management and the board, and between the board and its committees.
- **Preparing and Supporting General Meetings** The Company Secretary is responsible for liaising with the company's shareholders, notifying them of company meetings and of proposed resolutions, distributing the annual financial statements and publishing statutory notices as required. The Company Secretary must ensure that procedures are properly followed and keep the minutes of company meetings.
- **Expectations around Compliance** The Companies Act 2014 removed the previous requirement for a Company Secretary to ensure the company's compliance with company law. This acknowledges that the role is essentially advisory and administrative; the Company Secretary lacks the authority to enforce compliance.
- **Other Tasks** The Company Secretary is also responsible for the custody and control of the company seal, maintaining the statutory registers, e.g. the shareholders' register (see **Chapter 12**), and ensuring that the company's letterhead stationery and website comply with statutory requirements.

---

[39] *UK Corporate Governance Code* (April 2016) B.5.

It is important that there are clear terms of reference for the Company Secretary so that they understand what duties, other than the statutory duties, have been delegated to them by the board. The role of Company Secretary is important and can be technical in nature. As a result, many companies subcontract this work to a company providing specialist corporate secretarial services.

Conclusion

In this chapter we have focused on the roles and responsibilities that the various types of director and officer play in the governance of a company. The greater the clarity there is about these roles and responsibilities in the governance structure, the easier it is for all directors and officers to be effective. It is helpful if clear job descriptions are written for all roles. However, it should be noted that the Companies Act 2014 does not differentiate between the responsibilities of non-executive and executive directors.

It has also been emphasised that good governance advocates chairman and non-executive director independence, allowing them to exercise impartial judgement in their decisions and conduct.

Finally, the Companies Act 2014 requires the board to ensure that whoever carries out the role of Company Secretary has the skills and experience to do it competently. Other than the statutory duties enumerated by the Act, there are a number of administrative duties frequently associated with the role of Company Secretary, so it is important that there are clear terms of reference.

10 KEY POINTS: ROLE OF THE BOARD AND INDIVIDUAL DIRECTORS

1. The role of the board is to lead the company by:
   - setting strategy;
   - approving policies;
   - managing risk;
   - monitoring performance;
   - setting the 'tone from the top';
   - being accountable to shareholders and other stakeholders; and
   - ensuring the appropriate governance is in place.

2. Shareholders delegate the running of the company to the directors and should not usurp their role.
3. The chairman manages the board and brings leadership to the company. He or she is pivotal in creating the conditions for overall board effectiveness.
4. As a company grows, it is worth considering bringing in an independent chairman and non-executive directors to provide impartial judgement.
5. The role of the chair and the CEO should be separate and their roles documented.
6. The CEO is the head of the executive management team and is responsible for the day-to-day running of the company.
7. In larger companies and in fully listed companies a senior independent director may be appointed from among the independent non-executive directors to act as a sounding board for the chairman and individual directors, and also be available to shareholders.
8. In law, a non-executive director has the same duties and responsibilities to the company as an executive director.
9. A company should review on a regular basis how independent their independent, non-executive directors are.
10. The directors need to ensure that the Company Secretary has the appropriate skills needed to discharge his or her duties and that these duties are clearly defined in their terms of reference.

10.
How the Board Works

- Introduction
- Composition of the Board
- The Board as a Team
- Proceedings of Directors
- Evaluating the Board
- Conclusion
- Key Points

Introduction

The previous chapter explained the various roles of the board; this chapter will look at the composition of the board and achieving the right balance among directors to enable it to support the company in a collegiate manner. We will look at how the board should operate and the importance of accurate information to enable the directors to do their job.

Composition of the Board

Size and Structure of the Board

The size and structure of the board should be proportionate to the size and activity of the company. New companies do not need the overhead of being over-governed, whereas as companies grow, their governance structures will need to become more sophisticated. Governance issues that need to be considered as companies grow include:
- How many directors are required?
- Do the roles of chair and CEO need to be separated?
- How many non-executives are required, and when?
- What skills and experience are required?
- What committees are required?

By law there is no set number as to how many directors should be on the board of a company. However, the minimum number of directors for a LTD company is one and two for a DAC under the Companies Act 2014.

In more mature companies, the board is normally made up of a chairman, a number of non-executive and executive directors and a Company Secretary, who may also be a director (a Company Secretary cannot operate in a dual capacity unless there is more than one director in that company). The composition of the board depends on the stage of evolution of the company, its size and its ambitions. For example, a smaller board is effective for fast decision-making.

The *UK Corporate Governance Code* addresses the composition of a board as follows:

> "The board and its committees should have the appropriate balance of skills, experience, independence and knowledge of

the company to enable them to discharge their respective duties and responsibilities effectively."[1]

The Code also states that the board should:
- be of sufficient size for the business requirements[2];
- "have an appropriate combination of executive and non-executive directors (and, in particular, independent non-executive directors) such that no individual or small group of individuals can dominate the board's decision taking"[3];
- be able to allocate sufficient time to discharge its responsibilities effectively.[4]

Thus, the size of the board is very much left to each individual company. However, companies should be wary of large boards as they can be unwieldy, difficult to manage and get decisions made.

Succession Planning

It is the responsibility of the board to ensure that there is a succession plan in place in the event of the sudden departure or ill health of a key individual at executive management level. Such an event may lead to a crisis in the company. Succession planning starts with ensuring that, as far as possible, there are executives who could step up to fill vacant senior executive roles if need be. If this is not the case, then having a recruitment plan to replace key individuals is critical.

Succession planning for the board is the responsibility of the nominations committee, which is discussed in **Chapter 11**.

Balance and Diversity on the Board

Board diversity will contribute to a broader spectrum of ideas and perspectives in the boardroom. The board should have the skills and experience to support the company as it goes through its various stages of growth, providing appropriate oversight and guidance to the executive management team. Diversity considers factors like the age, gender, ethnicity, educational background and professional qualifications of the

---

[1] *UK Corporate Governance Code* (FRC, April 2016), B.1.
[2] *Ibid.*
[3] *Ibid.*
[4] *Ibid.*, B.3.

directors to make the board less homogenous. The greater the range of diversity in the boardroom, the greater the range of views.

Board composition should be regularly reviewed by the nominations commitee and renewed as appropriate, otherwise the board will not have the perspective that is required to ensure that it can support the strategy of the company. Board homogeneity can be a real hindrance in an increasingly dynamic, digital and global business environment. Boards need to ensure they are fit for purpose to support the future direction of the company through ongoing and planned renewal.

> "It is the breadth of perspective, not the mere inclusion of various diverse traits for the sake of it, that benefits an organisation."
> **Russell Reynolds Associates** (www.russellreynolds.com)

Finally, many countries have introduced regulations and legislation in response to the under-representation of women on boards. While companies and their boards should, of course, be careful to avoid gender discrimination, having a regulation or quota system requiring companies to have a minimum number of women directors can be problematic. For example, it can leave the argument open that a woman will be chosen as a director because of her gender rather than on merit.

Allocation of Responsibilities

The allocation of responsibilities to board members should be carried out in a manner that is balanced and assists in board effectiveness. Roles should be documented in the board's terms of reference together with role descriptions of the individual directors.

As the company grows, specific committees can be put in place to carry out specific tasks (see also **Chapter 11**). Such board committees could include:
- audit;
- remuneration;
- nomination;
- governance;
- ethics;
- finance;
- risk; and
- strategy.

The number of committees that a board has depends on the workload of the board. Some committees have a longer lifespan than others. Some may be set up for a particular purpose and once that has been achieved or completed, it should be stood down, e.g. after a major acquisition. Each committee should have clear terms of reference that are reviewed regularly.

It should be clear what matters are reserved for the board to make decisions on and what decisions, if any, a board committee can make.

Matters Reserved for the Board

In this section we will focus on matters that are reserved for decision by the board rather than by the board committees, the CEO and/or executive management. Though these matters will vary in each company, depending on its size and the board committees in place, typically they might include:
- company strategy;
- approval of annual budgets and business plans;
- acquisitions and disposals of legal entities;
- transactions outside designated limits;
- approval of the directors' compliance statement relating to compliance with the Companies Act and tax laws (as discussed in **Chapter 14**);
- establishment of risk appetite and review, and approval of risk management approach;
- appointment and removal of directors or key senior personnel;
- terms of reference for board committees;
- significant company and board policies, including approval of remuneration and financial management policies; and
- agreeing the list of matters reserved for the board.

Directors need to consider what decisions should be made by the board and those that they consider can be delegated to the CEO/executive management team. This should be reviewed on an ongoing basis.

Decisions can be delegated by the board to individual directors or board committees, particularly those with responsibility for a particular function, such as finance, marketing, etc. However, these decisions will always have to be made in the context of the strategic/business plan and budget.

The board of directors can also authorise a person as being entitled to bind the company. This authorisation should be registered with the CRO.[5]

---

[5] Section 39 CA 2014.

The Board as a Team

A board may be composed of many different types of people and personalities who have a diverse range of backgrounds and skills. However, having talented board members around the table is no guarantee of success if the board does not function as a team.

One of the key leadership challenges for the chairman is to ensure the board takes a collegiate and productive approach to its work. The chairman should ensure that:
- independence and objectivity are encouraged at all times and that there is no danger of 'groupthink' emerging (when a group strives for consensus, valuing harmony over critical evaluation and proper analysis);
- the questioning spirit of the 'devil's advocate' is alive and well on the board, and challenging the status quo is considered healthy;
- cliques do not develop that damage collegiality;
- there are no hidden agendas;
- no single member of the board exercises undue influence or is too domineering;
- trust and mutual respect are developed among the board members;
- members live the ethics and values of the company (see **Chapter 8**).

The environment at board meetings should support rigorous and constructive debate focused on agenda matters, and encourage differences of opinion in the quest for common purpose. The board should not be distracted by items that are not relevant to the business of the meeting nor focus too much on operational matters.

Board Behaviour

The formal structure of the board is not nearly as important as its behaviour and diversity. A board is a collection of personalities and how the directors on a board behave as individuals and as a group determines its effectiveness. Board behaviour can be influenced by individuals' personal values, experience and relationships, and by perceptions of power and authority.

A key role of the chairman is to ensure that he or she encourages mutual respect and trust among the directors. Cohesion is generally poorer where there is conflict, where tasks are allocated without explanation or where progress is not being made.

As mentioned above, with any group there is a danger of 'groupthink', resulting in decisions being taken that have not been adequately challenged or discussed. Additionally, bias may result from personal history and experience affecting the judgement of directors, resulting in poor or illogical decision-making. Therefore, the chairman should try to influence board behaviours through:
- committed and demonstrated leadership;
- ensuring commitment to the ethics and values of the company;
- identifying and challenging 'groupthink';
- proactive management of meetings and keeping to the agenda;
- ensuring that all who wish to be engaged on a particular issue are engaged;
- understanding and accommodating personal agendas insofar as that is possible;
- managing existing or emerging cliques in the boardroom appropriately; and
- arbitrating between board members where necessary.

Thus, the actions and behaviours of the chairman, and how he or she carries out the role, will have an impact on the behaviour and conduct of meetings. The chairman should set the standard for the rest of the board to follow.

Proceedings of Directors

This section covers meetings of directors at board meetings and board committee meetings, and the practical guidelines provided by the Companies Act 2014 for their conduct.

The Companies Act 2014 codifies general procedures relating to notice, voting and resolutions at board meetings unless a company chooses to change these by including specific articles in its constitution.[6]

Subject to a company's constitution:
- the directors of a company may meet as they think fit;
- questions arising at any such meeting shall be decided by majority and if there is a tie the chairman shall have a casting vote;
- a director may at any time call a meeting of the directors;
- all directors shall be entitled to reasonable notice of any meeting of the directors;
- the quorum necessary may be fixed by the directors;

[6] Section 157 CA 2014.

- the directors may elect a chairman of their meetings and determine the period for which he or she is to hold office;
- the directors may establish one or more committees consisting in whole or in part of members of the board of directors;
- a board committee may meet and adjourn as it thinks proper;
- questions arising at any meeting of a committee shall be determined by a majority of votes of the members present and, if there is a tie, the chairman shall have a casting vote.[7]

The Companies Act 2014 allows for board decisions to be taken by written resolution instead of holding a formal board meeting. A resolution in writing signed by all the directors of a company who are entitled to receive notice of a board or committee meeting shall be as valid as if it had been passed at a meeting of the directors duly convened and held.[8]

Location of Board Meetings

Within reason, the timing and location of board meetings should be convenient for all directors. Physical board meetings, i.e. where members attend in person, should always be preferred as they provide not only an opportunity for board members to meet but to interact before and after. This helps to engender familiarity, collegiality and trust in fellow board members. It also helps the chairman to read and understand the body language around the boardroom table during discussions.

At the same time, all companies should have a provision in their constitution for directors to 'dial in' to meetings by conference call, videolink or any other appropriate electronic means. Given the increasing use of communications technology for meetings, it is relatively easy for directors to participate by conference call or video link. However, as expressed above, there should be preference and requirement for a certain number of meetings to be held in person. For example, chairing a meeting remotely is much more difficult as there may be a delay in speech because of a poor connection, and the inability to view body language, etc.

The use of conference calls may be appropriate for emergency meetings that have been called at short notice and where some of the board members are based in another country. The Companies Act 2014 allows for board or committee meetings by conference call between some or all of

---

[7] Section 160 CA 2014.
[8] Section 161 CA 2014.

the directors, provided each is able to speak to each of the others and to be heard by each of the others.[9]

The Board Workplan

The chairman, with the input of the Company Secretary, should plan the work for the board for the year. Such a workplan for the board would consider the:
- work to be completed during the year (see below);
- responsibilities at board or committee level;
- timing of board, committee meetings and 'away days';
- role of board committees;
- information requirements to assist all the directors in carrying out their statutory responsibilities; and
- resource availability at executive level to support the committees.

The work to be completed during the year could include:
- approving strategic plans, annual business plans and budgets;
- reviewing and approving the statutory financial statements;
- preparation work for the annual strategy away day with the board and the executive management team;
- spotlight reviews of specific interest, e.g. expansion plans into another product/market;
- items requiring a special focus, such as risk management, e.g. cyber risk;
- work to be carried out by specific board members and/or committees;
- recruitment of new directors;
- review of executive compensation structures; and
- governance and ethics training for the board.

This workplan determines the board's calendar for the year, how many board and committee meetings are required, and the workload of the Company Secretary to support this level of activity. The workplan should be presented to the board for review and approval.

Agendas for Board Meetings

Agendas for board meetings should be drawn up by the chairman with input from the CEO and Company Secretary, along with consideration

---

[9] Section 161(6) CA 2014.

of requests from other directors or the executive management team. The chairman should ensure that the agenda is balanced between the strategic and the operational, and that there is time for adequate discussion of each item. The agenda should adhere to the board workplan for the company. On receiving the agenda, a director should prepare accordingly, so that he or she can contribute actively at the meeting.

Many boards spend too much time on management and operational issues at their meetings and not enough time on the future direction of the company. Board agendas should bring a balance in terms of their focus. Potential agenda items might include:
- minutes of the last meeting;
- action points that have not been completed from previous meetings;
- CEO report and related functional issues;
- financial accounts;
- performance against the strategic and annual business plan;
- board committee reporting;
- capital expenditure;
- compliance issues;
- health and safety issues;
- shareholder or other stakeholder issues; and
- actions going forward.

When the agenda is drafted, adequate time should be allowed for each agenda item. The board meeting agenda should be circulated to appropriate executives of the company as far in advance as possible to give time to prepare appropriate board papers for their specific agenda item and circulation later to the board members. The agenda and board pack should be made available physically or via an online board portal to the members at least five working days in advance of the meeting.

Chairing and Conducting the Board Meeting

The chairman must actively manage board meetings to ensure that they are effective and that time is not wasted. All directors should understand the role of the chairman and the processes that underpin the operation of a board meeting so that they can make timely and suitable contributions.

When preparing for a meeting, the chair should meet the CEO and the Company Secretary separately a week in advance. This is useful for understanding any issues on which the CEO will be seeking input from the board and any other matters that may require consideration by the chairman, such as potential conflicts of interest. This preparatory work should also involve determining the appropriate amount of time to allocate to agenda items.

It is the role of the chair to control and manage the meeting as per the agenda, allowing appropriate time for discussion of each item and ensuring that every board member is given an opportunity to contribute. He or she may need to manage any dominant personalties and facilitate the meeting to reach decisions. At the end of the meeting, it is useful to summarise any key decisions made and ensure that the Company Secretary has properly recorded them.

The chairman should also take a lead in arranging for the board members to have meals together occasionally to give directors a chance to interact informally and exchange ideas.

Minutes of Board Meetings

Once a board meeting is over, it is the Company Secretary's role to record the minutes. This should be done as soon as possible after the meeting to ensure accuracy. Accurate minutes are vital for ensuring that every director clearly understands the decisions taken and actions required.

While the Company Secretary usually performs the role of board secretary, this is not a statutory duty of Company Secretaries. Where the Company Secretary plays an active role in board meetings, e.g. where they are directors or, alternatively, where the Company Secretary is not a board member, it is advisable that there is a separate secretary to the board.

The Companies Act 2014 states that a company must record minutes of "proceedings of directors" showing:
- all appointments of officers made by its directors, such as new directors;
- the names of the directors present at each meeting and of any committee of the directors; and
- all resolutions and proceedings at all meetings.[10]

These minutes need to be available for inspection by the ODCE. Failure to maintain minutes or make them available for inspection is classed as a Category 4 offence (section 166(6) CA 2014).

---

[10] Section 166 CA 2014.

The *UK Corporate Governance Code* also highlights the importance of recording difficult issues in the board minutes:

> "Where directors have concerns which cannot be resolved about the running of the company or a proposed action, they should ensure that their concerns are recorded in the board minutes. On resignation, a non-executive director should provide a written statement to the chairman, for circulation to the board, if they have any such concerns."[11]

Board minutes should follow the agenda, recording the key points and anything that the chairman specifically requests to be included. They should not be a detailed account of 'who said what'. The chairman should conclude on each issue and each issue should result in an action point or a decision, unless the item was included for information only.

Ideally, minutes should be as short as possible with clear decisions and actions. However, there may be circumstances in which more detailed minutes should be kept; for example, if the company is in financial difficulty. Consequently, the rationale for the board's decisions and actions should be recorded in greater detail.

The minutes should be reviewed by the chairman, then circulated to the rest of the board. If a director has an issue with the minutes, or any part of them, this should be raised at the start of the next board meeting or directly with the chairman. (Remember: a decision of the board is a collective decision and each board member is responsible for the decision whether or not they voted for it.)

There is no general legal requirement for the board minutes of companies to record dissenting views (though a dissenting director can write to the chairman or the Company Secretary setting out his or her views on a particular issue). In certain regulated sectors, however, detailed minutes are mandatory, including the recording of dissensions, negative votes, etc. For example, the Central Bank of Ireland's corporate governance code for credit institutions states that:

> "Detailed minutes of all board meetings shall be prepared with all decisions, discussions and points for further actions being documented. Dissensions or negative votes shall be documented in terms acceptable to the dissenting person or negative voter."[12]

---

[11] *UK Corporate Governance Code* (April 2016) A.4.3.
[12] *Corporate Governance Requirements for Credit Institutions* (Central Bank of Ireland, 2015) para. 16.3.

Board 'Away Days'

Typically a day-long programme held away from the boardroom, an 'away day', allows the board take time out from its normal meetings routine to focus on particular issues, e.g. strategy and planning. They are also a good way of building team spirit at board level. It is useful if the executive management team attend some or all of the board away days so that the board can get to know them better, and vice versa. Away days are particularly effective in organisations with executive management and/or directors based at diverse locations. The programme for an away day needs to be carefully considered and planned to ensure that there is constructive output and that the time is productive.

Confidentiality

The chairman must insist that what is discussed in the boardroom is treated in confidence. A breach of confidentiality is a breach of a director's duties as it may harm the company.

For example, directors must ensure that all shareholders are treated fairly in relation to any **price-sensitive information**, which is factual and precise information that has the potential to influence a particular company's share price. Price-sensitive information must be disclosed to shareholders as soon as practicable. In public companies this is particularly important, as a person who takes advantage of inside knowledge can be convicted for insider trading.

Information for the Board

Without timely, accurate and relevant information that is well structured and presented, the board cannot carry out its statutory role, let alone add value in advising and supporting executive management. This section provides a guide on what information the board may require.

The information that goes to a board is generally in the form of a board pack, which allows each director to prepare for the next board meeting. A typical board pack contains the following information:
- agenda for the next meeting;
- minutes of the previous meeting, with a schedule of follow-up actions;
- CEO's report, including a review of operational and functional areas and issues, e.g. production, sales, health & safety (see below);
- financial director's report;

- board committee reports;
- items for noting, discussion or decision.

The CEO's Report The CEO's report should bring the board up to date on all matters for which the CEO is responsible in a clear and concise manner. It should also be used to flag issues on which the CEO wants the board's opinion and advice. The content of the CEO's report will differ by company, depending on the nature of its activities, its scale, geographic focus, etc. Typically, the main items included in the CEO's report are:
- current significant issues for discussion;
- matters for approval;
- strategic/business plan update;
- update on key performance indicators;
- risk and compliance update; and
- matters for noting.

The CEO's report takes into account the reports made to him or her by the various functions in the organisation.

Categories of Information Information is included in the board pack for various reasons. Being clear about why certain information is included, i.e. its purpose, will help in assembling the board pack as well as in preparing effectively for the meeting and the conduct of that meeting. The information included may be for:
- **Decisions** Issues brought to the board for decision should be supported by sufficient information for directors to make informed decisions. This process could take a number of meetings.
- **Discussion and Monitoring** The board needs to see how the company is performing against agreed key performance indicators (see **Chapter 13**). This information should be in a form that makes it easy for board members to compare planned with actual performance.
- **Noting** This involves contextual information, allowing the board to have an understanding of the market environment in which the company operates, the day-to-day work of the company and a greater insight into what key staff and units/divisions do. This could cover regulatory developments, competitor activity, market research, etc.

All information presented should be concise, relevant and reliable. It is useful if appropriate comparative data is included, e.g. prior-period figures, forecasts, information about competitors, etc.

Finally, the executive management team should aim to deliver documentation for review to the board in a timely manner and provide any important material information without delay. The presentation of board papers should be in a standardised report format. Directors must insist that board papers enable them to do their job effectively and efficiently. It is a waste of time and money for directors to have to work with poorly presented board papers.

Evaluating the Board

This chapter has highlighted that there are a myriad of moving parts that contribute to the success of a board. The constituent elements need to be evaluated regularly to ensure that the board is operating well. The need to evaluate the board depends on the size and stage of development of the company.

Though the Companies Act 2014 does not require regular, formal evaluation of board performance, it is still good practice to do so. The *UK Corporate Governance Code* states that:

> "The board should undertake a formal and rigorous annual evaluation of its own performance and that of its committees and individual directors."[13]

It is worth noting also that the Central Bank makes an annual evaluation mandatory for credit institutions, stating that:

> "The board shall formally review its overall performance and that of individual directors, relative to the board's objectives, at least annually. The review shall be documented. Every three years an evaluation by an external evaluator shall be undertaken."[14]

The *UK Corporate Governance Code* sets out the purpose of a board evaluation:

> "Evaluation of the board should consider the balance of skills, experience, independence and knowledge of the company on the board, its diversity, including gender, how the board works together as a unit, and other factors relevant to its effectiveness.

---

[13] *UK Corporate Governance Code* (April 2016) B.6.
[14] *Corporate Governance Requirements for Credit Institutions* (Central Bank of Ireland, 2015) para 14.6.

The chairman should act on the results of the performance evaluation by recognising the strengths and addressing the weaknesses of the board and, where appropriate, proposing new members be appointed to the board or seeking the resignation of directors.

Individual evaluation should aim to show whether each director continues to contribute effectively and to demonstrate commitment to the role (including commitment of time for board and committee meetings and any other duties)."[15]

The Code also recommends that the non-executive directors, led by the senior independent director (see **Chapter 9**), should be responsible for evaluating the performance of the chairman, taking into account the views of executive directors.

The chairman is responsible for the overall process of board evaluation; he or she should choose an appropriate approach and act on its outcomes. The evaluation may be carried out by using one or a combination of the following methods:

- **Self-assessment Questionnaire** Board members could be asked to complete a customised self-assessment questionnaire, the main purpose of which is to make board members more aware of their own performance and how they can contribute to overall board performance. (This will have limited value as it is very subjective.) A further step could be sharing all the individual responses to the questionnaire with a nominated director, who would collate them and feed them back to the board for discussion and actions.

    Alternatively, board members can be asked to complete a customised questionnaire, returning it to a board member nominated to carry out the review. The prime concern here will be that the confidentiality of board members' views will be maintained by the board member nominated to carry out the review. On completion, the nominated board member will summarise the responses and feed them back to the board, for discussion and action.

- **Interviews and Feedback** These could be conducted by the chair, Company Secretary or an agreed non-executive director. Members would be interviewed individually and the summarised results fed back to the board for discussion and action. The choice of interviewer would be vital for members to have confidence in the process. This

---

[15] *UK Corporate Governance Code* (April 2016) B.6.

process is often preceded by the use of the type of questionnaire described above.
- **Boardroom Discussion** This could be led by the chair or an independent facilitator.
- **External Evaluation** This is the most rigorous method as an independent external evaluator, experienced in assessing the performance of boards, will bring greater objectivity. This approach is likely to involve a combination of questionnaires and individual interviews.

Items raised during a board evaluation need to be dealt with sensitively and are generally fed back to the chairman in the first instance, and then to the board.

The evaluation should look at:
- the balance of the board's composition in terms of skills, experience and diversity;
- length of service of board members;
- the performance of the board as a collective unit – how it is run and boardroom practices;
- attendance record of directors;
- the individual performance of each member of the board, including the chairman;
- key board relationships, e.g. between the CEO and the chair, or the board and stakeholders;
- the effectiveness of board committees;
- the board's performance of its key functions – devising company strategy, managing risk and establishing ethical principles and values;
- the quality of information provided to the board;
- induction and professional development for directors; and
- succession planning.

Conclusion

This chapter has outlined how boards work and the component parts that need to be put in place to ensure that directors can carry out their role. It is up to the directors to ensure that there is an appropriate balance on the board. Balance involves a diversity of skills, experience and perspective influencing how best to govern the company and support the executive. The chair plays a vital role in managing the conduct of board meetings and ensuring that the company benefits from the talent around the boardroom table. Key to this is regular evaluation of the board and its processes.

10 Key Points: How the Board Works

1. Under the Companies Act 2014 there is no mandatory board size or composition, except that an LTD may have just one director and all other types of company must have at least two.
2. The behaviour of the board as a whole, as well as its individual members, can have a profound impact on its efficiency and effectiveness. The chair plays a key role in controlling this.
3. The directors must ensure that there is a board and an executive management succession plan that allows the organisation to prepare for change and to select qualified, competent replacements.
4. The board of directors should decide what decisions cannot be delegated. This list of 'matters reserved for the board' should be reviewed on an ongoing basis.
5. The chair should plan the work for the board for the year.
6. The chair should control and manage board meetings as per the agenda, encouraging constructive debate and ensuring that every member is given a chance to contribute.
7. The Companies Act 2014 codifies procedures relating to meetings, voting and resolutions of directors, and committee meetings unless a company, in its constitution, chooses to change these.
8. What is discussed in the boardroom should be confidential unless it is agreed otherwise.
9. Directors must ensure that they receive timely, accurate and relevant information.
10. The board should undertake a formal and rigorous annual evaluation of its own performance and that of its committees and individual directors on a regular basis.

11.
Board Committees

- Introduction
- Purpose of Board Committees
- The Audit Committee
- The Nomination Committee
- The Remuneration Committee
- Conclusion
- Key Points

Introduction

Committees, reporting to the board, are part of the infrastructure of the board. They are put in place to provide a particular focus on topics that need specialist attention and time outside of normal board time. Board committees may ask external specialists to attend their meetings.

Commonly there are three board committees to be found in larger companies, as recommended by governance codes such as the *UK Code of Corporate Governance*: the audit, nomination and remuneration committees. Other, separate committees may be set up to cover strategy, mergers and acquisitions, governance, ethics, etc.

Board committees are usually chaired by a member of the board assisted by one or two other non-executive directors who are preferably independent.

Before accepting such a responsibility, the director should ensure that he or she has the necessary time and is prepared to put in the extra effort to fulfil the purpose of the committee.

The board should approve the terms of reference of each board committee, making sure that it reports regularly and that the committee's recommendations are considered and, where appropriate, acted upon.

The Purpose of Board Committees

The purpose of a board committee is to consider complex and/or sensitive issues in detail and then report to the board. The requirement for a committee, its size and composition, depends on the type and size of the company and its stage of development, unless there are specific rules required by statute or corporate governance codes.

Many of the recommendations made in this chapter are from the *UK Corporate Governance Code*. The FRC adopts a very practical approach as to the arrangements that need to be put in place for board committees. For example, with regard to audit committees it observes that "arrangements need to be proportionate to the task, and will vary according to the size, complexity and risk profile of the company".[1]

It is recommended that board committees are made up entirely, or mainly, of independent non-executive directors wherever possible to avoid conflicts of interest.

---

[1] FRC, *Guidance on Audit Committees* (April 2016) para. 1.2. Available at https://www.frc.org.uk/Our-Work/Publications/Corporate-Governance/Final-Draft-Guidance-on-Audit-Committees-2016.pdf

Committee Terms of Reference

Terms of reference are vital to any committee, setting out its purpose and the scope of its mandate. The board is responsible for approving a committee's terms of reference. Terms of reference should be in writing and cover, at a minimum:
- committee's purpose;
- membership;
- meetings;
- reporting;
- duties;
- appointments;
- remuneration and expenses of committee members;
- skills and training;
- reviews of its performance;
- resources;
- authority; and
- period for next review of the terms of reference.

The membership of a committee, the profile of its knowledge and experience, will depend on the purpose of the committee. The committee should be left to work within its terms of reference without interference from the board. In relation to who can attend committee meetings, the *UK Corporate Governance Code* states:

> "No one other than the committee chairman and members are entitled to be present at a meeting of the nomination, audit or remuneration committee, but others may attend at the invitation of the committee."[2]

The board should review the terms of reference of its committees regularly and assess the effectiveness of each committee.

The Audit Committee

The Role of the Audit Committee

The audit committee works to ensure the effectiveness of both the company's internal and statutory auditors, that the financial statements are properly prepared and that effective internal controls are in place to ensure the integrity of the accounting systems that support the

---

[2] *UK Corporate Governance Code* (FRC, April 2016) B.1.

production of the financial statements. While the board cannot delegate its responsibility, it can request the audit committee to have a close look at these areas and report back to it. All directors are involved in the approval of the financial statements and the work of the audit committee can provide greater assurance to the board when signing off.

While audit committees are not mandatory for most companies, and indeed their scale would not justify one, the Companies Act 2014 requires an audit committee for large companies. A large company is defined as a company with a balance sheet total (i.e. total assets less liabilities) of €25 million and turnover of over €50 million.[3] If a 'large company' does not have an audit committee, it must explain to its members in its statutory and financial statements why it does not have one.[4]

The role and responsibilities of the audit committee, according to the Companies Act 2014, are to monitor the:
- financial reporting process and the integrity of the financial statements;
- effectiveness of the company's systems of internal control, internal audit and risk management;
- statutory audit of the company's statutory financial statements; and
- independence of the statutory auditors and the provision of additional services to the company.[5]

The audit committee needs to take a tactful approach in their work to develop a relationship of mutual respect with both the executive management team, the internal audit function (if there is one) and the statutory auditors to ensure they can carry out their role. The ability to be both challenging and understanding is part of the skillset required of the audit committee.

Additionally, the audit committee should review arrangements in place at the company for good faith reporting (whistleblowing) (see **Chapter 8**). Members of staff should be able to raise concerns about possible improprieties and know that these will be investigated in a proportionate, independent and appropriate manner.[6]

---

[3] Section 167(1) CA 2014. This requirement also applies to a company that has one or more subsidiaries, which, in combination, meet these financial thresholds.
[4] Section 167(3) CA 2014.
[5] Section 167(7) CA 2014.
[6] *UK Corporate Governance Code* (April 2016) C.3.5.

Membership of the Audit Committee

Section 167 of the Companies Act 2014 requires the members of the audit committee of a 'large' company to include at least one independent, non-executive director who at no time during the three years preceding his or her appointment has had a material business relationship with the company or a position of employment in the company. It is interesting that this is the only place in the Act where there is a reference to a non-executive director. Clearly, the aim of the legislation was to ensure that at least one audit committee member possesses the requisite degree of independence to contribute effectively to the committee's functions. Furthermore, the Act requires that at least one independent non-executive director on the audit committee have "competence in accounting or auditing".[7]

A company which is not a 'large company' does not have to comply with this section of the Act and does not have to adhere to the *UK Corporate Governance Code*. However, it would be good practice and advisable to do so if the resources are available.

The *UK Corporate Governance Code* makes the following important recommendation with regard to the membership of the audit committee:

> "The board should satisfy itself that at least one member of the audit committee has recent and relevant financial experience."[8]

In the author's opinion, this experience and skill set is essential, as much of the work of the audit committee is in interpreting technical, financial information.

A new member of the audit committee should be informed as to:
- details of the business and the inherent financial risks;
- the business's regulatory environment;
- market practice and current trends; and
- current accounting and audit issues.

The audit committee role is an onerous one in that the members of the committee must understand the financial statements and be prepared to challenge both the executive management team and the auditors. To be satisfied as to the integrity of the financial statements requires

---

[7] Section 167(4), (5) and (6) CA 2014.
[8] *UK Corporate Governance Code* (April 2016) C.3.1.

a high level of competence. Relevant and regular training is important for a director to be effective in this role.

Financial Reporting Process and the Integrity of the Financial Statements

An important role of the directors of a company, and in particular the audit committee, is to ensure the integrity of the financial reporting process, i.e. that the financial statements really do give a true and fair view of the financial position of the company as well as its financial performance (profit/loss) for the relevant period. The financial statements need to be reviewed to ensure that they are comprehensive and not misleading. Reviewing the integrity of the financial statements is a task for all directors, although it is usually delegated to the audit committee, where there is one.

It is the responsibility of the board/audit committee to review areas that are more vulnerable to potential misstatement/manipulation, such as:
- revenue recognition;
- recognition of expenses;
- capitalisation of expenses;
- under- or overstatement of asset values;
- understatement of liabilities; and
- limited disclosure of key information, e.g. executive remuneration.

The Effectiveness of the Company's Systems of Internal Control, Internal Audit and Risk Management

The company's executive management should report to the audit committee on the key internal controls that they have introduced. The committee should consider the effectiveness of the controls and the conclusions of any relevant work carried out by internal auditors.

The management of risk is becoming increasingly important and may be delegated to a separate risk committee. It should also be noted that risk does not only relate to financial risk.

Where there is a separate committee for risk, there should be clear demarcation of responsibilities with the audit committee to avoid duplication of effort or omissions. Often, the chair of one committee sits on the other committee. In a smaller company, there may not be a separate risk committee and the audit committee may take on this role.

Effectiveness of Internal Audit The board and/or its audit committee needs to assess the costs/benefits of having an internal audit function, bearing in mind the risks the company faces and its risk tolerance. The decision to carry out this assessment may come about as a result of heightened awareness from monitoring of controls or a specific incident.

Internal audit may be internally or externally resourced. If there is no internal audit function, the board or its audit committee should assess whether it has sufficient and objective assurance that internal controls are functioning. The statutory (external) auditors may highlight weaknesses that they noticed during their audit in their management letter, but an internal audit function would focus in more detail on internal controls. Statutory auditors only look at internal controls that are relevant to the audit of financial statements.

The Statutory Audit and the Independence of the Statutory Auditors

The role of the statutory (external) auditor is a fundamental element of corporate governance. Their primary role is to report to shareholders, and not the management, on the financial statements that are laid before the members of the company, and the directors must give them all the information they require. (It is the internal auditors who report to the board (or to the audit committee if there is one) and management on internal controls and how to make the company more efficient.)

The board or its audit committee ensures that the statutory auditors make an independent report to the shareholders, forming an opinion on whether the accounts show a true and fair view.

Generally, the members vote in general meetings for the appointment or removal of the auditors on the advice of the board.

With the increasing concentration of audit practices into a 'Big 4', the issue of the independence of auditors has become increasingly relevant and difficult. Independence is a core principle of the profession's Code of Ethics; indeed, external auditors are also subject to a specific ethical standard (in Ireland, the Ethical Standard for Auditors is issued by the Irish Auditing & Accounting Supervisory Authority). If an audit firm gets a disproportionate amount of fees from one client, e.g. from non-audit work such as taxation advice, consultancy services, etc., this could jeopardise their independence.

Reporting of the Audit Committee

The audit committee reports in the first instance to the board. A separate section of the company's annual report should describe the work of the committee in discharging its responsibilities.[9] This is important in ensuring that shareholders understand the role and value of the work that the audit committee is performing. According to the *UK Corporate Governance Code*:

> "The terms of reference of the Audit Committee, including its role and the authority delegated to it by the board, should be made available."[10]

Indeed, as well as the audit committee, it would be good practice for the terms of reference of all board committees to be made available on the company's website.

In summary, the audit committee's role is very important. Membership of the audit committee is a key role and responsibility for non-executive directors and should not be treated lightly. Non-executive directors should only go on to the audit committee if they have the skills and experience to do so.

The Nomination Committee

The Role of the Nomination Committee

The nomination committee is a board committee whose role is to lead the process for identifying and making recommendations to the board in relation to candidates for board positions and executive management. The committee considers the composition of the board and succession plans, and may also be responsible for evaluating the performance of the board (see **Chapter 10**). Its aim is to improve or maintain directors' effectiveness. This evaluation role can also be performed by the chairman and independent consultants. What is key is that there is "a formal, rigorous and transparent procedure for the appointment of new directors to the board".[11]

The *UK Corporate Governance Code*, which recommends that there should be a nomination committee, envisages that the nomination committee should:

---

[9] *UK Corporate Governance Code* (April 2016) C.3.8.
[10] *Ibid.*, C.3.3.
[11] *Ibid.*, B.2.

- "lead the process for board appointments and make recommendations to the board[12];
- "evaluate the balance of skills, experience, independence and knowledge on the board and ... prepare a description of the role and capabilities required for a particular appointment."[13]

It is the responsibility of the nomination committee to ensure that the directors have the right skills and experience to lead and support the company as it goes forward. In recruiting appropriate directors, the nomination committee considers the skills currently around the boardroom table and the skills that may be needed to support the strategic direction of the company. The *UK Corporate Governance Code* provides the following advice:

> "The search for board candidates should be conducted, and appointments made, on merit, against objective criteria and with due regard for the benefits of diversity on the board, including gender."[14]

When considering a candidate, the nomination committee should consider:
- What skills and experience are required to support the future direction of the company?
- How will they complement the skills and experience of the current board?
- Does the candidate have time to commit to the job?
- What skills need to be replaced or enhanced due to the board's rotation policy?

A board will generally have in its Code of Governance its policy on rotation and renewal of directors. This would normally stipulate that directors can only serve a single maximum term; six to nine years would be normal. The *UK Corporate Governance Code* states in relation to the nomination committee that:

> "Non-executive directors should be appointed for specified terms subject to re-election and to statutory provisions relating to the removal of a director. Any term beyond six years for a non-executive director should be subject to particularly

---

[12] *UK Corporate Governance Code* (April 2016) B.2.1.
[13] *Ibid.*, B.2.2.
[14] *Ibid.*, B.2.

rigorous review, and should take into account the need for progressive refreshing of the board.[15]

The nomination committee may use external search consultancies and advertising to assist in the search for new directors. Accurate selection criteria are essential.

If the director to be recruited is to be an independent non-executive director, the nomination committee should consider whether or not the candidate is truly independent (broadly meaning that the candidate has had no previous business or family relationship with the company).

Membership of the Nomination Committee

The *UK Corporate Governance Code* details the composition of the nomination committee as follows:

> "A majority of members of the nomination committee should be independent non-executive directors. The chairman or an independent non-executive director should chair the committee, but the chairman should not chair the nomination committee when it is dealing with the appointment of a successor to the chairmanship."[16]

The nomination committee must work closely with the board and yet maintain an independent view. Members of the committee need to be clear about the skills that the company requires in the future and have a deep understanding of the company's strategy. In this, they may get push back from other board members who may not have the same vision of what the company needs, for example a new non-executive director who has a thorough knowledge of digital marketing.

Induction of New Members to the Nomination Committee

In addition to its terms of reference, to be effective, new members of a nomination committee should be provided with information on:
- composition of the board, current succession planning and board rotation policy;

---

[15] *Ibid.*, B.2.3.
[16] *Ibid.*, B.2.1.

- evaluations of the current board in order to be able to assess strengths and weaknesses;
- recruitment advisors the company uses and their track record;
- training and development programmes for the current members and the impact they have had;
- current performance or other issues with existing board members;
- shareholder concerns with the composition of the current board.

Reporting of the Nomination Committee

The nomination committee reports in the first instance to the board. The work of the committee should also be set out in the company's annual report to ensure that shareholders understand the role and value of the work that the committee is performing. The *UK Corporate Governance Code* provides guidance on what should be reported:

> "The nomination committee should make available its terms of reference, explaining its role and the authority delegated to it by the board."[17]

Furthermore:

> "A separate section of the annual report should describe the work of the nomination committee, including the process it has used in relation to board appointments. This section should include a description of the board's policy on diversity, including gender, any measurable objectives that it has set for implementing the policy, and progress on achieving the objectives."[18]

The Remuneration Committee

The Role of the Remuneration Committee

The role of the remuneration committee is to ensure that the company has an appropriate remuneration policy to recruit, motivate and retain directors and senior management. The remuneration policy should be in line with the company's strategy and correctly disclosed in the financial statements.

---

[17] *Ibid.*, B.2.1.
[18] *Ibid.*, B.2.4.

In its annex summarising the principal duties of the remuneration committee, the Higgs Report (2003) proposed the following duties for the committee:

"• determine and agree with the board the framework or broad policy for the remuneration of the chief executive, the chairman of the company and such other members of the executive management as it is designated to consider. At a minimum, the committee should have delegated responsibility for setting remuneration for all executive directors, the chairman and, to maintain and assure their independence, the company secretary. The remuneration of non-executive directors should be a matter for the chairman and executive members of the board. No director or manager should be involved in any decisions as to their own remuneration;
- determine targets for any performance-related pay schemes operated by the company;
- determine the policy for and scope of pension arrangements for each executive director;
- ensure that contractual terms on termination, and any payments made, are fair to the individual and the company, that failure is not rewarded and that the duty to mitigate loss is fully recognised;
- within the terms of the agreed policy, determine the total individual remuneration package of each executive director including, where appropriate, bonuses, incentive payments and share options;
- in determining such packages and arrangements, give due regard to the comments and recommendations of the Code …;
- be aware of and advise on any major changes in employee benefit structures throughout the company or group;
- agree the policy for authorising claims for expenses from the chief executive and chairman;
- ensure proper disclosure of remuneration; and
- control use of remuneration consultants."[19]

When recommending a remuneration package, the committee should consider the scope of the role, the size of the business and the business sector. Sector is significant, as similar roles may pay better in some sectors than others, e.g. a profit-orientated business compared to mission-based companies. Independent remuneration consultants may provide comparable market data, although this can also have the effect

---

[19] Derek Higgs, *Review of the role and effectiveness of non-executive directors* (January 2003), Annex E. Available at www.ecgi.org/codes/documents/higgsreport.pdf

of ratcheting up salaries as companies chase the median. (**Chapter 16** looks at director and executive remuneration in detail.)

Again, the *UK Corporate Governance Code* offers some good advice in developing a remuneration policy:

> "There should be a formal and transparent procedure for developing policy on executive remuneration and for fixing the remuneration packages of individual directors. No director should be involved in deciding his or her own remuneration."[20]

The remuneration committee has:

> "Delegated responsibility for setting remuneration for all executive directors and the chairman, including pension rights and any compensation payments. The committee should also recommend and monitor the level and structure of remuneration for senior management. The definition of 'senior management' for this purpose should be determined by the board but should normally include the first layer of management below board level."[21]

Even in a small company, the process relating to remuneration should be formalised as this is a sensitive area, indeed often one of contention, as the board and the executive may contain a mixture of shareholders and non-shareholders.

Where consultants are used, such consultants should be engaged on terms agreed directly by the remuneration committee.

In CLGs and PLCs the remuneration of the directors should be determined in general meeting, unless the constitution of the company states otherwise.[22] The chair of the board should ensure that the chair of the remuneration committee communicates as required with its principal shareholders about remuneration. It is critical that there is a process that is agreed by the board and communicated to all who need to know, e.g. the CEO and other senior executives. It is even more important that the process is followed.

Membership of the Remuneration Committee

Membership of this committee should, if possible, be confined to the independent non-executive directors. In its provisions on remuneration,

---

[20] *UK Corporate Governance Code* (April 2016) D.2.
[21] *Ibid.*, D.2.2. The execution of this delegated responsibility will be subject to the requirements of section 291(2) CA 2014, which requires a resolution of the members to compensate a director for his or her loss of office.
[22] Sections 1092 and 1197 CA 2014.

the *UK Corporate Governance Code* details the composition of the remuneration committee as follows:[23]

> "The board should establish a remuneration committee of at least three, or in the case of a smaller company, two, independent non-executive directors. In addition the company chairman may also be a member of, but not chair, the committee if he or she was considered independent on appointment as chairman."

The role of chairman of the remuneration committee can be a difficult one. Clearly, he or she needs to ensure that there are no conflicts of interest with the executive management team, while remaining diplomatic, i.e there is no past or current relationship which may impair judgement. The committee chairman must balance the expectations of the directors and senior management against the demands of shareholders and the realities of the market for talent. Toughness, independence and the ability to listen are key attributes.

Induction of New Members to the Remuneration Committee

In addition to its terms of reference, a new member of the remuneration committee should receive information on:
- the company's legal and tax environment;
- the market and the industry;
- current issues, including any shareholder concerns;
- the company's remuneration consultants.

It is recommended here that a new member of the remuneration committee should have:
- copies of committee meeting minutes for the last five years;
- all contracts and side letters for those within the scope of the committee;
- history of pay in the company for the last five years;
- Investment Association recommendations (see **Chapter 16**);
- reports of the remuneration consultants;
- details of who appointed the consultants.

It is vital that members are properly informed and that their knowledge base is kept up to date by formal and informal training.

---

[23] *UK Corporate Governance Code* (April 2016) D.2.1.

Reporting of the Remuneration Committee

The remuneration committee reports in the first instance to the board. Furthermore,

> "The remuneration committee should make available its terms of reference, explaining its role and the authority delegated to it by the board. Where remuneration consultants are appointed, they should be identified in the annual report and a statement made as to whether they have any other connection with the company."[24]

In addition, the Companies Act 2014 requires detailed disclosure and reporting of directors' remuneration and benefits[25] and the members of the remuneration committee should ensure that the disclosures are accurate.

Conclusion

In most companies over a certain size there will be a committee structure to help the directors on the board to carry out their functions more effectively. Directors must ensure that these committees adhere to their terms of reference and deliver value to the company. All directors on the board, however, must be aware that they cannot delegate responsibility. Therefore, each director must approve of the work and give due consideration to committee recommendations. It is important that the board's committee structure and committees' terms of reference are reviewed regularly.

10 KEY POINTS: BOARD COMMITTEES

1. A board committee is a committee set up by the board to work on and report on a specific topic or issue, to enable it to be dealt with in greater depth.
2. The three most common committees, and those strongly recommended by corporate governance codes, are the audit, nomination and remuneration committees.

---

[24] *UK Corporate Governance Code* (April 2016), D.2.1.
[25] Sections 305–311 CA 2014.

3. The terms of reference of a committee should be approved by the board and reviewed regularly.
4. A director should ensure that he or she has the necessary time, skills, experience, and is prepared to put in the extra effort to fulfil committee roles.
5. The requirement for a committee and the size of that committee depends on the type and size of the company and its stage of development.
6. The board can delegate work or tasks to a committee but cannot delegate responsibility. The board remains responsible for the decisions taken.
7. The responsibilities of the audit committee are to monitor the:
    - financial reporting process and the integrity of the financial statements;
    - effectiveness of the company's systems of internal financial control, internal audit and risk management (unless there is a separate risk committee);
    - conduct of the statutory audit of the company's statutory financial statements;
    - appointment, reappointment and removal of the statutory auditors; and
    - independence of the statutory auditors and the provision of additional services to the company.
8. At least one member of the audit committee should have "competence in accounting or auditing".
9. The nomination committee should lead the process for board and senior management appointments and make recommendations to the board on potential candidates. It should also evaluate the balance of skills, experience and independence required on the board in the recruitment process.
10. The remuneration committee is responsible for developing policy on executive remuneration. Even in a small company the processes relating to remuneration should be formalised, as this is a sensitive area.

12.
General Meetings, Resolutions and Registers

- Introduction
- Meetings of Members
- Resolutions
- Registers and Letterheads
- Conclusion
- Key Points

Introduction

A meeting of the members of a company is termed a 'general meeting'. The members of the company are the owners of a company. Therefore, in a company with shares the members are the shareholders. 'Members' is simply a broader term than shareholders and includes companies in which there are no shares, for example a company limited by guarantee (CLG).

The board is accountable to the members in general meeting. It is a fundamental principle of corporate governance that the directors, having been elected by the members to run the company, must report to the members annually.

As we have seen, the directors are required to act in accordance with the Companies Act, the constitution of the company and resolutions of the members in general meeting. These resolutions are instructions to the directors. In addition, all directors must understand what they as a board can approve and what matters must be approved by the members in general meeting. There are certain decisions that the directors of a company are not allowed to take, for example the reduction of share capital.

This chapter discusses general meetings of members and the processes involved. It also sets out the registers and other information that directors must make available to members and the public.

Meetings of the Members

General meetings are meetings of the members of a company. The annual general meeting (AGM) involves certain specific resolutions that need to be passed concerning, for example, the approval of its financial statements. The AGM is when the directors account to the shareholders. All other meetings are called extraordinary general meetings (EGMs). Both AGMs and EGMs can be described as general meetings, as they are a general meeting of members of the company. At either AGMs or EGMs, decisions taken by the shareholders are in the form of resolutions.

Annual General Meetings

The AGM is the main forum for the assessment by shareholders of the performance of the company and, in particular, the directors. The Companies Act 2014 sets out legal requirements for the holding of an

AGM and directors need to ensure that the AGM is run accordingly. It is important that all legal requirements are met and that decisions cannot be queried or challenged later.

A company must hold its first AGM within 18 months of incorporation and subsequently not more than 15 months should elapse between meetings.[1] A private company limited by shares (LTD) with only one shareholder does not have to call an AGM as it can deal with issues such as the approval of accounts, removal of a director or an auditor by written resolution.[2]

The agenda of an AGM should include:
- consideration of the company's statutory financial statements and the directors' report and, unless the company has availed itself of an audit exemption, the report of the statutory auditors on those statements and report;
- review by the members of the company's affairs;
- appointment of the statutory auditors, unless the company has availed itself of an audit exemption (see **Chapter 14**).[3]

In addition, and unless the company's constitution states otherwise, the AGM should also cover:
- declaration of a dividend (if any) of an amount not exceeding the amount recommended by the directors;
- authorisation of the directors to approve the remuneration of the statutory auditors;
- election and re-election of directors; and
- remuneration of the directors.

If an AGM is overdue, a member of the company can ask the Director of Corporate Enforcement to call or direct the calling of a meeting.[4]

At an AGM, the directors of the company lay before the shareholders the statutory financial statements and other reports. The shareholders consider them, but do not have to approve them. In order to approve the accounts the shareholders may ask for more information and hopefully at that stage they can be approved.

---

[1] Section 175(1) CA 2014.
[2] Section 196 CA 2014. (Note: this does not apply exclusively to single-member companies – see section 175(3) CA 2014.)
[3] Section 186 CA 2014.
[4] Section 175(5) CA 2014.

Shareholders can also exercise their power in not reappointing directors up for re-election or, if allowed by the company's constitution, in not approving the remuneration of the directors. Similarly, they can choose to change the company's auditors.

The shareholders should be allowed sufficient time before the AGM to consider the performance of the directors. Therefore, the statutory financial statements, together with the directors' report and the auditor's report (see **Chapter 13**), should be sent to all shareholders and debenture holders 21 days before the AGM.[5] These parties can otherwise demand a copy of the financial statements and it is potentially an offence on the part of the company and its officers not to supply same.

Annual General Meeting of a LTD Company A LTD is an exception in that it is not required to hold an AGM in any year where all the members entitled to attend and vote at the AGM sign, before the latest date for the holding of that meeting, a written resolution:
- acknowledging receipt of the financial statements that would have been laid before that meeting;
- resolving all such matters as would have been resolved at that meeting;
- confirming no change is proposed in the appointment of the statutory auditor.[6]

This is a welcome innovation of the Companies Act 2014, reducing the administration burdens of the simplest form of company. It recognises the reality that many LTDs are director/shareholder companies, i.e. the directors are also the shareholders.

Extraordinary General Meetings

A meeting of members other than an AGM is an extraordinary general meeting (EGM). Most issues can be dealt with at an AGM. However, there are certain issues that may need to be addressed urgently, and actions taken, that cannot wait for the convening of the AGM. In this case, an additional meeting is called, an EGM.

Examples of reasons to hold an EGM include:
- approving the appointment of a liquidator;
- initiation of a creditors' voluntary winding up of the company (see **Chapter 18**);

---

[5] Section 181(1) CA 2014.
[6] Section 175(3) CA 2014.

- amending the authorised share capital of the company;
- removal of a director;
- removal of the auditor.

An EGM can be convened by the directors of a company whenever they see fit[7] or if they are requisitioned by 10% of voting members of the company.[8] Members with not less than 50% of the paid-up voting share capital[9] can also convene a general meeting. In the case of a PLC, a member or members may request that the directors convene an EGM if they hold at least 5% of the paid-up share capital.[10]

Notice of General Meetings

Unless the constitution of a company determines otherwise, 21 days' notice must be given for an annual general meeting or an extraordinary general meeting where a special resolution (see below) is to be passed. Any other general meeting, e.g. one prompted by a particular event, members must be given at least seven days' notice[11] or, in the case of a PLC, 14 days' notice.[12] Shorter notice can be given if agreed by all members and the auditors.[13]

Notice must be sent to every member, the representatives of deceased members and the assignee in bankruptcy of bankrupt members.[14] *Note:* every member, whether voting or non-voting, should receive notice, regardless of what is stated in the company's constitution. Similarly, formal notice of the meeting should be given to all directors of the company and the Company Secretary. Notice should also be sent to the auditors, unless the company is availing of an audit exemption (see **Chapter 14**).[15]

Notice of a general meeting should state:
- its place, date and time;
- the purpose of the meeting;
- details of any special resolutions to be passed;
- details about the use of proxies (see below).[16]

---

[7] Section 177(2) CA 2014.
[8] Section 178(3) CA 2014.
[9] Section 178(2) CA 2014.
[10] Section 1101 CA 2014.
[11] Section 181 CA 2014.
[12] Section 1098 CA 2014.
[13] Section 181(2) CA 2014.
[14] Section 180 CA 2014.
[15] Section 180(6) CA 2014.
[16] Section 181(5) CA 2014.

12. GENERAL MEETINGS, RESOLUTIONS AND REGISTERS

If a shareholder intends tabling a resolution to remove a director[17] or the incumbent auditors,[18] they must give the company extended notice of 28 days.

If a company's constitution permits, notice of meetings may be served on shareholders electronically.[19]

The required notice periods must be strictly observed.

Quorum and Attendance

A general meeting cannot proceed unless a quorum is present. Unless the company's constitution provides otherwise, two members of a company present in person or by proxy shall be a quorum; in the case of a single-member company, one member shall be considered a quorum.[20] If the quorum is not present within 15 minutes of the commencement of the meeting, the chairman must adjourn the meeting.[21]

While general meetings need not be held in the State, if a company holds an annual meeting outside of the State, unless all of the members entitled to attend and vote at such a meeting consent in writing to its being held outside of the State, the company must make arrangements to ensure that members can, by technological means, participate in the meeting without leaving the State.[22]

Proxies

Any member of a company entitled to attend and vote at a meeting of the company shall be entitled to appoint another person (whether a member or not) as his or her proxy to attend and vote instead of him or her.[23]

The chairman of a meeting may require a person claiming to be an authorised person of a corporate shareholder to produce evidence of the person's authority.[24]

A proxy is a person who may attend and vote at a general meeting to exercise the rights of a member. The authority must be given on a proxy

---

[17] Section 146(3) CA 2014.
[18] Section 396(2) CA 2014.
[19] Section 218(4) CA 2014.
[20] Section 182 CA 2014.
[21] Section 185(2) CA 2014
[22] Section 176 CA 2014.
[23] Section 183 CA 2014.
[24] Section 185(4) CA 2014.

form in writing and deposited at the registered office of the company at least 48 hours before the meeting.

Resolutions

Resolutions are instructions of the company's members to the directors.

Ordinary Resolutions

Most resolutions simply require a majority of votes. An ordinary resolution is "a resolution passed by a simple majority of the votes cast by members of a company".[25] Examples of ordinary resolutions include a resolution to vary the share capital of a company, i.e. to consolidate or divide the nominal value of the shares,[26] declare dividends[27] or increase or reduce the number of directors.[28]

Special Resolutions

For the protection of minority shareholders (members) and on more controversial issues, such as changing the constitution of the company, a greater majority of votes is needed. Special resolutions must be passed by at least 75% of the votes cast by shareholders/members. When a decision may have a significant effect on other members, a higher majority consensus may be required. For example, a special resolution is required for all types of company to commence a members' voluntary winding up[29] or a reduction of share capital.[30]

Certain resolutions must be filed with the Registrar of Companies within 15 days of the general meeting at which they were passed, e.g. special resolutions altering the share capital.[31]

In certain cases and decisions, a unanimous decision by shareholders in favour is required, e.g. the merger of two companies.[32]

---

[25] Section 191 CA 2014.
[26] Section 83 CA 2014.
[27] Section 124(2) CA 2014.
[28] Section 144(3) CA 2014.
[29] Section 200(1)(g) CA 2014.
[30] Section 200(1)(b) CA 2014.
[31] Section 198 CA 2014.
[32] Section 202(1)(a) CA 2014.

Written Resolutions

The options for companies to use written resolutions are useful to avoid the need for a general meeting to be held and not all members need to be in one place at one time. Thus, they can simplify the administration of a company.

Unanimous Written Resolutions

Section 193 of the Companies Act 2014 provides that:

> "A resolution in writing signed by all the members of a company shall be as valid and effective for all purposes as if the resolution had been passed at a general meeting of the company duly convened and held."[33]

The resolution is taken as passed on the date that the last member signed the resolution and all members must be notified of the passing of the resolution within 21 days. It cannot be used for the removal of a director or auditor, or for the acquisition by a company of its own shares.

If the members of a company decide that they do not wish to use unanimous written resolutions, they can preclude them by stating so in the company's constitution. For the LTD type of company, however, the use of unanimous written resolutions cannot be precluded in this way.

For a single-member company, a resolution may be taken by a decision in writing that is notified to the company.[34]

Majority Written Resolutions

Majority written resolutions can be used by LTDs and also by DACs, though, as with unanimous written resolutions, a DAC can choose to state in its constitution if it does not wish to avail of the use of majority written decisions. The use of majority written resolutions does not extend to CLGs[35] or PLCs.[36]

A resolution in writing may be an ordinary or special resolution if signed by the requisite majority of members of the company and delivered

---

[33] Section 193 CA 2014.
[34] Section 196 CA 2014.
[35] Section 1173 CA 2014.
[36] Section 1002 CA 2014.

to the company.[37] (As we have seen, an ordinary resolution requires a simple majority voting in favour to pass the resolution, whereas a special resolution requires a minimum of 75% voting in favour to pass it.) A resolution in writing is as effective for all purposes as if the resolution had been passed at a general meeting of the company duly convened and held.

Unlike unanimous decisions, there is a mandatory delay, unless waived by the members, for majority written decisions to come into effect. The delay is seven days for ordinary resolutions and 21 days for special resolutions after the last member has signed it in both cases.

Rights of Members

Directors should be aware of the rights of members, e.g. the right to serve notice to remedy a default, which might be exercised if the company is not complying with the Companies Act.[38] Members have the right to seek an investigation into the affairs of the company, e.g. if they are concerned about illegal or fraudulent activity.[39] In addition, members have the right to petition for the winding-up of the company.[40]

An important right of shareholders/members is the right to petition for relief in cases of oppression.[41] This right may be used if a member-director is excluded from management or if a member believes there are fraudulent or unlawful transactions (see **Chapter 4**).

Registers and Letterheads

Documents Available for Inspection

The performance of the directors and of the company is a matter of public record. The company must submit to the Registrar of Companies its annual return and financial statements.[42]

---

[37] Section 194 CA 2014.
[38] Section 797 CA 2014.
[39] Section 747 CA 2014.
[40] Section 571 CA 2014.
[41] Section 212 CA 2014.
[42] Section 348 CA 2014.

Certain documents and statutory registers must be kept by the company and made available for free to members, or other persons (only certain specific documents) on payment of the relevant fee,[43] including:
- copies of directors' service contracts[44];
- copies of instruments creating charges[45];
- a register of directors and secretaries, including their residential address and nationality (the address of a director or Company Secretary need not appear on the register if it is determined that their safety or security may be at risk)[46];
- a disclosable interests register showing where directors have a shareholding in the company (see **Chapter 5**)[47];
- a members' register[48]; and
- minutes of general meetings.[49]

Additionally, a member may request the minutes of general meetings of the company.[50]

Letterheads

On all business letters, order forms, invoices, website, etc. on which the company name appears, a company must show:
- the name and legal form of the company;
- its registration number and the address where it is registered; and
- the name, surname and nationality of all directors, including any former forenames or surnames.[51]

Conclusion

The members of a company meet to assess the performance of the company and to give instructions to the directors via resolutions. It is up to the directors to ensure that general meetings are run in accordance with the legal requirements set out in the Companies Act 2014.

---

[43] Section 216 CA 2014.
[44] Section 154 CA 2014.
[45] Section 418 CA 2014.
[46] Sections 149 and 150(11) and (12) CA 2014.
[47] Section 267 CA 2014.
[48] Section 169 CA 2014.
[49] Section 199 CA 2014.
[50] Section 216(9) and (11) CA 2014.
[51] Section 151 CA 2014.

Once a decision is taken by resolution in general meeting, it is for the directors to carry out those decisions. The directors must also be aware of the rights of members and of information that must be made available to members and the public.

10 Key Points: Meetings

1. All companies with more than one member must hold an annual general meeting (AGM) in person, except for a private company limited by shares (LTD).
2. A LTD need not hold an AGM in any year where all the members entitled to attend and vote at such general meeting sign a written resolution to that effect.
3. The AGM should cover: consideration of the company's statutory financial statements; the report of the directors and, if appropriate, the report of the statutory auditors; a review by the members of the company's affairs; and the appointment of the auditors.
4. A general meeting that is not the AGM is an extraordinary general meeting (EGM).
5. A resolution is a decision by the shareholders/members. An ordinary resolution is "a resolution passed by a simple majority of the votes cast by members of a company". A special resolution must be passed by 75% of the votes cast.
6. A resolution in writing signed by all the members of a company shall be as valid and effective for all purposes as if the resolution had been passed at a general meeting of the company. While unanimous written resolutions are valid for all types of company, for the LTD type of company the use of unanimous written resolutions cannot be precluded.
7. The required notice of an AGM or an EGM at which a special resolution is to be passed is 21 days. Otherwise, a general meeting can be called with seven days' notice. Extended notice of 28 days is required for general meetings to remove a director or to change the statutory auditors.
8. Unless the company's constitution provides otherwise, two members of a company present in person or by proxy shall be a quorum (except where the company has only one member).

12. GENERAL MEETINGS, RESOLUTIONS AND REGISTERS

9. General meetings can be held outside of Ireland, provided that technology means allow those members in the State to participate.
10. Certain company documents and registers must be available for inspection by the members. Letterheads and the website bearing the company name must show the directors' names, type of company, the company registration number and address of the company.

Part III

PRACTICAL ISSUES FOR DIRECTORS

No practical guide to being an effective company director can be complete without discussing directors' responsibilities for financial management and related matters.

By law, each and every director is responsible for the company's financial statements. The vast majority of directors are not accountants, so it is strongly advised that directors have adequate training, formal or informal, so that they understand the company's financial position on an ongoing basis.

It is a reality that companies, non-profit and public-sector entities are largely judged on their 'financials'. A director must be able to ask and understand the responses to questions such as:
- Is the company solvent?
- Is it profitable?
- Does it have adequate cash flow?
- Have margins decreased?
- What funds were received and how were they used?
- Did the business perform within its budget?

It is therefore fundamental that a director should have a reasonable understanding of financial statements.

Many companies employ people who in law have employment rights, including the right to a safe workplace. It is important that directors have a reasonable understanding of the key requirements of employment and health & safety law, and know when they need to ask for specialist advice.

The directors are ultimately responsible for the health and safety of the company's employees and it is recommended that this is on the agenda of every board meeting. Bullying, harassment and victimisation can cost a company time and stress. It is up to the directors to have the appropriate policies in place to prevent these issues arising and to address them if they do.

Director and executive remuneration is also an important area of which to be aware. The approach to executive compensation is an important corporate governance issue. To curb excessive risk-taking, the board should focus on transparency, accountability and fairness and look to the long-term success of the company.

In this Part III, therefore, we will look at directors' responsibilities regarding:

13. Financial Matters
14. Statutory Audit and Internal Audit
15. Employer Responsibilities
16. Directors' Remuneration.

13.
Financial Matters

- Introduction
- Statutory Accounting Requirements
- Directors' Duties with regard to Financial Matters
- Directors' Duties to Keep Adequate Accounting Records
- A Company's Accounts
- Management Accounts
- Statutory Financial Statements
- The Importance of 'True and Fair View'
- Further Requirements for Statutory Financial Statements
- Directors' Approval of the Statutory Financial Statements
- Obligation to have Statutory Financial Statements Audited
- Specific Considerations for Transactions involving Directors for Statutory Financial Statements
- Conclusion
- Key Points

Introduction

One of the key responsibilities of a non-executive director (NED) is that they must satisfy themselves as to the risk management processes and procedures of the company, with particular emphasis on risk when it comes to financial controls and the reporting of financial performance. Therefore, it is vital that all directors have strong and up-to-date knowledge of financial and accounting matters to discharge these responsibilities fully.

This chapter outlines important financial responsibilities of directors, including NEDs, e.g. ensuring that accounting records are properly maintained and that the annual statutory financial statements are correctly prepared.

It is important to note that these are areas in which all directors must be well informed. These are matters that cannot be the sole responsibility of the finance director as responsibility for the maintenance of a high standard of books and records rests equally with all directors. All directors should undertake regular professional development training in these areas of finance if they are not comfortable with their responsibilities and duties.

Statutory Accounting Requirements

As a company director, there is a myriad of requirements to be familiar with when it comes to accounting matters. These accounting and reporting requirements are dictated by the size and scale of the company in terms of its turnover, balance sheet total and employee numbers, as shown in **Table 13.1**.

TABLE 13.1: COMPANY SIZE CRITERIA

Company Size	Turnover does not exceed	Balance sheet total does not exceed[1]	Average no. of employees does not exceed
Micro[2]	€700,000	€350,000	10
Small[3]	€12 million	€6 million	50
Medium[4]	€40 million	€20 million	250

[1] The 'balance sheet' total is the total of a company's non-current assets and current assets (see section 297(4) CA 2014).
[2] Section 280D(3) CA 2014 as amended by section 15 of the Companies (Accounting) Act 2017 (C(A)A 2017).
[3] Section 280A(3) CA 2014 as amended by section 15 C(A)A 2017.
[4] Section 280F(3) CA 2014 as amended by section 15 C(A)A 2017.

As to whether a company is considered 'micro', 'small' or 'medium' will depend on it fulfilling at least two or more of the requirements for each in its first financial year or thereafter for two consecutive financial periods.

If a company does not meet any two of the above criteria, in other words it does not qualify as a micro, small or medium company, then it qualifies as a 'large' company.[5]

Note: these company size criteria apply irrespective of the company **type**, i.e. whether the company is a LTD, DAC, CLG, etc.

Accounting Standards

Accounting standards specify how all business transactions that a company undertakes must be reflected in the books and records of the company. This ensures a standardisation of treatment of all business transactions. There are accounting standards that apply to sales (turnover), purchases, direct and indirect costs, as well as all assets and liabilities, and so forth.

There are three principal accounting standards frameworks that are used by companies in Ireland:
- International Financial Reporting Standards (IFRS);
- FRS 102 *The Financial Reporting Standard applicable in the UK and Republic of Ireland*;
- FRS 105 *The Financial Reporting Standard applicable to the Micro-entities Regime*.

There are very particular rules when it comes to applying these accounting standards to companies.

Public companies, i.e. companies that have a listing on any form of capital market, have no choice; IFRS must be applied. However, private companies have options on what accounting standards to apply, depending on their size as set out above. **Table 13.2** below summarises the requirements and the options.

---

[5] Section 280H C(A)A 2017.

13. FINANCIAL MATTERS

TABLE 13.2: ACCOUNTING STANDARDS TO APPLY

Public or Private Company	Company Size	Mandatory accounting standards	Optional accounting standards	Level of Complexity
Public	Any	IFRS	None	Very High
Private	Large	None	IFRS or FRS 102	High
Private	Medium	None	IFRS or FRS 102	Medium
Private	Small	None	IFRS or FRS 102	Medium
Private	Micro	None	IFRS or FRS 102 or FRS 105	Low

The larger the company, the more complex the accounting standards that must apply. These complexities focus primarily on the accounting and disclosures required for areas that tend to be of a more commercially sensitive nature, including:
- revenue recognition, including a geographical analysis of revenue;
- key components of operating profits;
- directors' remuneration, including shares held, share option entitlements and bonus arrangements;
- transactions with fellow group companies;
- transactions with companies or entities classified as 'related parties';
- disclosure of remuneration for audit, audit-related and non-audit work;
- information on arrangements not included in the balance sheet.

Directors' Duties with regard to Financial Matters

It is the duty of each director of a company to ensure that the company complies with the Companies Act.[6] Furthermore, as 'officers' of the company,[7] directors are considered in default if they are in breach of their duty as an officer of the company or authorise or permit a default to take place.[8] A default includes a refusal to comply with, or a contravention of, a provision of the Companies Act.

---

[6] Section 223 CA 2014.
[7] Section 2(1) CA 2014.
[8] Section 270 CA 2014.

Where a director, in purported compliance with any provision of the Companies Act, answers a question, provides an explanation, makes a statement or completes, signs, produces, lodges or delivers any return, report, certificate, balance sheet or other document that is false in a material particular, and he or she knows that it is false or is reckless, they are in breach of the Act and are guilty of a Category 2 offence.[9]

Where an officer (in this case a director) of a company destroys, mutilates or falsifies, or is privy to the destruction, mutilation or falsification, of any book or document affecting or relating to the property or affairs of the company or makes a false entry in any such document, they are in breach of the Companies Act and are guilty of a Category 2 offence[10].

Where an officer of a company fraudulently parts with, alters or makes an omission in any book or document affecting or relating to the property or affairs of the company or are party to the fraudulent parting with, fraudulent altering or fraudulent making of an omission in any such book or document, they are in breach of the Companies Act and again are guilty of a Category 2 offence.[11]

Directors' Duties to Keep Adequate Accounting Records[12]

Every company is obliged to keep or cause to be kept adequate accounting records. It is a criminal offence for any director of a company to fail to take all reasonable steps to ensure compliance with this requirement.

Adequate accounting records are those that are sufficient to:
- correctly record and explain the transactions of the company;
- enable, at any time, the assets, liabilities, financial position and profit or loss of the company to be determined with reasonable accuracy;
- enable the company's directors to ensure that the statutory financial statements of the company required to be prepared comply with the Companies Act, and the relevant accounting standards;
- enable those statutory financial statements of the company so prepared to be properly audited, if required (see **Chapter 14**).

The accounting records must be kept on a continuous and consistent basis, i.e. the entries made in them must be made in a timely manner and be consistent from one period to the next. If those records are not kept by making entries in a bound book but by other means, adequate

---

[9] Section 876(1) CA 2014.
[10] Section 877 CA 2014.
[11] Section 878 CA 2014.
[12] Section 281 CA 2014.

precautions must be taken for guarding against falsification and facilitating discovery of such falsification, should it occur.[13]

The accounting records kept must contain[14]:
- entries from day to day of all sums of money received and expended by the company and the matters in respect of which the receipts and expenditure takes place;
- a record of the company's assets and liabilities;
- if the company's business involves dealing in goods (i.e. stocks):
  - a record of all goods purchased and sold (except those goods sold for cash by way of ordinary retail trade) showing the goods, sellers and buyers in sufficient detail to enable the goods, sellers and buyers to be identified and a record of all the invoices relating to such purchases and sales; and
  - a statement of stock held by the company at the end of each financial year and all records of stock-takes on which such statements are based;
- where the company's business involves the provision or purchase of services, a record of the services provided or purchased, to whom they were provided or from whom were purchased (unless provided or purchased by way of ordinary retail trade) and all the invoices relating thereto.

The accounting records should be kept at the company's registered office or at such other place as the directors think fit (such as its main place of business if it differs from the company's registered office).[15] Where records are stored outside the State, the directors must ensure that they keep at a place in the State such information as will allow the assets, liabilities, financial position and profit and loss of the company to be reasonably determined.[16]

A Company's 'Accounts'

'Accounts' is a rather loose, colloquial term referring to a broad range of financial information and reporting prepared for different purposes or under different rules. It is important that directors understand and appreciate the specific 'accounts' that companies prepare, which are of two distinct types:
- management accounts; and
- statutory financial statements.

---

[13] Section 282(2) CA 2014.
[14] Section 282(3) CA 2014.
[15] Section 283 CA 2014.
[16] Section 283(2) CA 2014.

Table 13.3 below sets out the significant differences between management accounts and statutory financial statements. In particular, this table highlights the matters that should be of principal concern to NEDs, i.e. those under the Statutory Financial Statements column.

TABLE 13.3: KEY DIFFERENCES BETWEEN MANAGEMENT ACCOUNTS AND STATUTORY FINANCIAL STATEMENTS

	Management Accounts	Statutory Financial Statements
Of importance to a NED	Yes (e.g. at board meetings, to assess how the company is performing)	Yes
Frequency of preparation	Weekly, monthly or quarterly	Annually
For use by	Board and internal management	Shareholders and external stakeholders (such as lenders)
Information used	Current	Historic
Legal requirement to prepare	None	Yes, under the Companies Act
Standard format to be followed	No	Yes
Profit and loss account	Included, in great detail	Yes
Balance sheet	Summary items included	Yes
Cash-flow statement	Summary items included	Yes[17]
Statement of changes in equity	Not required	Required[18]
Comparison of actuals vs budget	Yes	No
Variance analysis	Yes	No
KPIs	Yes	No

[17] Not required for small or micro companies.
[18] Not required for micro companies.

Management Accounts

Management accounting is concerned with providing information to users within the company to assist with effective and efficient management of the business. Management accounting involves applying accounting and financial management principles to the provision of information to the managers of a company to help them plan and control the company's activities and to make business decisions.

Management accounts typically include:
- A comparison of actual versus budgeted performance for the month/week/quarter/year in question and a detailed explanation of the reason for the differences (commonly referred to as 'variances').
- A comparison of actual versus budgeted performance for the year to date and a detailed explanation of the variance.
- A comparison of the current week/month/quarter versus the same week/month/quarter last year and a detailed explanation of the variance.
- A comparison of the year-to-date performance versus the same period in the previous year and a detailed explanation of the variance.

Key Performance Indicators (KPIs) Typically, companies will incorporate another business measurement performance tool as part of their management accounts. Known as key performance indicators ('KPIs'), these measure how effectively a company is achieving its performance objectives.

KPIs are effective at highlighting key issues succinctly and usually consist of figures and ratios that show the performance of the company.

Typical KPIs include unit cost of production against budget, the liquidity ratio, average debtor days outstanding, sales per employee, profit per employee, product profit margin, capacity usage of a machine, staff turnover, number of workplace accidents, etc.

The KPIs used will depend on the nature of the business and should be aligned with the annual business plan and strategic plan. Directors must understand how KPIs are calculated to understand any limitations or assumptions they need to be aware of in interpreting them.

Statutory Financial Statements

A company's statutory financial statements serve a different purpose to its management accounts. One of their principal purposes is to fulfill a compliance requirement of the Companies Act, which provides that the directors of a company are required to prepare financial statements in respect of each financial year.[19] The annual statutory financial statements are prepared from the information contained in the company's accounting records and other relevant information.

Statutory financial statements set out the financial performance and position of the company for and at the end of the most recent financial year, typically in **four 'primary statements'**:
- a 'profit and loss account', which is a statement of performance of the company showing revenue, expenses, gains earned and losses incurred by the company during a certain period;
- a 'balance sheet', which is a statement of the company's assets, liabilities and financial position at its financial year end;
- a 'cash-flow statement' showing how the cash generated by the company during the year was utilised, spent, or reinvested;
- a 'statement of changes in equity', which is a table disclosing movements in the various capital components of the company during the previous year, e.g. any new shares issued or any share premium received on shares issued.[20]

The Importance of 'True and Fair View'

This is an important concept in the preparation of statutory financial statements and one that any NED needs to understand. The statutory financial statements of the company must faithfully represent the financial performance of the company for the year and the financial position (in terms of assets and liabilities) of the company at its (chosen) year end. These statutory financial statements must also be free from any material error, omission or misstatement.

In order for a set of financial statements to give a 'true and fair view', they must:
- be prepared using accounting policies that are appropriate in the circumstances of the company;
- incorporate explicit disclosures on judgements used throughout the statutory financial statements (see the section on 'Notes to the Financial Statements' below);

---

[19] Sections 290 to 295 CA 2014, as amended.
[20] Not all companies are required to present these four financial statements. For example, companies reporting under the small and micro regimes are exempt from preparing a cash-flow statement.

- be prudent in the consideration of matters of judgement in the financial statements, especially where there is uncertainty; and
- ensure that the financial statements reflect the commercial substance of transactions, and not just their legal form.

The directors must not approve the financial statements of a company unless they are satisfied they give a 'true and fair view' of the assets, liabilities and financial position as at the financial year end and profit or loss for the financial year.[21]

Further Requirements for Statutory Financial Statements

As noted above, the directors of a company are required to prepare statutory financial statements in respect of each financial year. They are referred to as 'statutory' financial statements as their preparation, format and contents must comply with the following:
- the Companies Act 2014, as amended;
- a relevant financial reporting framework (i.e. accounting standards).

(Sample formats for the four primary financial statements as set out by CA 2014 are included as appendices to this chapter.)

The Companies Act 2014 sets out the format of the balance sheet and the profit and loss account, as well as the requirement to include the following in the statutory financial statements.

Accounting Policies

A company is required to disclose[22] in the notes to the financial statements (see below) the accounting policies adopted by the company in determining the items and amounts to be included in its profit and loss account and its balance sheet.

Notes to the Financial Statements

The 'notes to the financial statements' contain more detailed information relating to figures appearing in the profit and loss account, balance sheet, cash-flow statement, or statement of changes in equity, e.g. analysis of fixed assets and depreciation, analysis of the creditors' figure, etc.

---

[21] Section 289(1) CA 2014.
[22] Section 321 CA 2014.

Directors' Report

The directors of a company (for companies of all types and sizes) are obliged to prepare a report each financial year for the members, though the extent of the content and commentary of the directors' report will depend on the size of the company.[23] The directors' report must be approved by the board of directors and signed on behalf of the board by two directors, or if there is only a single director, by that director. The report should deal with general matters of the company, a business review, information on the acquisition or disposal of shares, and relevant audit information. The directors' report is required to address certain matters, namely:

- **Directors' report: general matters**, which include[24]:
    - the names of the directors during the financial year, the principal activities of the company, a statement in relation to compliance with keeping of accounting records and the exact location of those records and amounts paid, if any, as interim or final dividend;
    - particulars of any important event affecting the company since the financial year end, activities if any in the field of research and development, an indication of the existence of branches outside the state and disclosure of any political donations;
    - description of the use of financial instruments by the company and, in particular, financial risk management objectives and policies, including the policy of hedging forecasted transactions and exposure of the company to price risk, credit risk, liquidity risk and cash-flow risk.
- **Directors' report: business review**[25]:
    - the directors' report will contain a fair review of the business of the company, and a description of the principal risks and uncertainties facing the company;
    - the review should be a balanced and comprehensive analysis of the performance of the business and the assets and liabilities and financial position of the company at the end of the financial year, consistent with the size and complexity of the business.
- **Directors' report: interests in shares and debentures**[26]:
    - the report should list shares and debentures held by the directors any interests in share options and any acquisition or disposal by directors of their shares or debentures during the year.

---

[23] Section 325 CA 2014.
[24] Section 326 CA 2014.
[25] Section 327 CA 2014.
[26] Section 329 CA 2014.

- **Directors' statement on relevant audit information**[27]:
  - the directors' report will contain a statement to the effect that as far as the directors are aware, there is no relevant audit information of which the company's statutory auditors are unaware; and
  - the directors have taken all the necessary steps to ensure that the company's statutory auditor is aware of any relevant audit information of the company.

Directors' Responsibility Statement

The directors are responsible for preparing the statutory financial statements in accordance with CA 2014 and accounting standards. It is best practice that a statement to this effect be included in the statutory financial statements. An example of a directors' responsibility statement is set out below:

> "The directors are responsible for preparing the directors' report and the statutory financial statements in accordance with applicable Irish law and generally accepted accounting practice in Ireland, including the accounting standards issued by the Financial Reporting Council. Irish company law requires the directors to prepare statutory financial statements for each financial year.
>
> Under company law, the directors shall not approve financial statements unless they are satisfied that they give a true and fair view of the assets, liabilities and financial position, as at the end of the financial year, and profit or loss, for the financial year and otherwise comply with the Companies Act 2014.
>
> In preparing those financial statements, the directors are required to:
> - select suitable accounting policies and then apply them consistently;
> - make judgements and estimates that are reasonable and prudent;
> - state whether the statutory financial statements have been prepared in accordance with applicable accounting standards, identify those standards and note the effect and the reasons for any material departure from those standards;
> - prepare the statutory financial statements on the going concern basis, unless it is inappropriate to presume that the company will continue in business.

---

[27] Section 330 CA 2014.

The directors are responsible for ensuring that the company keeps or causes to be kept adequate accounting records that correctly explain and record the transactions of the company, enable at any time the assets, liabilities, financial position and profit or loss of the company to be determined with reasonable accuracy and enable them to ensure that the statutory financial statements and directors' report comply with the Companies Act 2014.

They are also responsible for safeguarding the assets of the company and hence for taking reasonable steps for the prevention and detection of fraud and other irregularities."

Directors' Compliance Statement

For all public companies, as well as companies that have an annual turnover in excess of €25 million and total assets in excess of €12.5 million,[28] CA 2014 introduced a new obligation on company directors to include a 'Directors' Compliance Statement' as part of the company's annual statutory financial statement disclosures in the Directors' Report.

In simple terms, section 225 CA 2014 sets out three requirements:
1. the drawing up of a statement setting out the company's policies (that, in the directors' opinion, are appropriate to the company) respecting compliance by the company with its relevant obligations;
2. the putting in place of appropriate arrangements or structures that are, in the directors' opinion, designed to secure material compliance with the company's relevant obligations; and
3. the conducting of a review, during the financial year, of any arrangements or structures referred to above that have been put in place.

The 'relevant obligations' referred to encompass all Irish tax legislation and company law, where a breach constitutes a serious offence. (*Note*: there are no new tax or legal requirements introduced by this Directors' Compliance Statement requirement.)

A failure to include a Directors' Compliance Statement or a statement that assurance measures have been undertaken (or explained if not) in the Directors' Report carries a maximum personal fine for each of the directors of €5,000 and/or a maximum prison sentence of six months.

Accordingly, NEDs of companies to which section 225 applies should ensure that they can identify those Irish tax law and company law

---

[28] Section 225 CA 2014. Note: these criteria were not amended by the Companies (Accounting) Act 2017.

obligations that are in scope. They should then review the company's existing compliance processes and procedures, how effectively they are being implemented and monitored, and rectify any failings.

Directors' Approval of the Statutory Financial Statements

The statutory financial statements must be approved by the board of directors and signed on behalf of the board by two directors or, if there is only a single director, by that director.[29]

The signature or signatures evidencing approval of the financial statements by the board should be inserted onto the balance sheet page of the statutory financial statements.[30]

If the statutory financial statements are approved but did not give a true and fair view or otherwise comply with the requirements of the Companies Act, every director of the company who is party to their approval, and who knows that they do not give a true and fair view or otherwise comply, or is reckless as to whether that is so, shall be guilty of a Category 2 offence.[31]

Every director of such a company at the time its statutory financial statements are approved will be a default party to their approval unless they show that they took all reasonable steps to prevent their being approved.[32]

Obligation to have Statutory Financial Statements Audited

The directors of a company are obliged to arrange for the company's statutory financial statements to be audited by a statutory auditor, unless the company is entitled to, and chooses to avail itself of, audit exemption (see **Chapter 14**).[33] A statutory audit is an independent examination of the financial statements by an independent professional (an auditor). Having conducted an examination of the financial statements, the auditor is required to report to the members of the company. In that report, the auditor is required to form an opinion on a number of matters, including, for example, whether the financial statements

---

[29] Section 324(1) CA 2014.
[30] Section 324(4) CA 2014.
[31] Section 324(6) CA 2014.
[32] Section 324(7) CA 2014.
[33] Section 333 CA 2014.

give a true and fair view[34] and whether the financial statements are in agreement with the underlying accounting records. (This is discussed in more detail in **Chapter 14**.)

Specific Considerations for Transactions involving Directors for Statutory Financial Statements

As discussed in more detail in **Chapter 5**, there are two areas that require considerable attention by all company directors:
- substantial non-cash transactions involving directors;
- loans to directors and connected persons.

From a statutory financial statements perspective, all directors must be aware that:
- the Companies Act 2014 requires explicit disclosure of transactions with directors (executive and non-executive) in the annual statutory financial statements;
- breaches of the relevant sections of the Companies Act are reportable by the company's auditors to the Office of the Director of Corporate Enforcement (see also **Chapter 14**);
- there are potential tax issues and consequences for both the company and the director(s) involved (discussion of which are beyond the scope of this guide).

Taxation

It is essential that all directors satisfy themselves that the company is tax compliant, particularly given the need to make a statement to that effect as part of the 'Directors' Compliance Statement' referred to above.

Companies pay corporation tax. Corporation tax is charged on all profits (income and gains), wherever arising, of companies resident in Ireland (with some exceptions) and non-resident companies who trade in Ireland through a branch or agency.

Corporation tax is charged on the company's taxable profits, which include both income and chargeable gains. A company's income for tax purposes is calculated in accordance with the income tax rules. Chargeable gains are calculated in accordance with the capital gains tax rules.

---

[34] Section 336(3) CA 2014.

There are two rates of corporation tax:
- 12.5% for trading income (unless the income is from an 'excepted trade', in which case the rate is 25%);
- 25% for non-trading income (e.g. investment income, rental income).

'Excepted trades' include certain land-dealing activities, income from working minerals and petroleum activities.

Close Companies

Most Irish resident companies are 'close' companies. A close company is a company that is controlled by five or fewer participators, or is controlled by any number of participators who are directors. The definition of a close company includes a company where, on distribution of its full income, more than 50% goes to five or fewer participators or participators who are directors. A 'participator' is a person having an interest in the income or capital of the company.

The close company provisions set out in the Taxes Consolidation Act 1997 have four main implications for a company and its participators/directors:
- certain benefits-in-kind and expense payments to participators or associates will be treated as distributions;
- interest in excess of a specified rate paid to directors or their associates will be treated as distributions;
- loans to participators or their associates must be made under deduction of tax and, if the loan is forgiven, the grossed-up amount is treated as income in the hands of the recipient;
- a surcharge of 20% is payable on the total undistributed investment and rental income of a close company. Close 'service' companies are also liable to a surcharge of 15% on one-half of their undistributed trading income.

Conclusion

Under company law, there is no distinction between an executive and a non-executive director. Consequently, NEDs must have a strong and up-to-date knowledge of financial and accounting matters to fully discharge their responsibilities in these areas. It is important for each director to have a reasonable financial knowledge of a company's affairs to do their job. This responsibility cannot be delegated.

In the next chapter, we will look at the requirement for a company to have an external, statutory audit, the criteria for audit exemption and other areas of importance for directors, such as internal audit.

10 Key Points: Financial Matters

1. It is the responsibility of the company to keep adequate accounting records and these are onerous requirements.
2. A director may be held personally liable if the absence of adequate accounting records contributes to the failure of the company.
3. All directors, and not just the finance director, are responsible for the company's annual statutory financial statements.
4. There are significant differences between the company's statutory financial statements and management accounts.
5. The board is collectively responsible for preparing and approving the statutory financial statements.
6. The Directors' Compliance Statement, required for large companies, includes compliance with all tax and company law.
7. The directors must have the statutory financial statements audited each year, unless the company is eligible to avail of audit exemption.
8. These statutory financial statements must faithfully represent the financial performance and position of the company.
9. Company auditors have extensive third-party reporting obligations.
10. A director should make every effort to understand the taxes to which a company is liable and the tax position of the company, even if he or she is not from a financial background.

Appendix 13.1: Profit and Loss Account – Sample Format

Typical Company Limited
PROFIT AND LOSS ACCOUNT
for the financial year ended 31 December 2017

	Notes	Year ended 31/12/2017 €'000	Year ended 31/12/2016 €'000
Continuing operations			
Revenue		X	X
Cost of sales		X	X
Gross profit		X	X
Distribution expenses		X	X
Administration expenses		X	X
Finance costs		X	X
Share of profits of associates		X	X
Profit before tax		X	X
Income tax expense		X	X
		X	X
Profit for the year		X	X

Appendix 13.2: Balance Sheet – Sample Format

Typical Company Limited
BALANCE SHEET
as at 31 December 2017

	Notes	31/12/2017 €'000	31/12/2016 €'000
Assets			
Non-current assets			
Property, plant and equipment		X	X
Investment property		X	X
Goodwill		X	X
Other intangible assets		X	X
Investments in associates		X	X
Other assets		X	X
Total non-current assets		X	X
Current assets			
Inventories		X	X
Trade and other receivables		X	X
Current tax assets		X	X
Other assets		X	X
Cash and bank balances		X	X
Assets classified as held for sale		X	X
Total current assets		X	X
Total assets		X	X

Equity and liabilities

Capital and reserves

Issued capital	X	X
Reserves	X	X
Retained earnings	X̲	X̲
Amounts recognised directly in equity relating to assets classified as held for sale	X̲	X̲
Equity attributable to owners of the company	X	X
Non-controlling interests	X̲	X̲
Total equity	X̲	X̲

Non-current liabilities

Borrowings		
Other financial liabilities	X	X
Retirement benefit obligation	X	X
Deferred tax liabilities	X	X
Provisions	X	X
Deferred revenue	X	X
Other liabilities	X̲	X̲
Total non-current liabilities	X̲	X̲

Current liabilities

Trade and other payables	X	X
Borrowings	X	X
Other financial liabilities	X	X
Current tax liabilities	X	X
Provisions	X	X
Deferred revenue	X	X
Other liabilities	X̲	X̲
	X	
	X	
Liabilities directly associated with assets classified as held for sale	X̲	X̲
	X	X
Total current liabilities	X̲	X̲
	X	X
Total liabilities	X̲	X̲
	X	X
Total equity and liabilities	X̲	X̲

Appendix 13.3: Cash-flow Statement – Sample Format

Typical Company Limited
CASH-FLOW STATEMENT
for the financial year ended 31 December 2017

	Year ended 31/12/2017 €'000	Year ended 31/12/2016 €'000
Cash flows from operating activities		
Profit for the financial year	X	X
Adjustments for:	X	X
Depreciation of property, plant and equipment	X	X
Amortisation of intangible assets	X	X
Profit on disposal of property, plant and equipment	X	X
Interest paid	X	X
Interest received	X	X
Taxation	X	X
Decrease/(increase) in trade and other receivables	X	X
Decrease/(increase) in inventories	X	X
Increase/(decrease) in trade payables	X	X
Cash from operations		
Interest paid	X	X
Income taxes paid	X	X
Net cash generated from operating activities	X	X
Cash flows from investing activities		
Proceeds from sale of equipment	X	X
Purchases of property, plant and equipment	X	X
Purchases of intangible assets	X	X
Interest received	X	X
Net cash from investing activities	X	X

Cash flows from financing activities

Issue of ordinary share capital	X	X
Repayment of borrowings	X	X
Dividends paid	X	X
Net cash used in financing activities	X̲	X̲
Net increase/(decrease) in cash and cash equivalents	X	X
Cash and cash equivalents at beginning of year	X	X
Cash and cash equivalents at end of year	X	X

Appendix 13.4: Statement of Changes In Equity – Sample Format

Typical Company Limited
STATEMENT OF CHANGES IN EQUITY
for the financial year ended 31 December 2017

	Share Premium €'000	Share Capital €'000	Profit and Loss Account €'000
At 1 January 2017			
Issue of shares	X	X	X
Profit for the financial year	X	X	X
Dividends paid	(X)	(X)	(X)
As at 31 December 2017	X	X	X

14.

The Audit of Statutory Financial Statements and Internal Audit

- Introduction
- Statutory Audits and Auditors
- Appointment of Statutory Auditors
- What do Statutory Auditors Do during the Audit?
- Audit Rotation
- Removal of Auditors
- Resignation of Auditors
- The Rights of Auditors
- The Auditor's Report
- Other Reporting by Statutory Auditors
- Audit Exemption
- Internal Audit
- Conclusion
- Key Points

Introduction

In the previous chapter, we looked at the responsibilities and requirement of directors relating to the statutory financial statements of a company, as well as other responsibilities, such as the responsibility to maintain adequate books and records. In addition to these requirements, the Companies Act 2014, as amended, requires companies over a certain size to have an independent external audit of their financial statements carried out on an annual basis. (Public quoted companies must have their statutory financial statements audited annually by an independent external auditor.)

This chapter looks at these requirements and other related matters when it comes to appointing and retaining auditors. The chapter also considers the reporting obligations of auditors, as well as audit exemption, and when a company can avail of it. Finally, the nature and role of internal audit function is examined and how it relates to and compares with external audit.

Statutory Audits and Auditors

A statutory or external audit (often referred to simply as an 'audit') is an independent examination of a company's statutory financial statements as prepared by the directors of the company.

The purpose of an audit is to enhance the degree of confidence of intended users in the statutory financial statements of a company. These intended users include the company's shareholders, its stakeholders (such as lenders) and the Revenue Commissioners. This is achieved by the expression of an independent opinion by an auditor on whether the financial statements are prepared, in all 'material respects', in accordance with the accounting standards that the company applies (see **Chapter 13**).

An auditor is an independent professional person qualified to audit a company's statutory financial statements. A qualified accountant, or firm of accountants, can act as a company's auditor. They must hold a valid practicing certificate from a recognised accountancy body (RAB), such as Chartered Accountants Ireland.

A 'statutory auditor', under the Companies Act, means an individual or a firm that is approved as a statutory auditor or statutory audit firm.[1]

---

[1] Section 2(1) CA 2014.

A list of auditors and audit firms entitled to act as auditors is available on the website of the Companies Registration Office, www.cro.ie.

To ensure that the audit is truly independent, auditors of companies cannot be:
- a director or employee of the company; or
- a family member, partner or employee of a director; or
- a bankrupt while their debts remain unpaid or until a court excuses them from paying those debts;
- found guilty by a court of fraud or serious misconduct.

Appointment of Statutory Auditors

It is the role of the members of the company in general meeting, not the directors, to appoint the statutory auditors.[2]

The board of directors or its audit committee may draw up selection criteria against which to judge the auditing firms bidding for the work and may make a recommendation to the general meeting.

The first auditors of the company may be appointed by the directors before the AGM[3] and can hold office until the conclusion of that first AGM.[4] Subsequent appointments of auditors are made at the AGM by the members. This is an important right of the shareholders/ members.

Matters to Consider in Choosing a Company's Auditors

There are a number of important matters that must be considered in not only appointing the auditors in the first place, but also when it comes to retaining them year on year.

It is the responsibility of the directors, and the audit committee (if there is one), to ensure that the company's statutory auditors remain independent and objective at all times. The independence of statutory auditors is vital if they are to give an impartial opinion on a company's financial statements.

---

[2] Section 383 CA 2014.
[3] Section 382(1) CA 2014.
[4] Section 382(2) CA 2014.

Professional auditors must adhere to ethical standards which provide them with rules and procedures for avoiding any threats to their objectivity and independence.

Examples of potential threats to an auditor's independence and objectivity are:
- the influence of other professional services that the audit firm may have provided the company during the year;
- existing personal or business relationships between the company's directors (including NEDs) and the auditors;
- 'management threats', which arise where partners or employees of the auditor make judgements or take decisions on behalf of the management of the audited entity;
- advocacy threats, which arise when the auditor undertakes work that involves acting as an advocate for an audited entity and supporting a position taken by management in an adversarial context.

In essence, it is imperative that the board of directors (or the audit committee) is satisfied that the statutory auditor is independent and not subject to any influence that may impair their judgement.

To allow shareholders to be able to monitor the independence of auditors, the Companies Act 2014 requires that information on the remuneration of the auditors of a company be disclosed in the notes to its financial statements, categorised as follows:
- audit of the entity's (company's) financial statements;
- other assurance services;
- tax advisory services; and
- other non-audit services, e.g. IT services.[5]

Directors need to be aware of the total fees paid for non-audit services to an audit firm in order to ensure that the quantum will not influence the auditors' ability to provide an independent and objective opinion on the accounts.

The board of directors need to consider the independence and objectivity of the company auditors on an annual basis.

What do Statutory Auditors Do during the Audit?

The auditors will determine the work they need to do on a company-by-company basis; this will be influenced by factors such as the size

---

[5] Section 322(3) CA 2014.

of the company, the complexity of its operations and the risks that the auditors believe affect the company (either now or in the future).

In broad terms, the following matters will be actioned by the auditors on all audits:
- regular meetings with the company's directors and executive management to understand the company's business and areas of financial statement risk;
- identification of areas of the statutory financial statements that may be misstated;
- checking the accuracy of a wide range of transactions (such as sales, purchases, wages);
- checking the accuracy of the representation of the company's assets and liabilities at its balance sheet date;
- deciding if the company's accounting policies are reasonable and appropriate;
- testing that the company's internal financial controls are effective and working properly;
- assessing the reasonableness of directors' estimates and judgements;
- evaluating any significant events that have occurred since the statutory financial statements were completed and determining if they impact on the financial statements;
- verifying certain matters in the statutory financial statements with third parties, such as the company's bankers and solicitors, for example the company's bank balance or any threatened litigation against the company.

The purpose of the auditors' procedures is to allow them issue an independent auditor's report on the company's statutory financial statements (this is discussed later in this chapter).

Audit Rotation

Familiarity and self-interest are some of the key arguments for the regular rotation of the statutory audit of a company to another audit firm, for example every five years.

Under an Irish statutory instrument giving effect to an EU Directive and Regulation on audits carried out in Europe, it is mandatory for the statutory audit of public-interest entities (PIEs) to be rotated to another audit firm after 10 years (the legislation allows for transitional arrangements).[6]

---

[6] European Union (Statutory Audits) (Directive 2006/43/EC, as amended by Directive 2014/56/EU, and Regulation (EU) No 537/2014) Regulations 2016 (S.I. No. 312 of 2016).

14. THE AUDIT OF STATUTORY FINANCIAL STATEMENTS AND INTERNAL AUDIT

PIEs include entities with transferable securities listed on an EU-regulated market as well as credit institutions and insurance companies.

Despite the counter-argument to rotation that it may significantly increase the cost of the audit, regular auditor rotation can assist with greater audit independence and provide greater reassurance to the shareholders.

Removal of Auditors

A company may, by ordinary resolution at a general meeting, remove a statutory auditor and appoint, in his or her place, any other (qualified) auditor. This facility to remove an auditor is subject to some stringent conditions, including:
- the removal is without prejudice to any rights of the statutory auditor;
- there must be good and substantial grounds for the removal related to the conduct of the auditor with regard to the performance of his or her duties as auditor of the company, or otherwise; and
- the passing of the resolution is, in the company's opinion, in the best interests of the company.[7]

Note: the decision to propose the removal of the auditors by the directors should be taken with great care.

Resignation of Auditors

Statutory auditors of a company may, by notice in writing served on the company and stating their intention to do so, resign from the office of statutory auditors to the company.[8] The resignation will take effect on the date on which the notice is served, or on a later date as specified in the notice. This notice shall contain either:

"(a) a statement to the effect that there are no circumstances connected with the resignation to which it relates that the statutory auditors concerned consider should be brought to the notice of the members or creditors of the company, or

(b) a statement of any such circumstances as mentioned in paragraph (a)."

---

[7] Sections 394 and 395 CA 2014.
[8] Section 400 CA 2014.

The incoming statutory auditors of the company may carefully consider such a statement and the grounds as to why the previous auditors resigned.

The Rights of Auditors

Statutory auditors have the right to:
- access the accounting records of the company[9];
- information and explanations as appear to the auditors to be within the knowledge of company's officers and directors[10];
- information concerning subsidiary undertakings of the company[11];
- be notified of company general meetings, and attend and address the meetings;[12] and
- explain at a general meeting the circumstances of any proposal to remove them as auditor and to contest their removal.[13]

The Auditor's Report

The company's auditors will express an independent opinion on whether the financial statements are prepared, in all 'material respects', in accordance with the accounting standards that the company has applied (see **Chapter 13**) and with company law.

The phrase 'material respects' is important: a statutory audit includes examination, on a test-basis only, of evidence relevant to the amounts and disclosures in the financial statements. The auditors do not test or validate every transaction that the company has undertaken.

The format and content of the auditor's report, as set out by International Auditing Standard (Ireland) 700, can be perceived as rigid, and can be subjected to criticisms by shareholders as a result. However, the auditor's report to the members of the company must be made in accordance with section 336 CA 2014. The auditor's report is required to state:
- whether the board of directors has given the auditors all the information they sought;
- whether the board has provided the auditors all the explanations they sought;

---

[9] Section 386 CA 2014.
[10] Section 387 CA 2014.
[11] Section 388 CA 2014.
[12] Section 180(6)(a) CA 2014.
[13] Section 180(6)(c) CA 2014.

- whether the statutory financial statements have been properly prepared in accordance with the company's chosen accounting standards;
- whether the company maintained proper books and records during the year under audit;
- whether the balance sheet of the company as at the end of the financial period is 'true and fair';
- whether the profit or loss of the company for the financial year is 'true and fair';
- whether the information given in the directors' report for the financial year is consistent with the statutory financial statements.

There are a number of opinions that can be issued by the auditors in their report, as shown in **Table 14.1**.

TABLE 14.1: TYPES OF AUDITOR'S OPINION AND WHAT THEY MEAN

Auditor's Opinion	What does this opinion mean?
Clean, or Standard, Opinion	The statutory financial statements prepared by the directors: (a) comply in all material aspects with CA 2014, as amended, and the relevant accounting standards; (b) represent fairly the results of the company for the year (i.e. its profit or loss before and after corporation tax is fairly stated); (c) represent fairly the assets and liabilities of the company at its year end.
Adverse Opinion	The statutory financial statements prepared by the directors: (a) DO NOT comply in all material aspects with CA 2014, as amended, and the relevant accounting standards; **or** (b) DO NOT represent fairly the results of the company for the year (i.e. its profit or loss before and after corporation tax is fairly stated); **or** (c) DO NOT represent fairly the assets and liabilities of the company at its year end. In other words, the statutory financial statements are not true and fair.

Disclaimer of Opinion	The auditors are unable to issue an opinion on the overall statutory financial statements due to: (a) the absence of necessary supporting documentary evidence; **or** (b) they have been unable to perform the necessary audit procedures they want to perform.
Qualified Opinion	**On one particular matter only**, the statutory financial statements prepared by the directors: (a) DO NOT comply in all material aspects with CA 2014, as amended, and the relevant accounting standards; (b) DO NOT represent fairly the results of the company for the year (i.e. its profit or loss pre- and post-corporation tax is not fairly stated); **or** (c) DO NOT represent fairly the assets and liabilities of the company at its year end. **However**: The rest of the statutory financial statements: (a) comply in all material aspects with CA 2014, as amended, and the relevant accounting standards; (b) represent fairly the results of the company for the year (i.e. its profit or loss before and after corporation tax is fairly stated); (c) represent fairly the assets and liabilities of the company at its year end.
Emphasis of Matter	The statutory financial statements prepared by the directors: (a) comply in all material aspects with CA 2014, as amended, and the relevant accounting standards; (b) represent fairly the results of the company for the year (i.e. its profit or loss before and after corporation tax is fairly stated); (c) represent fairly the assets and liabilities of the company at its year end.

	However: There is a significant uncertainty that the company is dealing with presently and the directors are unable to determine with any certainty the outcome of this matter, Such significant uncertainties typically include: • the outcome of a court case; • the outcome of a tax audit; • the renewal of banking facilities; • the renewal of significant customer contracts.

Other Reporting by Statutory Auditors

While the main objective of the auditor's report is to issue an audit opinion on the statutory financial statements (as outlined above), auditors have some further reporting obligations, as set out in **Table 14.2** below.

TABLE 14.2: EXAMPLES OF MATTERS ON WHICH STATUTORY AUDITORS MUST REPORT

Matter giving rise to reporting obligation	Required by	Reported to
Deficiency in internal financial controls	International Standard on Auditing (Ireland) 265	Shareholders and Board of directors
Suspected breach of the Companies Act by the company	Companies Act 2014, as amended	Office of the Director of Corporate Enforcement (see below)
Company officers have knowingly or willingly filed incorrect tax returns or failed to make tax payments	Taxes Consolidation Act 1997, as amended	Revenue Commissioners

(Continued)

Matter giving rise to reporting obligation	Required by	Reported to
• Failure to comply with relevant banking and finance • Failure to comply with the requirements of company law • Money laundering • Fraud • Corruption • Competition • Consumer protection • Cybercrime	Criminal Justice Acts	An Garda Síochána

Specific Consideration of Reporting Company Law Offences

Of particular interest and importance to NEDs is the obligation of company auditors to report suspected breaches of the Companies Act 2014 to the Office of the Director of Corporate Enforcement (ODCE).

If, in carrying out an audit of the statutory financial statements of the company, information comes into the possession of the statutory auditors that leads them to form the opinion that there are reasonable grounds for believing that the company, or an officer or agent of it, has committed an offence, the statutory auditors must immediately report the suspected breach to the ODCE.[14]

Audit Exemption

Historically, a criticism of doing business in Ireland was the need for smaller companies to incur the cost of having an independent external audit completed on their annual statutory financial statements. It was not until the enactment of the Companies Amendment Act (No. 2) 1999 that the possibility of an exemption from this annual audit requirement was introduced. While this Act is now replaced by the Companies Act 2014, provisions for audit exemption remain.

There are certain advantages to availing of audit exemption, including avoiding the costs of statutory audit and freeing up directors' time from dealing with the auditors.

[14] Section 393(1) CA 2014.

A company can apply for an exemption from statutory audit if it meets certain criteria. The principal criteria are:
(a) it must be either a 'small' company or a 'micro' company[15] (see **Chapter 13**);
(b) it cannot be a public company;
(c) the company must have has filed its annual return on time.[16]

If availing of the audit exemption, the directors must record the decision in the board minutes and notify the members of the company's intention to avail of the audit exemption.

If the members want to object, they must do so one month before the financial year end to which the exemption is to be availed of.[17] The directors must then proceed to terminate the contract with the company's auditors.

If the company is availing of the audit exemption, the directors must still assert that they:
- keep adequate accounting records and prepare financial statements that give a true and fair view of the assets, liabilities and financial position of the company at the end of its financial year and of its profit or loss for such a year; and
- otherwise comply with the provisions of the Companies Act 2014, as amended, relating to financial statements so far as they are applicable to the company.[18]

Charities and Not-for-profits

Many charities and not-for-profit organisations are incorporated as guarantee companies without a share capital (CLGs). Such companies can avail of an audit exemption unless one member objects.[19] However, the directors of a charity may prefer not to avail of an exemption so that they can be seen by their donors and beneficiaries as accountable. Charities with a gross annual income of over €100,000 are currently required to file audited accounts with the Charities Regulator.

---

[15] Section 358(1) CA 2014.
[16] Section 363 CA 2014.
[17] Section 334 CA 2014.
[18] Section 335(d)(i) and (ii) CA 2014.
[19] Section 1218 CA 2014.

Internal Audit

The statutory auditors report to the members and are, therefore, also referred to as the 'external auditors'. In contrast, the internal auditors report to the board of directors and are a fundamental part of corporate governance and risk management, particularly of large companies and public sector organisations.

Ensuring corporate governance and risk management is in place is an ongoing challenge for all directors, including NEDs. Internal audit assesses the key risks facing a company and what is being done to manage those risks effectively. Implementing a robust, transparent and effective internal audit function assists the NEDs in discharging their duties in understanding and managing risks. Internal audit function operates independent to all other areas of the company, including the finance department.

The Institute of Internal Auditors defines internal audit as follows:

> "Internal audit is an independent, objective assurance and consulting activity designed to add value and improve a company's operations. It helps an organisation accomplish its objectives by bringing a systematic, disciplined approach to evaluate and improve the effectiveness of risk management, control, and governance processes."[20]

The Financial Reporting Council states that:

> "The need for an internal audit function will vary depending on company specific factors including the scale, diversity and complexity of the company's activities and the number of employees, as well as cost/benefit considerations. Senior management and the board may require objective assurance and advice on risk and control."[21]

An adequately resourced internal audit function (or its equivalent where, for example, a third party is contracted to perform some or all of the work concerned) may provide such assurance and advice.

Internal auditors should report to the board or the audit committee. They should not report to the finance director; otherwise some of their objectivity may be lost. Their role is to provide assurance on risk management

---

[20] See https://na.theiia.org/standards-guidance/mandatory-guidance/Pages/Definition-of-Internal-Auditing.aspx (accessed July 2017).

[21] Financial Reporting Council, *Guidance on Audit Committees* (2012) para 4.42.

and internal controls, with the aim of improving systems. Internal auditors need to have an independent and constructive approach. If the internal audit function does not have sufficient authority, resources or the appropriate reporting lines to the board or the audit committee to do its job effectively, the board and/or its audit committee should intervene and resolve the issues that are impacting its functioning.

For most small companies a separate internal audit function would not be cost-effective, as the number of processes to monitor is small. The company's external auditors may point out any internal control weaknesses they notice during their audit; however, it is the responsibility of the directors to ensure there are adequate controls, particularly segregation of duties and safeguarding of assets. As observed by the FRC in the quote above, a third party may be "contracted to perform some or all of the work concerned".

As a company increases in size, it may make sense to put an internal audit function in place. However, it can be difficult to justify the cost of maintaining a full-time internal audit function as well as keeping the internal audit's knowledge and skills up to date. As a result, many companies contract out internal audit until such time as it is cost-effective and more efficient to bring it in-house. There is a benefit to outsourcing in that it is not a fixed cost and the internal auditors can be changed, if necessary.

Terms of Reference

Finally, an internal audit function, whether in-house or outsourced, should have clear terms of reference and reporting lines. The overall role and responsibilities of the internal audit function should be formalised by way of clearly documented terms of reference, and approved by the board, normally recommended by the audit committee. These should then be communicated throughout the company to the relevant departments.

Internal audit's terms of reference should provide clarity about its:
- overall strategy and objectives;
- annual workplan;
- role and responsibilities;
- scope of its work;
- accountability to the audit committee;
- accessibility to the board and the audit committee.

The scope of internal audit can extend beyond financial matters. The scope may include the company's operations, IT, prevention and detection of fraud, and human resources.

Conclusion

Directors must be familiar with the role and responsibilities of external statutory auditors, as well as the nature and limitations of that external audit process.

If a company meets certain criteria as defined in the Companies Act 2014, as amended, it can avail of an exemption from the necessity to have an annual external audit carried out.

Directors should be aware of the types of opinion external auditors can include in their reports, as well as other types of reports that the external auditors can issue, and the implications of each of these.

The establishment of an internal audit function can greatly assist directors in discharging their roles and responsibilities with regard to corporate governance and risk management, including internal financial controls.

10 KEY POINTS: STATUTORY AUDIT AND INTERNAL AUDIT

1. An audit is an independent examination of a company's statutory financial statements prepared by the directors of the company under the Companies Act 2014.
2. The purpose of an external audit is to enhance the degree of confidence of intended users in the statutory financial statements as well as to fulfill this directors' obligation under CA 2014.
3. An auditor must be an independent qualified professional person.
4. The auditors can issue a variety of audit opinions on a company's statutory financial statements.
5. There are a number of important matters that must be considered in not only appointing the auditors in the first place but also when it comes to retaining them year on year.
6. A company can apply for an exemption from statutory audit if it meets certain robust criteria.
7. Statutory external auditors have reporting responsibilities to third parties, including the ODCE, the Revenue Commissioners and An Garda Síochána.
8. Internal audit is a function that operates within a company.
9. A key function of internal audit is to assess the robustness of internal financial controls within a company.
10. NEDs must be familiar with the differences between internal and external audit and their responsibilities with regard to each.

15.
Employer Responsibilities

- Introduction
- Employment Law
- Pensions
- Health and Safety
- Conclusion
- Key Points

Introduction

Employment is a difficult and complex area in which the law changes frequently and about which directors must remain informed. This chapter will highlight the areas of employment, pensions and health & safety legislation with which a director should be familiar.

Employment costs in many companies are often among its highest expenses and therefore need to be actively managed. Employee-related claims, such as for bullying, can take up a huge amount of management time and be very stressful for all parties concerned. The directors of a company are required by law to provide staff with a safe place to work.

Employment Law

If employee-rated matters are not handled appropriately, it can be extremely time-consuming and costly. While the more important issues for directors to consider are outlined below, specialist advice is also strongly recommended.

The directors should ensure that the company has an employee handbook containing all relevant policies, which all employees receive on joining the organisation and which is updated regularly according to changes in policies or the law. If certain contract terms are contained in the handbook, the handbook must be provided to the employee when they receive a copy of the employment contract for signature. Otherwise the terms are not part of the employment contract. The company's policies should also be explained to new employees as part of the induction process and made available on the company's website or intranet.

Contracts of Employment

An employer must, not later than two months after the commencement of an employee's employment, provide him or her with a statement in writing containing certain particulars, the main contents of which are outlined below:
- full names of both employer and employee;
- address of the employer in the State;
- the place of work, or where there is no fixed or main place of work, a statement specifying that the employee is permitted to work in various places;
- title of the job or the nature of the work;
- date of commencement of the contract of employment;

- in the case of temporary contracts, the expected duration thereof or, if the contract of employment is for a fixed term, the date on which the contract expires;
- method of calculation of the employee's remuneration;
- length of the intervals between the times at which remuneration is paid;
- terms and conditions relating to:
    - hours of work (including overtime),
    - paid leave (other than paid sick leave),
    - incapacity for work due to sickness or injury and paid sick leave;
- details of pension arrangements; and
- period(s) of notice which the employee is required to give and entitled to receive, whether by statute or contract;
- reference to any collective agreements (union agreements) which directly affect the terms and conditions of the employee's employment.[1]

Directors should ensure that there is a standard contract that suits the business of the company and that every employee is issued with and signs one of these.

Working Time

There are detailed rules relating to employee work periods and it is useful for a director to have a working knowledge of the legislation. The law is mainly set out in the Organisation of Working Time Act 1997,[2] which deals with minimum rest periods, holidays and the maximum average working week. It also sets out rules in relation to rest and intervals at work, weekly working hours, night working hours, as well as entitlements to annual leave and public holidays.

For many employees, the 1997 Act states that the maximum *average* working week cannot exceed 48 hours, the average being calculated in one of the following ways:
- over a four-month period for most employees;
- over a six-month period for employees working in the security industry, hospitals, prisons, gas/electricity, airport/docks, agriculture and employees in businesses that have peak periods at certain times, e.g. tourism; and
- over a 12-month period where there has been an agreement between the employer and the employees to this effect, approved by the Labour Court.

---

[1] Section 3 of the Terms of Employment (Information) Act 2015.
[2] Organisation of Working Time Act 1997.

The calculation of 48 hours does not include annual leave, sick leave or maternity/adoptive/parental and paternity leave. Also, there are exceptions in that the provisions of the 1997 Act do not apply to all employees, for instance they do not apply to members of An Garda Síochána, the Defence Forces, employees who control their own working hours or family employees on farms or in private homes. There are separate regulations governing trainee doctors, employees involved in road transport activities and those working at sea.

Equality

Given the increasingly diverse nature of the workforce in Ireland, equality is an area of increased focus and one of which the directors of a company should be aware. The Employment Equality Acts 1998 to 2015 aim to:
- promote equality;
- prohibit discrimination (with some exemptions) across nine grounds as follows:
    - gender;
    - marital or civil status;
    - family status;
    - age;
    - race;
    - religion;
    - disability;
    - sexual orientation;
    - membership of the Traveller Community.

Discrimination may relate to dismissal, equal pay, sexual harassment, working conditions, promotion, access to employment, etc. Giving an equal chance to all is important. Directors should take positive action to ensure a safe environment without harassment or victimisation for all and that there is appropriate access, participation and training for people with disabilities.

Unfair Dismissal

The objective of the Unfair Dismissals Acts 1977–2015 is "to provide for redress for employees unfairly dismissed from their employment".[3] Whenever a company terminates an employee's contract, with or

---

[3] Unfair Dismissals Act 1977.

without notice, there is a risk of it being sued for unfair dismissal. Similarly, an unfair dismissal claim is very likely if there has been a 'constructive dismissal', i.e. when the behaviour of the employer is such that it is reasonable for the employee to terminate the contract.

Dismissal of an employee is likely to be judged unfair if it results from their:
- membership of a trade union;
- religious or political opinions;
- civil or criminal proceedings against the employer;
- race;
- sexual orientation;
- age;
- unfair selection for redundancy;
- taking part in a lawful industrial action against the employer;
- the employee's participation (or threat to participate) in legal proceedings against the employer;
- pregnancy or they have exercised their rights under the Adoptive Leave Act 2005 or the Parental Leave Act 1998;
- exercise of rights under the National Minimum Wage Act 2000 or the Protected Disclosures Act 2014.

The Unfair Dismissal Acts do not usually apply to a person employed for less than a year. (There are exceptions to this service requirement where the dismissal arises as a consequence of the employee's pregnancy, trade union membership or activities, exerting their rights under the Minimum Wage Act 2000 or the Protected Disclosures Act 2014.)

The Unfair Dismissal Acts set out two core principles:
- there must be substantive grounds to justify the termination of a contract of employment; and
- fair procedures must be followed when effecting the termination of employment.

The existence of a formal contract with a clear or ascertainable date for the end of employment, e.g. a fixed-term contract for one year, and written policies setting out under what terms an employee may be dismissed, as well as the procedures that will be utilised to effect this dismissal, may alleviate many issues.

Disciplinary and grievance policies must be in place and should be contained in an employee handbook (see above). Directors should ensure that such a handbook is readily available.

Redundancy

Redundancy occurs when there is the dismissal of an employee by an employer and the dismissal results 'wholly or mainly' from one of the following situations:
- where an employer has ceased, or intends to cease, to carry on the business for the purposes for which the employee was employed by the company;
- where the requirements of that business for an employee to carry out work of a particular kind in the place where he or she was so employed have ceased or diminished or are expected to cease or diminish;
- where the employer has decided to carry on the business with fewer or no employees;
- where an employer has decided that the work for which the employee has been employed (or had been doing before his or her dismissal) should henceforth be done in a different manner for which the employee is not sufficiently qualified or trained;
- where an employer has decided that the work for which the employee has been employed (or had been doing before his or her dismissal) should henceforth be done by a person who is also capable of doing other work for which the employee is not sufficiently qualified or trained.[4]

(*Note:* specialist advice is recommended before taking action on any matter relating to redundancy.)

Transfers of Undertaking

If a company (employer) acquires another company and the employees from that company become employees of the acquiring company with no change to their working conditions, then this is not a redundancy situation but rather a 'transfer of undertaking'.[5] The employees' continuity of service, i.e. length of time worked, is carried into the new employment. The employees are entitled to the same terms and conditions of employment with the new employer or to terms no less favourable than those they enjoyed with their previous employer.

---

[4] Section 7(2) of the Redundancy Payments Act 1967, as amended.
[5] European Communities (Protection of Employees on Transfer of Undertakings) Regulations 2003 (S.I. No. 131 of 2003).

Pensions

Types of Occupational Pension

There are a variety of different types of pension arrangement that can be put in place by employers. It is imperative that directors are aware of the company's financial and legal commitments connected to any arrangement when putting such schemes in place. This is a highly specialist area and directors are strongly advised to take professional advice.

There is no legal requirement for a company to provide an employee with a pension, but there is an obligation on all employers to give each employee access to a personal retirement savings account (PRSA). If the employee chooses to avail of a PRSA, the employer must facilitate the deduction of pension contributions through the company's payroll.

Some companies provide occupational pension schemes, often described as a company pension. These are set up by employers to deliver benefits to employees on their retirement or to nominated individuals on the employee's death. Such schemes are set up under trusts that have to be approved by the Revenue Commissioners. The investments of the pension fund do not incur income or capital gains tax. Retirement benefits paid to employees are subject to PAYE, with the exception of a certain amount, which can be paid as a lump sum tax free on retirement or death. This is a complex area and requires specialist advice.

There are two main types of occupational pension scheme:
- **Defined Benefit Schemes** A defined benefit scheme is where the beneficiary knows what their pension will be in cash terms, i.e. the benefit is defined. The pension is usually defined by earnings and length of service. Contributions required may vary to ensure that the fund can meet the requirements.
- **Defined Contribution Schemes** A defined contribution scheme is where contributions are fixed but the beneficiary depends on the performance of the fund and does not know what pension they will receive on retirement.

Furthermore, occupational pension schemes may be:
- **non-contributory schemes** where only the employer pays in contributions;
- **contributory schemes** where the employer and the employee pay contributions into the scheme.

Occupational schemes operated by companies are funded, meaning that the contributions build up a fund and benefits are paid from that fund.

The trustees of an occupational pension scheme must ensure that an annual report is prepared. This allows the beneficiaries to assess the strength of their pension scheme. Directors should also monitor the success of company pension schemes to ensure that the fund is being well run and that it is adequately funded.

Underfunded Pension Schemes

As a result of the economic crisis, a significant number of defined benefit occupational pension schemes are underfunded. Their liabilities, i.e. the money needed to cover current and future employee benefits, are greater than their assets. This means that employees may not receive the pension they have been promised.

This is an extremely complex and sensitive area for many companies and their directors. The director's duty is to the company. On the other hand, the welfare of employees and retirees may well depend on the pension scheme.

Understanding the extent of the deficit is not simple and involves considerable judgement. A small change in major assumptions, such as discount rates or inflation, can have a significant effect on the level of liability estimated.

If a company has an underfunded pension scheme, the directors should ensure that they understand the implications and sensitivities of the judgements that they are being asked to make. Any liability must be disclosed in the accounts and the directors are required to sign off on the accounts as being true and fair.[6]

This is a good example of a significant company liability that may be understated in the company's accounts. As the figures are usually material, all directors, and in particular the audit committee, should challenge the assumptions and ensure that they are satisfied that the figures give a true and fair view.

Health & Safety

Health & safety is a key consideration for company directors. Section 80 of the Safety, Health and Welfare at Work Act 2005 states that when an offence under the health and safety legislation is committed by a business, and the acts involved were authorised or consented to, or were

---

[6] International Accounting Standard (IAS) 19 *Employee Benefits* and FRS 102 Section 28.

attributable to connivance or neglect on the part of a director, manager or other similar officer in the undertaking, both the person and the business will be guilty of an offence and liable to be proceeded against and punished as if the person was guilty of the offence committed by the business. The maximum penalties where prosecuted on indictment include fines not exceeding €3 million and/or a term of imprisonment not exceeding three years. Relevant case law in this areas includes: *HSA v. Technical Engineering and Tooling Services Limited & Others* (2011) and *DPP v. Kildownet Utilities Ltd, Cormac Building Contractors Ltd, Byrne & Molloy* (2006).

Health & safety legislation is embodied in a number of Acts and statutory instruments, some of which relate to specific industries, e.g. quarries, construction, etc.

This is a complex area and needs the attention of the board at all times. Health & safety is not only for companies engaged in hazardous activities; the welfare of staff should always be on a board's agenda. For example, fire drills with staff should be carried out regularly, according to a predetermined and communicated evacuation plan.

Employer's Duties regarding Health & Safety

Employers are required by law to:
- provide and maintain facilities and arrangements for the welfare of their employees at work;
- carry out a risk assessment and prepare a 'safety statement';
- prepare and revise adequate plans and procedures to be followed and measures to be taken in the case of an emergency or serious and imminent danger;
- report any accident that causes an employee to lose three consecutive days, excluding the day of the accident, as well as any accident causing death or a dangerous occurrence, to the Health and Safety Authority.[7]

The Health & Safety Authority (HSA) is the body responsible for workplace health & safety in Ireland. Its role is to ensure that "those affected by work activity are protected from work-related injury and ill health". They do this by enforcing occupational health and safety law, promoting accident prevention, and providing information and advice across all sectors.[8]

---

[7] Section 8(2) (f), (h), (j) and (k) of the Safety, Health and Welfare at Work Act 2005.
[8] See www.hsa.ie/eng/About_Us

Companies employing more than three people must have a safety statement. A company employing three or fewer people does not need to draft a safety statement and can instead adopt the Code of Practice relating to Safety Statements, prepared by the Health & Safety Authority for the relevant sector or work activity. Compliance with that Code is sufficient to discharge its obligations regarding a safety statement.[9]

Company directors as employers have clear duties under the health & safety legislation. The following duties must be implemented "so far as is reasonably practicable":
- manage and conduct work activities in such a way as to ensure the safety, health and welfare at work of employees;
- ensure the safety, health and welfare at work of employees;
- prevent any improper conduct or behaviour;
- ensure the design, provision and maintenance of the workplace;
- prevent any risk from noise, vibration or ionising or other radiations or physical agents;
- plan, organise, perform, maintain and revise systems of work;
- provide the information, instruction, training and supervision to ensure the safety, health and welfare at work of employees;
- provide and maintain suitable protective clothing and equipment; and
- obtain the services of a competent person for the purpose of ensuring the safety, health and welfare at work of employees.[10]

Employers must not make the employee pay for health & safety equipment or protective clothing. Employers should set the tone; for example, they should always, no matter what the circumstances, insist on the use of seat belts in cars and other road vehicles or refuse to talk to anyone who is using a mobile phone while driving. The employer should continually assess safety procedures and ensure that they remain appropriate.

Employees' Duties regarding Health and Safety

Not only do employers have responsibility in relation to health & safety, employees also have duties in this regard, including:
- to take reasonable care to protect the health & safety of themselves and of other people in the workplace;
- not to be under the influence of alcohol or drugs in the workplace;

---

[9] See section 20(8) of the Safety, Health and Welfare at Work Act 2005.
[10] Section 8 of the Safety, Health and Welfare at Work Act 2005.

- not to engage in improper behaviour that will endanger themselves or others;
- to co-operate with their employer or any other person so far as is necessary to enable the employer or the other person to comply with the law; and
- to report to his or her employer any defects in the place of work or equipment that might be a danger to health & safety.[11]

Employees are under a duty to take reasonable care for their own safety. For instance, they should avail of any protective equipment supplied.

Corporate Manslaughter

'Corporate manslaughter' is an offence that occurs where an 'undertaking' causes the death of a person by gross negligence. The definition of an 'undertaking' in this regard is very broad, encompassing "a person being a body corporate or an unincorporated body of persons engaged in the production, supply or distribution of goods or the provision of a service whether carried on for profit or not including those which are Government departments and statutory bodies, whether carried on for profit or not, as well as faith based organisations and groups".[12]

While corporate manslaughter is an indictable offence (crime) in England and Wales,[13] prosecutions in Ireland are currently taken under Safety, Health and Welfare at Work Acts. However, a Bill before the Oireachtas at the time of writing, the Corporate Manslaughter (No. 2) Bill 2016, will create the "indictable offence of corporate manslaughter by an undertaking" and "the indictable offence of grossly negligent management causing death by a high managerial agent of the undertaking".[14] A "high managerial agent" could be a director.

The Bill is intended to introduce the law on corporate manslaughter to ensure that undertakings or persons can be held accountable when deaths of workers are caused by neglect of workplace health & safety, whether it is through established bad practice or mismanagement. "As outlined in the explanatory memorandum, the Bill is based on the Law Reform Commission Report on Corporate Killing

---

[11] Section 13 of the Safety, Health and Welfare at Work Act 2005.
[12] Section 1 of the Corporate Manslaughter (No. 2) Bill 2016. Available at www.oireachtas.ie
[13] Corporate Manslaughter and Corporate Homicide Act 2007 (UK).
[14] See www.oireachtas.ie/viewdoc.asp?DocID=33374&&&CatID=59 (accessed December 2016).

of October 2005, which recognised that current legislation was deficient and recommended that a new offence of corporate manslaughter be created."[15]

Under the Bill, if a company is found guilty, the directors may also be presumed guilty unless they can prove otherwise. Director culpability is likely if they have taken risks to save costs or that there are repeated failures that are not addressed. The key responsibility for directors is to ensure that they provide a safe place and that they are not grossly negligent which could lead to the death of a staff member. Sanctions can range from fines to up to 12 years in prison.

Bullying, Harassment, Violence and Victimisation

Another aspect of ensuring that employees have a safe and healthy environment in which to work is to ensure that they are not subject to bullying, harassment, violence or victimisation from other staff members. In this context the employer has a duty to:
- prevent improper conduct or behaviour;
- establish procedures to deal with complaints;
- prevent harassment in the workplace, including harassment relating to gender, civil status, marital status, family status, sexual orientation, age, disability, race, religious belief or membership of the Traveller Community;[16]
- as far as possible, ensure proper safeguards to eliminate the risk of violence; and
- not penalise employees for exercising their rights under safety and health legislation.

Company directors, as employers, should not underestimate the amount of time that can be lost as a result of a careless remark or the stress that such incidences bring to both the accused and the accuser.

In today's workplaces, avoiding offence can be difficult. For example, some women may be annoyed if a man opens a door for them or even offers to carry a heavy load. Others may be offended if a man does not. Clear company protocols should be developed that are suitable to the local environment.

---

[15] See http://wdsolicitors.ie/corporate-manslaughter-bill-2016/ (accessed December 2016).
[16] Section 32 of the Employment Equality Act 1998.

Every company should have a written policy relating to bullying and harassment in the workplace and this should be brought to the attention of all employees at the time of joining and at regular intervals thereafter. Directors should ensure that there is adequate training and that the company's employee handbook is regularly updated.

Workplace Stress

An employer has a duty not to expose an employee to unreasonable levels of workplace stress. Where an employer is aware that an employee has a predisposition to workplace stress or there are prior indications of impending harm, they have a duty to take the steps which are reasonable in the circumstances, bearing in mind the magnitude of the risk of harm occurring, the gravity of the harm which may occur, the cost and practicability of preventing it, and the justifications for running the risk.

Risk Assessment

To reduce health and safety risks to employees, employers must carry out a risk assessment to identify measures to be enshrined in the company's safety statement. Such a risk assessment would look at:
- areas where risks are more likely to occur, e.g. use of machinery;
- employees that may be more at risk, such as those with a disability;
- safety measures that can be put in place to reduce risk, such as 'hi-vis' jackets for those who work outdoors near roadways;
- reviewing previous accident records;
- reviewing similar workplaces and activities with the same risk profile;
- identification of potential risks, the reasons for them and their probability;
- implementation of remedial procedures and the cost of same;
- provision of training, support and advice to staff; and
- testing the effectiveness of procedures.

Thus, the risk assessment identifies the hazards, determines the risks and then puts in place appropriate measures.

The company's safety statement should outline measures to reduce the risks identified. These may be simple, such as:
- provision of protective equipment (headgear, footwear, eyewear, gloves, etc.), together with training on how to use it, where necessary;
- communicating to staff that abuse or violence will not be tolerated;

- use of coded locks on doors that access the workplace;
- installing CCTV; and
- use of cash-free systems and time-locked safes.

The resources devoted to risk management and the approach taken depend on the nature of the working environment. Clearly, measures will be different for an office, a retail shop or a high-tech manufacturing operation, though the same law applies to them all.

Conclusion

Employing staff involves a myriad of responsibilities, all of which need to be taken seriously by company directors. Employment law is complex, with many different Acts and Regulations to be observed. Directors must regularly check to ensure that the obligations of the company to its staff are being met. If issues are not addressed promptly, there is a real risk that they will cost the company more money at some stage in the future, or, worse still, a member of staff will be injured. Employment issues, if allowed to escalate, can be very stressful for all concerned.

10 KEY POINTS: EMPLOYEE MATTERS

1. Employment law is complex and directors must ensure that they are being regularly updated on changes.
2. Employers must promote equality and prohibit any discrimination in their workplaces.
3. Employees must be given a statement of prescribed particulars within two months of commencement of their employment.
4. The Unfair Dismissals Acts do not generally apply to somebody who has been employed for less than a year.
5. Redundancy occurs when there is the dismissal of an employee by an employer under the Redundancy Act, where the employee's position no longer exists.
6. The European Communities (Protection of Employees on Transfer of Undertakings) Regulations 2003 protect the rights of employees where a business in which they are employed is transferred to a new owner.

7. A defined benefit occupational pension scheme is where the beneficiary knows what their final pension will be in cash terms. However, many defined benefit occupational pension schemes are underfunded at present. A defined contribution pension scheme is where contributions are fixed, but the amount of the pension will depend on the performance of the fund.
8. Company directors must understand the implications and sensitivities of the judgements they are being asked to make in assessing the company's liability to pension scheme funding in their financial statements.
9. Employers have clearly identified duties in relation to the health & safety of their employees, including providing and maintaining facilities, making arrangements for employees' welfare in the workplace, carrying out a risk assessment and preparing and adhering to a safety statement.
10. Every company should have a written policy relating to bullying and harassment in the workplace and this should be brought to the attention of all employees.

16.
Directors' Remuneration

- Introduction
- Developments in Executive Director Remuneration
- The Components of Remuneration
- Remuneration of Non-executive Directors
- Conclusion
- Key Points

Introduction

While the previous chapter looked at employee issues in general, this chapter addresses the remuneration of executive directors (the remuneration of non-executive directors is discussed towards the end of the chapter). The larger a company gets, the more complex executive directors remuneration packages can become. Elements of remuneration may include salary, bonuses, pensions, share options and benefits in kind.

Performance-based pay remains a popular approach to remuneration in companies. The rationale is that executive directors should be given appropriate incentives to ensure they implement and meet the strategic objectives of the business and that their interests are aligned with those of the company. However, after the financial and economic crisis, which exposed large bonuses being linked to excessive risk-taking, questions have arisen as to whether such incentives were properly structured and whether they truly align the interests of the directors with those of the company.

Developments in Executive Director Remuneration

The Emergence of Concern over Remuneration

In the 1990s, executive remuneration emerged as an important corporate governance issue. Performance-based pay became increasingly popular. At the same time, it should be noted that the quantum of pay also increased significantly.

As corporate governance evolved, the Hampel Report of 1998 brought guidlines on executive pay while the Higgs Report of 2003 brought greater formality to the role of non-executive directors. It is debatable as to whether these measures have worked; for example, some executive directors have been rewarded with very high remuneration packages for what would appear to have been excessive risk-taking, albeit condoned by their boards.

Issues Surrounding Executive Pay

In the UK, the High Pay Centre[1] was formed following the findings of the High Pay Commission,[2] which was an independent inquiry,

---

[1] "The High Pay Centre is an independent non-party think tank established to monitor pay at the top of the income distribution and set out a road map towards better business and economic success." See http://highpaycentre.org/
[2] High Pay Commission Report (2012).

commenced in 2009, into high pay and boardroom pay across the public and private sectors in the UK. Some of its more relevant findings include those relating to:
- Transparency:
  - executives should be paid a basic salary with one additional performance-related element only where it is absolutely necessary;
  - an anonymous list should be published of the top-10 highest paid employees outside the boardroom; and
  - remuneration reports should be presented in a standardised format.
- Accountability:
  - companies should implement defined and structured succession plans;
  - the recruitment of non-executives should be openly advertised; and
  - the extent and nature of all the services provided by remuneration consultants should be published.
- Fairness:
  - all publicly listed companies should publish fair pay reports (with the pay gap between highest paid and the company median open to scrutiny) as part of their remuneration reports to build trust in pay policies; and
  - a permanent body should be established to monitor pay trends.

Few of these findings have been implemented, and the issue of executive pay remains problematic.

The Investment Association, a leading source on remuneration guidelines, has proposed the following with regard to remuneration policies:

> "a. Remuneration policies should be set to promote value creation through transparent alignment with the agreed corporate strategy.
> b. Remuneration policies should support performance, encourage the underlying sustainable financial health of the business and promote sound risk management for the benefit of all investors, including shareholders and creditors.
> c. Undeserved remuneration undermines the efficient operation of the company.
> d. Excessive remuneration adversely affects its reputation and is not aligned with shareholder interests."[3]

---

[3] The Investment Association, *The Investment Association Principles of Remuneration* (October 2016). Note also: the Investment Association "do not support any retrospective changes to performance metrics or adjustments for exchange rate movements".

The Association of British Insurers (ABI) also supports performance-related pay:

> "A significant proportion of executive remuneration should be performance related, and tied to the achievement of the agreed corporate strategy and long-term value creation."[4]

The ABI also believe that:

> "Equity based long-term incentive schemes are the most effective way to align the interests of participants and shareholders."[5]

However, this approach requires some deeper consideration.

Focus on the Long-term Success of the Company

Today, the erstwhile whole-hearted endorsement of variable and performance-related pay has been tempered. The emphasis has moved away from rewarding the director in the short term to ensuring that remuneration is aimed at promoting the long-term success of the company. This is reflected in a shift in emphasis in the *UK Corporate Governance Code*, the 2012 version of which states the main principle on remuneration as follows:

> "Levels of remuneration should be sufficient to attract, retain and motivate directors of the quality required to run the company successfully."[6]

However, for the September 2014, and then the April 2016 versions of the Code, this had changed to:

> "Executive directors' remuneration should be designed to promote the long-term success of the company. Performance-related elements should be transparent, stretching and rigorously applied."[7]

While the *UK Corporate Governance Code* applies to listed companies, the principles are still valid for any size of company. Regardless of the size of the company, shareholders are uncomfortable when large rewards are made to executive directors while the company is failing to perform, or even when it is performing.

---

[4] Association of British Insurers, *ABI Principles of Remuneration* (2013) Section C.
[5] Ibid.
[6] *UK Corporate Governance Code* (FRC, 2012) D.1.
[7] *UK Corporate Governance Code* (FRC, 2014) D.1.

The Link to Corporate Strategy

The performance-related pay model assumes that remuneration policies for both executive directors and higher paid executives should be linked to the achievement of the company's corporate strategy. The logic is that if the shareholders benefit, so should the directors responsible for running the company.

However, selecting performance criteria that link remuneration to the long-term performance of the company is not easy. It means that the non-executive directors involved in deciding remuneration policy must understand the strategy of the company for value creation, the associated KPIs (see **Chapter 13**) and ensure that the performance-related remuneration scheme is designed to complement this.

In larger companies, this work is typically performed by non-executive directors on a remuneration committee. This can be extremely time-consuming and therefore costly, particularly in trying to agree bonus criteria to avoid windfall profits being paid to executive directors and/or where a director later disputes the assumptions influencing the criteria.

Realistically, there are few perfectly objective criteria for performance-related remuneration schemes. Even audited financial statements are dependent on subjective judgements that are made by the board. All too often the criteria may not be sufficiently defined at the outset and this will only become apparent when the results are challenged.

There are many approaches, both financial and non-financial, that can be used to develop criteria to underpin bonuses. No matter what method is chosen, it is essential to keep criteria straightforward and to avoid creating an expensive 'microindustry' in information preparation, collection and justification.

The Link to Corporate Risk Appetite

In setting bonus criteria, the board also needs to consider risk. In the aftermath of the financial crisis, there has been an increased emphasis and focus on risk and on curbing excessive risk-taking at board level. Executive remuneration flows from the corporate strategy, which reflects a certain risk appetite, so it is fundamental for executive remuneration to reflect this risk appetite.

This trend is reflected in the *UK Corporate Governance Code*, which states that: "Remuneration incentives should be compatible with risk policies and systems."[8] Similarly, the IBA states that "structure should be aligned with strategy and agreed risk appetite".[9]

The remuneration committee or NEDs involved in determining remuneration and the criteria for variable performance-related pay need to appreciate the risks to which the company is exposed and ensure that the criteria for variable pay do not exacerbate these risks.

Performance-related Pay

Though the trend for performance-related pay continues to be strong, a sizeable amount of academic research now questions its effectiveness and, post the financial crisis, the issue has become increasingly contentious.

The argument for performance-related pay includes claims such as:
- additional reward increases productivity;
- it allows the setting of objective criteria;
- it reduces favouritism; and
- any performance weaknesses result from poor implementation.

The argument against performance-related pay considers that:
- it does not work for cognitive or creative tasks;
- it encourages excessive risk-taking;
- it leads to a short-term focus at the expense of the longer-term strategic objectives of the company;
- people may behave differently from how performance-related pay policy assumes; and
- the criteria selected may produce unexpected results.

A company may have positive results simply because of a good economic climate rather than the effort of its directors. Conversely, a director may not be adequately rewarded where he or she has performed exceptionally in a poor economic climate.

Performance-related pay is based on the agency theory perspective,[10] i.e. that the relationship between the owner of capital and the executive

---

[8] *UK Corporate Governance Code* (April 2016) Schedule A: The design of performance-related remuneration for executive directors.
[9] Association of British Insurers, *ABI Principles of Remuneration* (2013), principle iii.b.
[10] Conceptualised by M. Jensen and W. Meckling in "Theory of the Firm: Managerial Behavior, Agency Cost, and Capital Structure" (1976) *Journal of Financial Economics*, 3: 305–360 (see also **Chapter 9**).

is one of principal and agent, and that the agent, i.e. the director, acts in his or her own interests unless he or she is motivated by pay to act in the interests of the principal, i.e. the shareholder.

However, as a model, performance-related pay may take a rather simplistic view of human behaviour and overestimate the motivational power of money. Many directors and senior executives are motivated by the satisfaction of doing a competent job, by the need for respect and status as a result of their achievements, or simply by the fact that their work may in some way contribute to something interesting resulting from it. People may passionately pursue a role because of their belief in the mission or vision of the company. They are not necessarily or exclusively driven by pay or self-interest.

Variable pay is still the norm for executive directors and senior executives. Such incentives often have unintended consequences, are expensive to administer and can even reduce motivation. A careful balance between fixed and variable pay needs to be considered and every effort made to construct performance-related pay schemes that are efficient and encourage appropriate behaviour.

Remuneration Benchmarking

There are organisations that provide benchmarking information for specific executive roles to assist companies in setting remuneration. If benchmarking, a company needs to select the appropriate peer groups to use for comparative purposes. It is is worth pointing out, however, that better disclosure, as initially demanded in 'The Greenbury Report' in 1995,[11] led to directors demanding higher salaries when they compared their remuneration to that of their peers.

The *UK Corporate Governance Code* appears to be wary of benchmarking, stating:

> "The remuneration committee should judge where to position their company relative to other companies. But they should use such comparisons with caution, in view of the risk of an upward ratchet of remuneration levels with no corresponding improvement in corporate and individual performance, and should avoid paying more than is necessary."[12]

---

[11] *Directors' Remuneration: Report of a Study Group Chaired by Sir Richard Greenbury* (Gee Publishing, 1995).

[12] *UK Corporate Governance Code* (April 2016) D.1.

There are risks with using remuneration consultants. If the consultant is employed by those whose remuneration they are assessing, this may clearly lead to a conflict of interest, particularly in the absence of a remuneration committee or input from non-executive directors. Such external advice should be used objectively and no increase should be made more than is necessary.

The Components of Remuneration

As we have seen, the role of the board, particularly the non-executive directors and/or the remuneration committee, is to ensure that the remuneration policy is appropriate for the company.

An individual executive director's total remuneration package may be made up of a number of elements, fixed and variable, annual and long term. The balance of the various elements is for each company to decide.

Remuneration is typically made up of:
- fixed elements:
  - base pay;
  - pension; and
  - other benefits, e.g. health insurance; and
- variable elements:
  - bonus; and
  - long-term incentive plans.

The *UK Corporate Governance Code* states that:

> "The remuneration committee should determine an appropriate balance between fixed and performance-related, immediate and deferred remuneration ... [and] ... consider whether the directors should be eligible for annual bonuses and/or benefits under long-term incentive schemes."[13]

The concept of balance is important. Executive directors and senior management are likely to seek a balance between basic pay and performance-related pay. They may also expect certain benefits in kind, e.g. a company car. While the company needs to ensure that executive directors or senior executives will work to the best of their ability, it should also be mindful of the cost of administering certain elements of remuneration, such as cars, pensions and health insurance.

---

[13] *UK Corporate Governance Code* (April 2016) Schedule A.

Base Pay

Base pay is important as it will be difficult to recruit the right talent at executive level if base pay is not set at a level that is competitive in the market. Input from recruitment and selection specialists will be helpful in establishing base pay for any particular position. Other considerations in developing base pay are set out by the Investment Association as follows:

> "Base pay should be set at a level which reflects the role and responsibility of the individual, whilst respecting the principle of paying no more than is necessary."[14]

> "Where Remuneration Committees seek to increase base pay, the reasons should be fully disclosed and justified. Salary decisions should not be taken purely on the basis of simple benchmarking against peer companies."[15]

> "Remuneration Committees should also be aware of the multiplier effect that increases in base pay have on the overall quantum of remuneration."[16]

Non-executive directors and/or remuneration committees need to decide what is best for the company. Companies should be wary of adhering to a perceived median as a benchmark in a sector as this has the effect of increasing salaries across the sector.

Pensions

First, it is important to note that the *UK Corporate Governance Code* states that "in general only basic pay should be pensionable",[17] rather than any performance-related pay.

Though pensions can be a significant cost to a company, they can also be overlooked when considering the quantum, or changes in the quantum, of an individual executive director's or senior executive's pay. Depending on the nature of the scheme, a change in base pay may change pension contributions for the company.

---

[14] The Investment Association, *The Investment Association Principles of Remuneration* (October 2016) Section B.1.
[15] Ibid.
[16] Ibid.
[17] *UK Corporate Governance Code* (April 2016) Schedule A.

Particular care should be taken when considering awarding salary increases to executive directors or senior executives who are close to retirement. This may not be in the company's interests where the company has a final salary pension plan. For example, the final pension could be based on the last three years' salary. However, every scheme is different and it is hard to generalise. Pension entitlements should not be excessive. Directors should consider the company's workforce as a whole and be prepared to justify any differing contribution rates for executives compared to employees. The Investment Association provides general guidance on this as follows:

> "The pension provision for executives should, where possible, be in line with the general approach to the employees as a whole. Any differences in pension contribution rates for executives and the general workforce should be disclosed and justified to shareholders."[18]

Benefits and Allowances

Where a director is given a benefit or an allowance, for example an allowance for accommodation or a company car, it should be justifiable and disclosed in the company's financial statements. The Investment Association highlights that:

> "Benefits should be fully disclosed and, where significant, viewed as an integral component of fixed remuneration."[19]

Adding that:

> "In general, the use of allowances as part of fixed pay goes against the spirit of simplicity, clarity and pay for performance."[20]

Directors should aim for remuneration packages to be simple and clear, without adding layers of administration. For instance, providing a car creates the need to ensure that the car is serviced and insured.

---

[18] The Investment Association, *The Investment Association Principles of Remuneration* (October 2016) Section B.2.
[19] *Ibid.*, Section B.3.
[20] *Ibid.*, Section B.4.

Bonuses

Bonuses are generally awarded to executive directors and senior management for exceeding objectives set down by the board, which involve a combination of short-term and long-term goals. The nature of these objectives needs to be carefully considered by the board to ensure that they are fair, realistic and that the underpinning criteria cannot be easily manipulated.

The Investment Association strongly supports bonuses:

> "Annual bonuses incentivise performance and reward achievement in line with the agreed corporate strategy.
>
> Annual bonuses exist to reward contribution to the business during the year above the level expected for being in receipt of a salary. They should be clearly linked to business targets, ideally through the KPIs reported in the Strategic Report. ...
>
> Deferring a portion of the bonus into shares can create a greater alignment with shareholders, particularly where there is no long term incentive. ...
>
> Shareholders discourage the payment of annual bonuses to executive directors if the business has suffered an exceptional negative event, even if some specific targets have been met. In such circumstances, shareholders should be consulted on bonus policy and any proposed payments should be carefully explained.
>
> Discretion should be retained to ensure that a payment that is inappropriate in all the company's circumstances is not made."[21]

A bonus should be payable for achieving 'stretch' objectives and not simply to pay the executive director or senior executive for doing their job. Other types of bonus, whether for the retention of a key client or the completion of an important transaction, need to be carefully thought through to ensure they result in the desired behaviour of the recipient.

Share-based Incentives

Long-term, share-based incentives are designed to reward executive directors and senior management with the successful implementation

---

[21] The Investment Association, *The Investment Association Principles of Remuneration* (October 2016) Section C.1.

of strategy and the creation of shareholder value over a period appropriate to the strategic objectives of the company.

According to the *UK Corporate Governance Code*:

> "The Remuneration Committee should consider requiring directors to hold a minimum number of shares and to hold shares for a further period after vesting or exercised, including for a period after leaving the company."[22]

It is in the company's interests to ensure that executive directors hold on to shares for an agreed period once they have received them (i.e. once they have been 'vested'). Early cashing in of shares may lead to market uncertainty and a lack of confidence in the management, or indeed the company.

Long-term, share-based incentives are more commonly used in PLCs, the shares of which are more tradable and the value of whose shares can be determined daily. The mechanism is less attractive for executive directors and senior executives in a private company where an independent valuation of the shares or a liquidity event, e.g. sale of the company, would be required.

Approval by Shareholders

It is good practice and good governance to seek shareholder approval for share-incentive schemes awarded/offered to executive directors and senior executives. Although the quantum may not be material in the context of the total shares in issue, it can have a dilutive effect on shareholdings and potential dividends.

The presentation of these share-based incentive schemes at company general meetings needs to be carefully thought through as shareholders may refuse to approve schemes if they have not been properly consulted.

On the one hand, remuneration of directors and senior executives may be seen as an operational issue that should be handled by the board of directors rather than shareholders. However, the trend towards shareholder 'say on pay' is becoming stronger as a result of the collapse of companies with highly paid executives and the perceived greed and self-interest of directors.

---

[22] *UK Corporate Governance Code* (April 2016) Schedule A.

LTD and DAC companies (see **Chapter 2**) may have the remuneration of directors decided by the board, unless their constitutions state otherwise.[23] However, PLCs[24] and CLGs[25] should have directors' remuneration decided by the members in general meeting, unless their constitution states otherwise.

There are, however, potential problems with shareholders having a binding vote in this regard. Certain shareholders may have a much shorter perspective than the long-term success of the company. Institutional investors or majority shareholders may have their own agenda. Paradoxically, 'say on pay' may in fact only serve to align remuneration with short-term company performance.

Clawback of Excessive Bonuses

If excessive bonuses have been paid to executive directors or senior management as a result of misstatement or misconduct when the company has performed badly and/or shareholder value has been lost, shareholders are likely to want to reclaim bonuses paid. The *UK Corporate Governance Code* approves of such clawbacks:[26]

> "Schemes should include provisions that would enable the company to recover sums paid or withhold the payment of any sum, and specify the circumstances in which it would be appropriate to do so."

This is a now a regular feature of executive director contracts.

Taxation

The remuneration committee and/or the non-executive directors need to be aware of the tax environment in which the remuneration policy is developed and implemented. However, policy should be developed regardless of an individual's tax status or changes to that status. While remuneration policy should take into account tax efficiency, it should not do so at an additional cost to the company.

According to the Investment Association in its *Principles of Remuneration*:

---

[23] Section 155 CA 2014.
[24] Section 1092 CA 2014.
[25] Section 1197 CA 2014.
[26] *UK Corporate Governance Code* (April 2016) D.1.1.

"Remuneration Committees should not seek to make changes to any element of executive remuneration to compensate participants for changes in their personal tax status.

Remuneration structures that seek to increase tax efficiency should not result in additional costs to the company or an increase in its own tax bill. Remuneration Committees should be aware of the potential damage to the company's and shareholders' reputation from implementing such schemes."[27]

In a multinational company, personal taxation issues may need to be considered when benchmarking salaries across different jurisdictions.

Pay on Termination of Employment

When an executive director or senior executive is leaving a company, an important component of remuneration policy is pay on termination or severance. However, companies should limit severance payments, particularly where they might be perceived as a reward for failure or under-performance.

Severance terms in a contract would include compensation for loss of office and a minimum period of notice. The risk of the role is theoretically included in the base pay and therefore high severance payments are arguably unnecessary. From a company perspective, the minimum period of notice should take into account the cost (i.e. money over time) and also the time required to transition to a new staff member. It should be a maximum of one year.[28]

The *UK Corporate Governance Code* provides that:

"The Remuneration Committee should carefully consider what compensation commitments (including pension contributions and all other elements) their directors' terms of appointment would entail in the event of early termination. The aim should be to avoid rewarding poor performance. They should take a robust line on reducing compensation to reflect departing directors' obligations to mitigate loss."[29]

---

[27] Investment Association, *The Investment Association Principles of Remuneration* (October 2016) Section A.7.
[28] *UK Corporate Governance Code* (April 2016) D.1.5.
[29] *Ibid.*, D.1.4.

Though confidentiality clauses in severance agreements are all too frequent, these are not appropriate in a listed company. Compulsory disclosures should negate much of the effect of a confidentiality agreement, but greater visibility of the constituent parts of a termination payment is desirable.

Directors should also be wary of the potential existence of side letters, a practice that should not be encouraged and may create issues for both parties if they become public. A 'side letter' is a document that is ancillary to another contract and may contain additional terms and conditions which may not be transparent to all those party to a contract. The key question wherever the content or effect of a side letter is disputed is whether or not the side letter is binding.

Section 251 CA 2014 states that it is not lawful for a company to make to any director of the company any payment by way of compensation for loss of office or as consideration for or in connection with his or her retirement from office, unless the following conditions are satisfied:
(a) particulars relating to the proposed payment (including the amount of it) are disclosed to the members of the company; and
(b) the proposal is approved by resolution of the company in general meeting.

Section 252 imposes the same obligations in the context of the transfer of the whole or any part of the undertaking or property of a company for any payment to be made to any director of the company by way of compensation for loss of office or as consideration for or in connection with his or her retirement from office.

Similarly, section 253 imposes the same obligations in relation to a payment to a director arising from the transfer of the whole or part of the shares of the company.

Breach is classed as a Category 3 offence.

Remuneration of Non-executive Directors

The discussion to date has focused on the remuneration of *executive* directors. We will now address the remuneration of non-executive directors, which is a matter for the remuneration committee and the board. This is normally a fixed fee and does not include a variable element, such as a performance-related bonus. Directors involved in deciding the remuneration of non-executive directors may wish to ensure that the quantum is enough to motivate the individual. On the other hand, it could be argued that the non-executive director, who is bringing specialist advice to the board, should be eligible for variable, performance-related pay, but this could impact their independence.

The *UK Corporate Governance Code* does not support performance-related pay for independent non-executive directors, the rationale being that NEDs are there to provide independent oversight; to control and temper the actions of the executive; and to help avoid decisions that may negatively affect shareholder value. They are also there to manage conflicts of interest and to provide vigilant monitoring on behalf of the shareholders. They should be able to take decisions that might impact on the short-term valuation or performance of the company.

The Code states:

> "Levels of remuneration for non-executive directors should reflect the time commitment and responsibilities of the role. Remuneration for non-executive directors should not include share options or other performance-related elements."[30]

Similarly, the Investment Association states that "shareholders consider it inappropriate for chairmen and independent directors to receive incentive awards geared to the share price or corporate performance."[31]

However, young companies, whether private or public, may wish to conserve scarce cash and instead award their NEDs with share options, which introduces a question of judgement and balance: should the NEDs accept performance-related pay? A new company may not have the funds to pay for their expertise, let alone the duties they take on. Reasonable share options may be the most sensible, cost-effective solution for the company. While the *UK Corporate Governance Code* specifically discourages share options for NEDs, it does recognise that they may be granted.

> "If, exceptionally, options are granted, shareholder approval should be sought in advance and any shares acquired by exercise of the options should be held until at least one year after the non-executive director leaves the board. Holding of share options could be relevant to the determination of a non-executive director's independence".[32]

---

[30] *UK Corporate Governance Code* (April 2016) D.1.3.
[31] Investment Association, *The Investment Association Principles of Remuneration* (October 2016) Section A.3.
[32] *UK Corporate Governance Code* (April 2016) D.1.3.

Conclusion

Establishing remuneration policies for the executive directors, senior management and non-executive directors of a company can be a complex task. In setting remuneration policy, those involved in the process, the remuneration committee, if one exists, or the independent non-executive directors, must balance the mix of incentives in the short term with creating shareholder value in the longer term. All remuneration policy should reflect corporate strategy.

Performance-related pay needs to be considered by those responsible for remuneration and they must assess to what extent it will be beneficial and what the desired outcomes are. Choosing criteria can be very difficult.

10 KEY POINTS: DIRECTORS' REMUNERATION

1. Remuneration of executive directors and senior executives is an important corporate governance issue. It should be transparent and fair.
2. Remuneration should be linked to the company's strategy and risk appetite.
3. Executive directors' remuneration should be designed to promote the long-term success of the company.
4. Executive pensions should only be calculated on base pay.
5. The rationale for performance-related pay is that executive directors' interests must be aligned with that of the company.
6. There should be an appropriate balance between fixed and performance-related remuneration, as well as immediate and deferred remuneration.
7. It may be extremely difficult to recruit the right executive director for the company without a performance-related pay structure.
8. Benchmarking and the use of remuneration consultants may serve to *increase* the quantum of remuneration.
9. In setting criteria for bonuses, it is important to keep them simple and easy to benchmark to avoid creating a 'micro-industry' and incurring disproportionate costs to support their measurement.
10. The *UK Corporate Governance Code* and Investment Association do not encourage performance-related pay for independent non-executive directors.

Part IV

FINANCIAL DIFFICULTY AND WINDING UP

There may come a time when the shareholders will consider winding up the company. This may be for trading reasons or as a result of financial difficulties. If a company is not in a position to pay its debts as they fall due, then the company cannot be considered a going concern. If there is a reasonable prospect of survival, examinership should be considered; if not, the company will need to be liquidated (wound up). Questions as to going concern and insolvency pose extreme risks for directors. It is here more than in any other area that there is a risk of personal liability.

If there are any concerns as to a company's solvency or its ability to continue as a going concern, it is strongly recommended that the issue is dealt with immediately at a board meeting and that external professional advice is taken. Where there is a going concern issue, directors may be tempted to try to trade out of the situation, but should not consider doing so if there is any risk that they could be involved in fraudulent or reckless trading.

Fraudulent trading is when someone knowingly carries on a business intending to defraud its creditors (section 722 CA 2014). Reckless trading, however, is more subtle. It is where a director ought to have known that their actions or those of the company would cause loss to the creditors of the company, but where there is no actual intent to defraud. A director of a company is knowingly a party to the carrying on of any business of the company in a reckless manner if:
- having regard to the general knowledge, skill and experience that might reasonably be expected of a person in that position he or she ought to have known that his or her actions, or those of the company, would cause loss to any creditor of the company; or
- he or she was a party to the contracting of new company debt and did not honestly believe on reasonable grounds that the company would be able to pay that other debt when falling due (section 610(3) CA 2014).

If in the course of the winding up of a company or examinership proceedings, or where an insolvent company is not being wound up but should be, it is found that any officer of the company was knowingly a party to the carrying on of the business in a reckless manner, then such person may be personally liable for all or any part of the debts or other liabilities of the company. If a director finds themselves in these circumstances, they could carry unlimited personal liability, which is unlikely to be covered by the company's D&O insurance policy (see **Chapter 6**).

Winding up a company, even if it is solvent, can be fraught with difficulties. For instance, Revenue may treat any debt forgiven as taxable income in the accounts of the company.

When a company becomes insolvent and it is wound up, it is likely that its directors will be restricted or disqualified for a period of five years. However, there is no maximum term of disqualification as it is at the discretion of the court. The liquidator of an insolvent company is obliged to apply for the restriction of all its directors and shadow directors who held that role within 12 months of the liquidation.

This fourth and final part of this guide, therefore, deals with the two very important areas for directors:

17. Financial Difficulty and Insolvency
18. Winding Up: Processes and Options.

17.
Financial Difficulty and Insolvency

- Introduction
- Financial Difficulty
- Going Concern
- Fraudulent Acts, Fraudulent Trading and Reckless Trading
- Examinership and Receivership
- Conclusion
- Key Points

Introduction

This chapter examines the situations in which a company can get into financial difficulties and the implications of this for the directors. It highlights the tell-tale signs of financial difficulties to which both executive and non-executive directors should be alert.

In the event of a company struggling and/or going out of business, this chapter outlines processes that directors need to be aware of, such as examinership and receivership, as well as risks such as unfair preference and reckless trading.

Financial Difficulty

When a company is in financial difficulty it can cause immense stress for all those involved – directors, management and staff. As profits decrease and/or losses increase, directors may be in denial about the situation and may not be aware of the options available to them. By the time they must address the issues, all too often the options they should have considered may no longer be available.

No one likes to fail and the reputational fallout from failure can be hard to cope with. However, as we move to a more entrepreneurial culture, initial failure can be part of the learning curve to success, providing, of course, that the lessons are learnt.

Failure is tough, particularly in a family business where the people have invested time and money over a long period in a business and perhaps the company is failing due to poor management, succession planning or decision-making. In situations like this, professional business advice is critical, but so is having people to talk to, be they family, friends or others, such as one's GP.[1]

Adequate Accounting Records

As discussed in **Chapter 13**, the directors, whether non-executive or executive, are responsible for ensuring that proper books and accounting records for the company are maintained.

---

[1] For advice on how to cope in such situations, see *A Professional's Guide to Understanding Stress and Depression* by Dr Claire Hayes, free to read and download from www.charteredaccountants.ie

In cases of financial difficulty, the directors' responsibility to have adequate accounting records is extremely important. In their annual statutory audit report, the company's auditors must state whether or not "the accounting records are sufficient to permit the financial statements to be readily and properly audited".[2]

A director may be guilty of a Category 1 offence and be held personally liable if inadequate accounting records:
- contribute to the company's inability to pay all of its debts;
- result in substantial uncertainty as to the assets and liabilities of the company;
- substantially impede the orderly winding-up of the company.[3]

Tell-tale signs of problems in relation to this responsibility include:
- accounts not being prepared on time;
- although prepared on time, accounts have material inaccuracies;
- annual budgets not being prepared for comparison purposes;
- cash flows not being produced and used as a management tool.

Even if a director does not have a financial background, it is strongly advised that he or she make an effort to understand the company's accounts and the problems faced by the finance director.

Unfair Preference

If a company is in financial difficulties, the directors need to be very careful in how they deal with payments to creditors, particularly prior to a winding up. All similarly ranked creditors must be treated equally and no one creditor at that ranking should be preferred over another of the same ranking.

A number of sections of the Companies Act 2014 address this issue.
- Preference of one creditor over other creditors in the six months prior to a winding up may be deemed as unfair preference and therefore invalid.[4] In effect, this means that if the status of a creditor is altered (such as from unsecured to secured) in the six months prior to liquidation, that debt can be declared void by the liquidator as an unfair preference. In practice, this may be difficult to prove as some creditors may be more proactive in pursuing payment than others.
- Any repayment of a debt by the company to a shareholder or a related party is likely to be examined carefully to ensure that no one

---

[2] Section 336(4)(b) CA 2014.
[3] Section 286 CA 2014.
[4] Section 604 CA 2014.

party was preferred over another prior to a winding up or a liquidation. The period in relation to payments to connected parties within the meaning of section 220 CA 2014 (such as a director's spouse, civil partner, parent, brother, sister or child) is extended to two years before the date of the winding up.[5]

Thus, if a company is in financial difficulty, directors should be careful as to which creditors are paid. If there is any doubt as to whether it could be considered unfair preference, professional advice should be taken. Some of the issues surrounding unfair preference were illustrated in the following cases. In *Re Creation Printing Company Limited*[6] the Court invalidated a floating charge in favour of a bank, which had been given in forbearance to a demand for the immediate repayment of monies due, on the grounds that the action amounted to an unfair preference and there was no evidence that the company was solvent immediately after the creation of the charge.

In contrast, in *Boylan v. Bank of Ireland*,[7] Laffoy J. in the High Court dismissed an application by the liquidator seeking a declaration that payments to Bank of Ireland were an unfair preference, on the grounds that there was insufficient evidence of a dominant intention to prefer the creditor.

Going Concern

For a company to be considered a 'going concern', it should be able to continue in business for the foreseeable future, i.e. it can pay its debts as they fall due in the ordinary course of trade. ISA (Ireland) 570 *Going Concern* defines 'going concern' as follows:

> "Under the going concern assumption, an entity is viewed as continuing in business for the foreseeable future. General purpose financial statements are prepared on a going concern basis, unless management either intends to liquidate the entity or to cease operations, or has no realistic alternative but to do so."[8]

---

[5] Section 604(4) CA 2014.
[6] [1981] I.R. 353.
[7] (2012) IEHC 386.
[8] International Standard on Auditing (Ireland) 570 *Going Concern* (ISA (Ireland) 570), para 3.

The judgement as to whether a company is a going concern or not ultimately rests with the directors of the company. This responsibility is re-iterated in the accounting standards, i.e. those rules by which a set of financial statements are drawn up:

> "When preparing financial statements, the management of an entity ... shall make an assessment of the entity's ability to continue as a going concern. An entity is a going concern unless management either intends to liquidate the entity or to cease trading, or has no realistic alternative but to do so."[9]

The *UK Corporate Governance Code*, under the section 'Accountability', states that:[10]

> "In annual and half-yearly financial statements, the directors should state whether they considered it appropriate to adopt the going concern basis of accounting in preparing them, and identify any material uncertainties to the company's ability to continue to do so over a period of at least twelve months from the date of approval of the financial statements."

The *UK Corporate Governance Code* sees the assessment of going concern as a fundamental part of risk management and internal control. Therefore:

> "The directors should explain in the annual report how they have assessed the prospects of the company, over what period they have done so and why they consider that period to be appropriate. The directors should state whether they have a reasonable expectation that the company will be able to continue in operation and meet its liabilities as they fall due over the period of their assessment, drawing attention to any qualifications or assumptions as necessary."[11]

The effect of the going concern principle in the financial statements is that "assets and liabilities are recorded on the basis that the entity will be able to realise its assets and discharge its liabilities in the normal course of business".[12] Thus, it can realise its assets (buildings, plant, debtors, etc.) for the value stated in the financial statements

---

[9] FRS 102 *The Financial Reporting Standard applicable in the UK and Republic of Ireland*, Section 3.8.
[10] *UK Corporate Governance Code* (April 2016) C.1.3.
[11] *Ibid.*, C.2.2.
[12] ISA (Ireland) 570, para 2.

and pay its bills as they fall due (trade creditors, VAT, PAYE, rent, bank loans, etc.).

If a company is not able to pay its debts as they fall due, it is insolvent and therefore is not a going concern. If the company is not a going concern, assets and liabilities must be shown at their break-up value.

Assessment of Going Concern

The assessment of going concern is one of the most important and difficult risk areas and it must always be addressed when managing risk (see **Chapter 6**).

If trading results are poor and cash flow is increasingly challenged due to ongoing losses, directors must regularly assess whether the company can continue in business. They may have to make judgements, perhaps daily, to assess this. It is therefore essential that decisions are documented as they may later protect the directors from accusations of reckless trading. In the event of insolvency, directors run the risk of personal liability if they are judged to have compromised the creditors.

The accounting standards suggest that directors use all available information to assess whether the company is a going concern.[13] This might include reviews of:
- cash-flow forecasts, particularly receipts from debtors;
- timing of payments to creditors, such as VAT, PAYE, etc.;
- credit terms;
- all aspects of the cost base, staff, premises, advertising, cost and source of raw materials, etc.;
- maturity dates of existing overdraft and loan facilities; refinancing possibilities, including invoice discounting;
- potential sources of equity.

Other available information that should be taken into account includes:
- market trends and forecast demand;
- emergence of a strong competitor;
- product issues, e.g. recalls due to poor quality, obsolescence, etc.;
- staff issues – pension liabilities, wage demands, loss of key staff and high rates of staff turnover;
- reputation and brand damage;
- litigation, e.g. due to inability to meet contract terms, poor product quality, etc.;

---

[13] FRS 102, Section 3.8.

- technological changes, e.g. impact of online sales from overseas competitors;
- supplier issues, such as late deliveries due to late payments by the company;
- customer issues, such as returns of faulty goods, poor service leading to delayed payments of invoices, etc.

The issues causing financial difficulties differ from company to company, as every company's circumstances are unique. However, the assessment process should always address "the company's borrowing requirements, the timing of cash flows and the company's exposure to contingent liabilities".[14]

Guidance on Going Concern

Determining whether a company is a going concern or not can be a complex issue. "The directors' going concern assessment process should be integrated with their on-going business planning and risk management processes" and include "a focus on both solvency and liquidity risks, whatever the business".[15]

In assessing whether or not a company has a going-concern issue, it is important to consider whether there are material uncertainties that directors should take into consideration:

> "Uncertainties ... should be considered material, and therefore disclosed, if their disclosure could reasonably be expected to affect the economic decisions of shareholders and other users of the financial statements.
>
> ...
>
> In determining whether there are material uncertainties, the directors should consider:
> - the magnitude of the potential impacts of the uncertain future events or changes in conditions on the company and the likelihood of their occurrence;
> - the realistic availability and likely effectiveness of actions that the directors would consider undertaking to avoid, or

---

[14] FRC, *Guidance on the Going Concern Basis of Accounting and Reporting on Solvency and Liquidity Risks* (April 2016) Section 5.2.
[15] *The Sharman Inquiry: Going Concern and Liquidity Risks: lessons for companies and auditors. Final report and recommendations of the Panel of Inquiry* (June 2012).

reduce the impact or likelihood of occurrence, of the uncertain future events or changes in conditions; and
- whether the uncertain future events or changes in conditions are unusual, rather than occurring with sufficient regularity to make predictions about them with a high degree of confidence."[16]

Assessing the existence of material uncertainties requires a high degree of judgement. It is important that directors can subsequently justify their decision as to why they judged there to be, or not to be, material uncertainties.

Period for Assessing Going Concern

The period for assessing the going concern assumption for a business is also a matter of judgement for the directors. The period will vary by market conditions, the size of company, its financial status, access to cash, attitude of its banks, etc. Access to cash at the end of the day will determine how much time the directors have to assess the going concern issue.

While the going-concern principle relates to the preparation of the financial statements, the concept is relevant to directors at all times. If they identify or foresee problems at any time, they must discuss these at board level and, where appropriate, external advice must be sought.

It is important to note that directors can only make judgements as to the future prospects of the business based on the information available to them. The more evidence-based the information provided is, the more informed their decisions will be.

Disclosures on Going Concern

According to guidance from the Financial Reporting Council:

"When there are material uncertainties that may cast doubt upon the company's ability to continue to adopt the going concern basis of accounting in the future, the financial statements should disclose clearly the existence and nature of the material uncertainty, including a description of the principal events or conditions that may cast significant doubt on the entity's ability

---

[16] FRC, *Guidance on Risk Management, Internal Control and Related Financial and Business Reporting* (September 2014) Appendix A, para 5.

to continue as a going concern and the directors' plans to deal with these events or conditions."[17]

Such disclosures should be included in the directors' report (see **Chapter 13**). Disclosure is key to enabling readers of the financial statements to understand the judgements that the directors have taken.

The FRC further guides that:

> "In the annual financial statements, three reporting scenarios follow from the directors' assessment of whether to adopt the going concern basis of accounting and whether there are material uncertainties".[18]

These three reporting scenarios are that the:
- going concern basis of accounting is appropriate and there are no material uncertainties; or
- going concern basis of accounting is appropriate but there are material uncertainties; or
- going concern basis of accounting is not appropriate.

If the directors conclude that the financial statements cannot be prepared on a going-concern basis, they must set out the reasons why. In reality, where a company prepares financial statements that are not on a going-concern basis, it is likely that steps have already been taken to consider examinership or a winding-up. If there are material uncertainties, the directors should explain and quantify these as far as possible and outline why they still believe that the financial statements can be prepared on a going-concern basis.

Auditors on Going Concern

The company's statutory auditors must consider the reasonableness of the going-concern judgement by the directors. Their duty is to review, test and challenge the directors' assumptions. According to the auditing standards, the auditors must:

> "obtain sufficient appropriate audit evidence about the appropriateness of management's use of the going concern assumption in the preparation and presentation of the financial statements

---

[17] FRC, *Guidance on the Going Concern Basis of Accounting and Reporting on Solvency and Liquidity Risks* (April 2016) Section 3.8.
[18] FRC, *Guidance on Risk Management, Internal Control and Related Financial and Business Reporting* (September 2014) Appendix A, para 9.

and to conclude whether there is a material uncertainty about the entity's ability to continue as a going concern."[19]

The auditors can reduce their risk by asking for directors' representations on specific matters and possibly letters of support from shareholding companies.

The auditors conclude their report by giving:
- an unqualified report; or
- an unqualified report with an 'emphasis of matter'[20]; or
- a qualified report.

This means that, in the auditor's judgement, the matter or disclosure so highlighted is so important that if it is missed, then users may be misled or may end up not understanding the financial statements accurately.

It is worth noting that just because the auditors have given a clean opinion or unqualified opinion does not mean that the company may not fail tomorrow. The auditors' report could well be based on the financial statements of six months ago and a lot can happen in six months. It is the duty of the directors, and not the auditors, to assess at all times if the company has the cash to pay its debts when they fall due and not only when the company is producing its financial statements.

Fraudulent Acts, Fraudulent Trading and Reckless Trading

Personal Liability

Fraudulent and reckless trading are extremely serious issues as they can expose the officers of the company to both personal liability under company law, and possible criminal proceedings. There is no limitation on a director's personal liability and an insurance policy may not always protect directors.

---

[19] ISA (Ireland) 570 *Going Concern*, para 6.
[20] According to ISA (Ireland) 706 *Emphasis of Matters Paragraphs and Other Matter Paragraphs in the Independent Auditor's Report*, an emphasis of matter is a "paragraph included in the auditor's report that refers to a matter appropriately presented or disclosed in the financial statements that, in the auditor's judgment, is of such importance that it is fundamental to users' understanding of the financial statements".

Fraudulent Trading

Fraudulent trading is when:

> "Any person is knowingly a party to the carrying on of the business of a company with intent to defraud creditors of the company or creditors of any other person or for any fraudulent purpose."[21]

Just one instance of fraudulent behaviour may suffice to constitute fraudulent trading. The case of *Re Hunting Lodge Limited*[22] involved a secret arrangement to divert half of the proceeds of the sale of the only remaining company asset to a building society account with fictitious names. The company was insolvent at the time. This single transaction was enough to constitute fraudulent trading by the directors.

Fraudulent trading is a Category 1 offence.[23] If there is a risk of fraudulent trading being considered or having taken place, every director must consider their personal position, as well as that of the company, and take legal advice.

Fraudulent Acts

Given the pressure and stress that a company and its directors may be under due to poor trading and a worsening financial position, the temptation to cut corners (e.g. not pay VAT or PAYE on time or to defer for a period in the hope that the business may be saved, may make a bad situation worse. The Companies Act 2014 is quite specific on the consequences of fraudulent acts. Specifically, the Act states that:
- Concealing, destroying, or falsifying any book or paper affecting or relating to the property or affairs of the company, making any false entry in any book or paper or omitting to make an entry within the period of 12 months ending on the commencement of the winding up or at any time thereafter are all Category 2 offences.[24]
- Officers must make full disclosure to the liquidator of all the property of the company and any disposals.[25] Concealing or not disclosing just €20 of debts or property is a Category 2 offence.[26]

---

[21] Section 722 CA 2014.
[22] *Re Hunting Lodge Limited* [1985] I.L.R.M 75.
[23] Section 722 CA 2014.
[24] Section 717 CA 2014.
[25] Section 716 CA 2014.
[26] Section 717 CA 2014.

In short, there is 'zero tolerance' for non-disclosure and directors should document every decision and the rationale for every decision when the company is in difficulty. This rationale may change day by day. Directors need to be able to demonstrate that they were not making false representations and regular legal advice is strongly recommended.

Reckless Trading

The risk of a charge of reckless trading should be of real concern to any director of a company that is in difficulty. According to the Companies Act 2014, an officer of a company shall be deemed to be carrying on the business of the company in a reckless manner if:
- the person was a party to the carrying on of such business and that "the person ought to have known" that their actions or those of the company would cause loss to its creditors; or
- the person was a party to the contracting of a debt by the company and "did not honestly believe on reasonable grounds that the company would be able to pay the debt when it fell due for payment".[27]

Of particular note, from section 610 CA 2014, are the phrases "the person ought to have known" and that the person "did not honestly believe on reasonable grounds", meaning that a third-party, objective test is applied as to what it is 'reasonable' to expect someone to have known. While failure to carry out a director's duties (see **Chapter 4**) may amount to recklessness, it may also be a defence to show that the director acted in an honest, responsible and reasonable manner.

The possibility of being charged with reckless trading and the dangers of unlimited personal liability mean that officers and directors need to tread carefully when a company is in financial difficulties. This is an area of extreme risk for all directors, no matter how honest or diligent.

Examinership and Receivership

If a company is in financial difficulty, it may consider the option of examinership or a lender may impose a receiver. Neither of these necessarily leads to the winding up of the company. Examinerships and receiverships are dealt with below. (Options for winding up are considered in **Chapter 18**.)

---

[27] Section 610(3) CA 2014.

Examinership

Examinership is a legal process whereby the protection of the court is obtained to assist the survival and restructuring of an insolvent company. The examinership process results in all assets of the company being protected from its creditors, so that hopefully a viable enterprise can be saved, thereby saving the jobs of the employees and giving creditors a greater return than would arise on a winding up.

The examinership process involves the appointment of a qualified person as 'examiner' by a judge of the Circuit Court[28] (or the High Court for large companies) to guide the company through a 'breathing space' from its creditors to enable a restructuring to take place.

The directors of a company or the company itself, a creditor or shareholder can petition the court to put a company into examinership. This gives a company protection from its creditors while an examiner assesses whether the company has a reasonable prospect of survival and prepares a proposal to be put before members, creditors and the court.

The petition is accompanied by a report in relation to the company, which is prepared by a person who is either the statutory auditor of the company or a person who is qualified to be appointed as an examiner of the company.[29]

Following a successful outcome to the court hearing, the company is under the protection of the court for 70 days. An extension of 30 days may be applied for.[30]

For as long as the company is under the protection of the court, the following are the key provisions that apply:
- no proceedings for the winding up of the company may be commenced;
- no receiver over any part of the property of the company shall be appointed;
- no attachment, sequestration, distress or execution shall be put into force against the property or effects of the company;
- no action may be taken to realise any claim against the company secured by a mortgage, charge, lien or other encumbrance;
- no steps may be taken to repossess goods in the company's possession; and
- no proceedings against a person who is liable to pay the debts of the company may be commenced.[31]

---

[28] Section 509(7)(b) CA 2014.
[29] Section 511 CA 2014.
[30] Section 534(3) and (4) CA 2014.
[31] Section 520 CA 2014.

The court can confirm a company's proposals for restructuring, modify them or refuse to confirm them.[32] The protection under the examinership and the appointment of an examiner cease on the coming into effect of a compromise or scheme of arrangement, or on such earlier date as the court may direct.[33] A 'scheme of arrangement' is a process used by a company in financial difficulty to reach a binding agreement with its creditors to pay back all, or part, of its debts over an agreed timeline.

If the company is not judged to have a reasonable prospect of survival as a result of the examinership process, it will be placed into liquidation (see **Chapter 18**).

Receivership

The appointment of a receiver can be sought by directors; however, a receiver is usually appointed on foot of a demand from a lender and therefore will act for and on behalf of that specific creditor. While there are no specific qualifications to be a receiver, a receiver **cannot be**:
- an undischarged bankrupt;
- a person who has been an officer or employee of the company in the last 12 months;
- a parent, spouse, civil partner, brother, sister or child of an officer of the company;
- a person who is a partner of, or in the employment of, an officer or employee of the company; and
- a body corporate.[34]

The court can remove a receiver and appoint another, if cause is shown.

A receiver is appointed as a result of a lender enforcing, for example, a fixed charge over an asset which is the security for a loan in default. The receiver acts in accordance with the lending documentation to generate sufficient funds to repay or maximise the repayment of the charge holder. For example, if a bank has lent money to a company, the bank may have taken a fixed charge over the property of the company until such time as all the money is paid back.

On the appointment of a receiver, the directors should ensure that all security documentation under which the receiver is appointed is valid,

---

[32] Section 541 CA 2014.
[33] Section 552 CA 2014. A 'scheme of arrangement' is a process used by a company in financial difficulty to reach a binding agreement with its creditors to pay back all, or part, of its debts over an agreed timeline.
[34] Section 433 CA 2014.

was properly and timely registered and that there is no unfair preference, i.e. another creditor who has a stronger claim.

If the receiver is appointed over the whole, or substantially the whole, of the company, the company must file a statement of affairs (with the receiver) together with an affidavit signed by one of the directors and the Company Secretary.[35]

> "The statement as to the affairs of a company required by section 430 (the 'statement') to be submitted to the receiver (or his or her successor) shall show as at the date of the receiver's appointment—
>
> (a) particulars of the company's assets, debts and liabilities,
> (b) the names and residences of its creditors,
> (c) the securities held by those creditors respectively,
> (d) the dates when those securities were respectively given, and
> (e) such further or other information as may be prescribed."[36]

The role of the receiver is to repay the charge/debenture holder and as a result he or she has extensive powers.[37] Where a receiver is acting under a floating charge, they must first discharge all 'preferential creditors'. Preferential creditors include all rates and taxes due to the Revenue and all wages or salary due to staff, including holiday entitlements.[38]

It is worth emphasising that the receiver is not working in the interests of the company but in the interests of a particular creditor. It is possible that the receiver does not understand the business and has little appreciation of the value of its assets.

While the receiver is obliged to obtain the best price on realisation of the assets, the wording in the Companies Act is 'soft':

> "A receiver of the property of a company shall, in selling property of the company, exercise all reasonable care to obtain the best price reasonably obtainable for the property as at the time of sale."[39]

The words "all reasonable care", "reasonably obtainable", "at the time of the sale" weaken the obligation to get the best price. The receiver is generally not interested in the business in the long term, so it is unlikely that they will

---

[35] Sections 430 and 431 CA 2014.
[36] Section 430(1) CA 2014.
[37] Section 437 CA 2014.
[38] Section 621 CA 2014.
[39] Section 439(1) CA 2014.

exert themselves to get the very highest price. In fact, a quick sale is more likely to be in the interests of the lender/creditor for whom they are acting.

However, receivers should be mindful of the decision in *Holohan v. Friends Provident and Century Life Office*[40] where a receiver sold a charged property (a building) without vacant possession (i.e. with tenants *in situ*). The issue that arose was whether the receiver had breached his duty by not waiting for the tenants to vacate the building or buying the tenants out of their contract, as a sale with vacant possession would have generated a higher price for the building. It was estimated that the sale value of the building would have increased threefold without the tenants. The Court held that the receiver had breached his duty of care as he had failed to consider alternatives, and in particular he had failed to investigate the possibility of buying out the tenants from their lease and the cost of this versus the benefits of selling with vacant possession.

On appointment, the receiver takes control of the assets charged to the appointing creditor and may attempt to continue to trade while seeking to recoup the monies under the charge or to offer the business and assets for sale as a going concern.

In addition, the receiver may well initiate proceedings against the directors for reckless trading or initiate restriction proceedings.

The directors are expected to co-operate with the receiver. The relationship can be extremely difficult, however, and it is important to keep the relationship professional. Even when the receivership is finished, it is the responsibility of the company and its directors to resurrect, sell or liquidate what remains.

Conclusion

This chapter has outlined the responsibilities of directors when a company is in financial difficulty, particularly the importance of directors understanding the 'going concern' concept and being able to assess if the company is, in fact, a going concern. To do this, the directors need to be well informed about all aspects of their business and have the right information to make that judgement.

If the directors decide to restructure the company (e.g. reduce its cost base by renegotiating expensive pre-recession lease costs), they may consider the option of an examinership to protect the company from its creditors and, at the same time, ensure that they cannot be accused

---

[40] [1966] I.R. 1.

of fraudulent or reckless trading. On the other hand, when a company is in difficulty and goes into default on a loan, it is likely that a lender will enforce a receivership. It is in these situations that directors are at the greatest risk and could face unlimited personal liability.

10 Key Points: Financial Difficulty and Insolvency

1. The 'going concern' concept involves an assessment as to whether the company can continue in business for the foreseeable future.
2. Directors are responsible for assessing the ability of a company to continue as a going concern. The auditors should review, test and challenge their assumptions.
3. It is the directors' obligation to keep proper books and accounting records. If not, and the company becomes insolvent, they risk personal liability for losses.
4. The preference of one creditor over other creditors in the six months prior to the winding up may be deemed as unfair preference and therefore invalid.
5. Fraudulent trading is defined as when "any person is knowingly a party to the carrying on of the business of a company with intent to defraud creditors of the company or creditors of any other person or for any fraudulent purpose". In this case, the directors may be held personally liable for the fraudulent trading of a company.
6. Reckless trading is where the director ought to have known that their actions or those of the company would cause loss to the creditors of the company. Directors may be held personally liable for reckless trading.
7. There is zero tolerance in company law for non-disclosure of assets to the liquidator of the company.
8. Examinership gives a company protection from its creditors while an examiner assesses whether or not the company has a reasonable prospect of survival and prepares a proposal to the court.
9. A receiver is appointed as a result of a lender enforcing a charge over an asset given as security. The receiver acts in accordance with the lending documentation to generate sufficient funds to repay or maximise the repayment to the charge holder.
10. If the company is in financial difficulty, take professional advice. Directors must be conscious of the possible personal toll and take steps to mitigate the effect on their health and family.

18.
Winding Up: Processes and Options

- Introduction
- Strike Off
- Members' Voluntary Winding Up
- Creditors' Voluntary Winding Up
- Winding up by the Court
- Liquidation
- Restriction and Disqualification of Directors
- Compliance and Enforcement
- Conclusion
- Key Points

18. WINDING UP: PROCESSES AND OPTIONS

Introduction

The members of a company may decide to close the company down possibly due to poor trading, ongoing financial difficulties or because the project or purpose for which the company was founded has been completed. This chapter will review the various methods by which a company may be wound up and the implications for directors.

A company that gets into financial difficulties may well survive and if it does, as many do, the lessons learned may make it more resilient in the future. However, if the company is solvent, the members can decide to cease trading and proceed with a members' voluntary liquidation. If the company is insolvent, then a creditors' voluntary liquidation applies.

The previous chapter addressed how a creditor/lender can call in a receiver to enforce a fixed or floating charge over an asset. If sufficient funds are not available to meet the charge, a receivership may often lead to the decision to seek a creditors' voluntary winding-up process.

It should be noted that whenever there is a deficiency of funds, the priority of debts on winding up is generally as follows:
- fixed charges (charges on a specific asset, such as a property);
- fees and expenses due to the liquidator;
- super preferential debts (unpaid employee PRSI);
- preferential debts (tax and employee liabilities);
- uncrystallised floating charges, in order of their creation;
- unsecured debts;
- deferred debts; and
- shareholders (if any surplus).[1]

Tax advice should be taken when seeking to wind up a company. In particular, two issues to bear in mind are:
- **Distributions to Shareholders** These are considered a disposal of shares and therefore are subject to capital gains tax rather than income tax.
- **Writing off of Loans** A loan that is written off by a creditor may be treated as income to the company and therefore be subject to corporation tax.

---

[1] Section 621 of the Companies Act 2014 (CA 2014).

Strike Off

Voluntary Strike Off

A company with no outstanding liabilities can choose to be struck off by the Register of Companies. This is usually the simplest and least expensive way of closing down a company. To have a company struck off **voluntarily**, directors must:
- show that the company has ceased its business;
- pass a special resolution (Form G1 H15) of the members at general meeting to request for the company to be struck off;
- file Form H15, which is the formal strike off request, with the Companies Registration Office (CRO);
- ensure all outstanding annual returns have been filed before the request for strike off is made;
- file Form H15 showing no assets or liabilities in excess of €150 and no litigation pending;
- produce confirmation from the Revenue that it has no objection to the company being struck off; and
- produce evidence of the company advertising its intention to be struck off.[2]

It is important to note, however, that even when a company has been dissolved, whether by way of strike off or liquidation, a director remains liable.[3] Thus, company dissolution, by whatever means, is not a way for the directors to avoid their liabilities.

> "The liability, if any, of every director, officer and member of the company shall continue and may be enforced as if the company had not been dissolved."[4]

A company cannot avail of voluntary strike-off if it has any assets or liabilities. On the other hand, if assets or liabilities emerge, it is possible, after a company has been struck off, to resurrect a company on application to the court if it has disadvantaged the applicant.[5]

---

[2] Section 731 CA 2014.
[3] Section 734(1) CA 2014.
[4] *Ibid.*
[5] Section 737 CA 2014.

Involuntary Strike Off

A company will be struck off the Register **involuntarily** if:
- it fails to make an annual return[6];
- it fails to deliver to the Revenue the company's particulars[7];
- it has no director resident in the EEA[8];
- the company is being wound up and the Registrar has reasonable cause to believe that no liquidator is acting[9]; or
- there are no persons recorded at the CRO as being current directors of the company.[10]

The consequences of a company being struck off involuntarily are serious[11] in that the assets of the company become the property of the State, the protection of limited liability is lost and a disqualification order may be made against the directors, effectively blocking their ability to continue acting as a company director. Directors may also be subject to disqualification orders by the courts under the terms of section 160 CA 2014. This applies where a person has been convicted of an indictable offence in relation to a company, involving fraud or dishonesty.

Members' Voluntary Winding Up

A members' voluntary winding up is the process of winding up a company that has sufficient assets to repay all of its creditors within one year of the liquidator's appointment. This may occur, for example, because the company has completed its purpose or the directors want to retire.

In a members' voluntary winding up, the liquidator is appointed by and reports to the company's shareholders/members. The key features of a members' voluntary winding up are:
- it is a solvent winding-up initiated by the shareholders with no creditor involvement;
- the company directors swear a declaration of solvency, stating that the company can pay any remaining debts in full within 12 months;

---

[6] Section 343 CA 2014.
[7] Section 726(b) CA 2014.
[8] Section 137(1) CA 2014.
[9] Section 726(e) CA 2014.
[10] Section 726(f) CA 2014.
[11] Section 734 CA 2014.

- after the company's creditors have been repaid in full, the liquidator distributes the balance of the company's assets to the company's members/shareholders;
- following completion of the liquidation the company is dissolved.

The Procedure for a Members' Voluntary Winding Up

To complete the process of a members' voluntary winding up the directors must follow a 'Summary Approval Procedure' as set out in the 2014 Companies Act. The directors must complete a declaration that summarises the company's assets and liabilities. The directors must also state that the company will be able to pay all of its debts in full within 12 months of the commencement of the liquidation. There may be serious consequences for the directors if they swear a declaration which is inaccurate.

The declaration must be:
- made in writing;
- by all or a majority of directors;
- at a meeting held not earlier than 30 days before the shareholders meeting called for the purposes of the voluntary liquidation;
- state the amount of the company's assets and liabilities;
- state that the company will be able to pay its debts in full within 12 months of commencement of winding up[12];
- accompanied by an auditor's report stating that the declaration is not unreasonable[13];
- appended to a shareholders' notice/resolution; and
- delivered to the CRO within 14 days.

Once the declaration is completed, a copy of it must be sent to all shareholders, together with a formal notice of the shareholders' meeting. At the shareholders' meeting, a special resolution must be passed, i.e. 75% of the shareholders voting must vote in favour of the resolution.

If a director makes a declaration of solvency without having reasonable grounds for believing the company is solvent, the court may declare the director to be personally liable, without limitation, for the debts of the company.[14]

The resolution for a members' voluntary winding-up must be published in *Iris Oifigiúil* (Irish State Gazette) within 14 days of the passing of the

---

[12] Section 207 CA 2014.
[13] Section 208 CA 2014.
[14] Section 210 CA 2014.

resolution.[15] To enable the winding up to be completed, the company must then appoint a liquidator in general meeting.[16]

Finally, another procedure to effect a members' voluntary winding-up is contained in section 580 CA 2014, which applies where the company was established for a fixed duration that has expired, or for a fixed purpose that has been achieved, subject to the requirement that the company is solvent.

Creditors' Voluntary Winding Up

While a members' voluntary winding up is a process for liquidating solvent companies, a creditors' voluntary winding up is a process used to deal with companies that are insolvent.

> "A company may be wound up voluntarily as a creditors' voluntary winding-up where the following circumstances occur:
> - the members of the company in general meeting resolve that the company cannot by reason of its liabilities continue its business and that it be wound up as a creditors' voluntary liquidation and a creditors meeting is held;
> - a members' voluntary liquidation is converted to a creditors voluntary liquidation ...; or
> - where a declaration in relation to a members voluntary winding-up is not made in accordance with the relevant provisions of the Companies Act."[17]

Creditors' Meeting

When the members of the company in general meeting resolve that the company cannot by reason of its liabilities continue its business and that it be wound up as a creditors' voluntary liquidation, a liquidator is usually appointed at the members' meeting, with a meeting of the creditors called on the same day or shortly thereafter. The company must also advertise the creditors' meeting in at least two daily newspapers in the vicinity of where the business is based, with at least 10 days' notice given.

---

[15] Section 581 CA 2014.
[16] Section 583 CA 2014.
[17] See www.odce.ie/en-gb/faq/windingupliquidations.aspx

The main difference between a creditors' voluntary winding up and a members' voluntary winding up is that in the former, the creditors can select the liquidator.

It is the responsibility of the directors to prepare and present a statement of the company's affairs, together with a list of creditors and of the amounts they claim are owed. It is up to the liquidator to call any further meetings and present his or her final account before the final meeting with the creditors and members.

The company will be dissolved when the liquidator's report is delivered to the CRO, three months after it has been delivered.

Winding Up by the Court

A company can be wound up under the supervision of the court. Usually, in such cases, the directors or shareholders petition the court to wind up the company, although the option is also available to individual creditors.

A company can be wound up by the court if the:
- company has, by special resolution, resolved that it is to be wound up by the court;
- company does not commence its business within a year after the date of its incorporation or suspends its business for a continuous period of 12 months;
- members of the company are all deceased or no longer exist;
- company is unable to pay its debts (as per section 570 CA 2014);
- court is of the opinion that it is just and equitable that the company should be wound up;
- court is satisfied that the company's affairs are being conducted, or the powers of the directors are being exercised, in a manner oppressive to any member or in disregard of his or her interests as a member;
- court is satisfied, on a petition of the Director of Corporate Enforcement (DCE), that it is in the public interests that the company should be wound up.[18]

Note: a court liquidation may be useful if there is a danger that the value of the company would diminish materially should it delay for the required 10 days to give notice to the members under a creditors' winding up. It is also useful in circumstances where there is a suspicion of wrongdoing on the part of company officers, as a compulsory liquidator has the power to investigate whereas a voluntary liquidator does not.

[18] Section 569 CA 2014.

Duties of Company Directors in a Winding Up

If a company is in liquidation, the directors must co-operate with the liquidator. If a director is found to have misapplied or wrongfully retained property of the company or if they have wrongfully exercised their powers, proceedings can be instituted for the recovery of the property or compensation for the property lost.[19]

Liquidators

Whether it is a voluntary or involuntary winding up, a liquidator is the officer of the company who has responsibility for realising the value of all of the assets of the company and making distributions to creditors in appropriate preference before dissolving the company.

On appointment, the liquidator gives notice of his or her appointment to the Registrar of Companies and takes control of the seal, books and accounting records of the company and all the property to which the company is or appears to be entitled.[20]

Under the Companies Act, a liquidator must be qualified and be a practising accountant, solicitor, or a member of a body recognised by the supervisory authority[21] or whose experience is recognised or is qualified under the laws of another EEA state.[22]

On the appointment of a liquidator, the powers of the directors cease, with the following exceptions:
- in a creditors' voluntary or court winding-up, the creditors, with the approval of the liquidator, may sanction the continuance of the directors' powers; or
- in a members' voluntary winding-up, the members may sanction the continuance of the directors' powers.[23]

To assist the liquidator in their work, the directors and/or Company Secretary must provide him or her with information enabling the completion of the statement of affairs and provide such assistance as they are in a position to give as may be reasonably required by the liquidator.[24]

---

[19] Sections 612 and 613 CA 2014.
[20] Section 596 CA 2014.
[21] Irish Auditing and Accounting Supervisory Authority (IAASA).
[22] Section 633 CA 2014.
[23] Section 677(3) CA 2014.
[24] Section 594(3) CA 2014.

Dissolution

As soon as the affairs of the company are completely wound up, the liquidator prepares an account of the winding up and how the property of the company has been disposed of. The liquidator then calls a general meeting of the company,[25] or of the creditors in a creditors' winding-up,[26] giving 28 days' notice. Within seven days after the date of that meeting, the liquidator sends to the Registrar of Companies a Final Statement of Account (Form E5). The company will be deemed to be dissolved three months after receipt by the Registrar of the Final Statement of Account.

Restriction and Disqualification of Directors

Restriction of Directors

Restriction orders apply to the directors of insolvent companies. The liquidator of an insolvent company is obliged to apply for the restriction of all directors and shadow directors within 12 months of appointment.[27] The Director of Corporate Enforcement or a receiver may likewise apply for the restriction of the directors.

The court will restrict the directors unless it is satisfied that:
"(a) the person concerned has acted honestly and responsibly in relation to the conduct of the affairs of the company in question, whether before or after it became an insolvent company;
(b) he or she has, when requested to do so by the liquidator of the insolvent company, cooperated as far as could reasonably be expected in relation to the conduct of the winding up of the insolvent company; and
(c) there is no other reason why it would be just and equitable that he or she should be subject to the restrictions imposed."[28]

The Registrar of Companies keeps a register of restricted persons under the Companies Act. This is a public document.

A restriction order means that a director of an insolvent company is not permitted, for up to five years, to be appointed or act in any way, directly

---

[25] Section 705 CA 2014.
[26] Section 706 CA 2014.
[27] Section 683 CA 2014.
[28] Section 819(2) CA 2014.

or indirectly, as a director or a Company Secretary or to be concerned in, or take part in, the formation or promotion of a company.[29]

The purpose of a restriction order was described by Mr Justice Shanley in *La Moselle Clothing Ltd. v. Soualhi* (1998) as:

> "the protection of the public from persons who, by their conduct, have shown themselves unfit to hold the office of a director and as a result represent a danger to potential investors and traders dealing with such companies."[30]

Mr Justice Shanley put forward five tests on which the responsibility of a director should be determined:
1. the extent to which the director has or has not complied with the Companies Act;
2. conduct so incompetent as to amount to irresponsibility;
3. responsibility for the insolvency of the company;
4. responsibility for a net deficiency in assets of the company; and
5. the extent to which the director has displayed a lack of commercial probity or want of proper standards.

A person who has been restricted can, within 12 months of the order, apply to the High Court for relief. Even if a director successfully defends against the imposition of a restriction order, it is likely that he or she will still be liable for costs, as it is up to the director to prove that he or she acted honestly and responsibly. This appears to be a situation where a director is presumed guilty unless they can prove otherwise.

Restriction is only effective after the DCE requires the liquidator to bring proceedings and the High Court has made a restriction order.

The Companies Act 2014 allows a person who is to be restricted to avoid a court appearance. In this case the person (i.e. the director) must sign and give to the DCE a restriction-acceptance document, which the DCE must then file.[31]

The inconvenience and cost of a restriction order is a key reason why shareholders, and particularly shareholder/directors, may prefer to inject sufficient funds into the company to allow for a members'

---

[29] Section 819(1) CA 2014, unless the company has allotted share capital of nominal value not less than €500,000 if it is a PLC or €100,000 if it is any other company (section 819(2)).
[30] *La Moselle Clothing Ltd. v. Soualhi* [1998] 2 I.L.R.M 345.
[31] Section 854 CA 2014.

voluntary liquidation rather than let the company become insolvent. Restriction is a powerful incentive for directors not to walk away from a company on the verge of insolvency.

The impact of a restriction order on non-executive directors from a professional background can be catastrophic and an unfortunate consequence of this is that many well-qualified people may shy away from sitting on boards where, in fact, their expertise would be most useful.

Disqualification of Directors

The court may make a disqualification order.[32] If a person is 'disqualified', they are not allowed to be appointed or act as a director or other company officer, statutory auditor, receiver, liquidator or examiner, or be any way, whether directly or indirectly, concerned or involved in the promotion, formation or management of a company.[33]

A person is automatically disqualified for five years if that person is convicted on indictment of any offence under the Companies Act 2014, or of any offence involving fraud or dishonesty.[34] The disqualification period covers a period which the DCE considers warranted in relation to the underlying facts and circumstances.[35] (All director disqualifications listed on the ODCE website are for five years or less.)

If there is a change in the circumstances of a director, the company must notify the Registrar, including if he or she is disqualified in a foreign jurisdiction.[36] As with restriction orders, the Companies Act 2014 allows a person who is to be disqualified to avoid a court appearance. In this case, the director must sign and give the DCE a disqualification acceptance document, which the DCE must then file.[37]

Enforcement of Restriction and Disqualification Orders

If a person acts contrary to a:
- restriction order, they are deemed guilty of a Category 2 offence and will be subject to a disqualification order;

---

[32] Section 842 CA 2014.
[33] Section 838 CA 2014.
[34] Section 839 CA 2014.
[35] Section 850(3)(b) CA 2014.
[36] Section 840 CA 2014.
[37] Section 854 CA 2014.

- disqualification order, they are guilty of a Category 2 offence and the disqualification order is extended for 10 years, or as decided by the court.[38]

A director who acts in accordance with the directions or instructions of another person knowing that that other person, in giving the directions or instructions, is acting in contravention of a restriction or disqualification order, is guilty of a Category 2 offence. If convicted, they too are disqualified.[39]

In addition, a person acting while restricted or disqualified may be held personally liable for the debts of the company should that company be found insolvent.[40]

While court cases have started to differentiate the role of non-executive directors,[41] a director cannot rely on this and the underlying law is that all directors are equally responsible. Thus, all directors may be subject to restriction and disqualification orders, even if they may not be involved in the day-to-day management of the company.

Conclusion

This chapter reviewed the various ways in which the life of a company may come to a legal end. Voluntary strike off is the easiest approach if the company has no assets or liabilities remaining. In an insolvency situation, it is likely that the directors may end up being restricted for five years.

10 Key Points: Winding Up: Processes and Options

1. Voluntary strike off is the simplest way of closing a company; however, the company must have ceased business and have no assets or liabilities.
2. There is a priority of debts where there is a deficit of funds in a winding up.
3. The consequences of involuntary strike off, e.g. for failing to make a return, may result in the assets of the company becoming the property of the State.

---

[38] Section 855 CA 2014.
[39] Section 856 CA 2014.
[40] Section 859 CA 2014.
[41] *Re Tralee Beef and Lamb Limited (In Liquidation)* [2008] 3 I.R. 347.

4. A members' voluntary winding up is used for the orderly liquidation of a solvent company.
5. A creditors' voluntary winding-up takes place where a company is insolvent.
6. The role of the liquidator is to realise the assets, pay the creditors according to their rights and then dissolve the company.
7. The liquidator of an insolvent company is obliged to apply for the restriction of all directors and shadow directors within 12 months.
8. Restriction means that a director of an insolvent company is not permitted to be appointed or act in any way, directly or indirectly, as a director or secretary of a company for five years.
9. If a person is 'disqualified', he or she is not allowed to be appointed or act as a director or other officer, statutory auditor, receiver, liquidator or examiner or be any way, whether directly or indirectly, concerned or involved in the promotion, formation or management of a company.
10. The result of a restriction is so strict that directors are strongly advised to take legal advice as to whether it is possible ensure that the company is solvent when it is wound up.

Index

accommodation
  benefit in kind 275
accounting records
  adequacy of 212, 213, 287, 288
  charities 22
  contents 213
  continuous and consistent basis 212
  directors' duties to keep 212, 213
  financial difficulties, importance of adequate accounting records 287, 288
  financial statements *see* financial statements
  key differences between management accounts and statutory financial statements 214
  management accounts 215
    differences between statutory financial statements and 214
    key performance indictors 215
    typical inclusions 215
  meaning of accounts 213, 214
  obligations 16, 24, 209
  personal liability of directors 224
  place of keeping 213
  standards *see* accounting standards
  types of accounts 213
accounting requirements
  accounting standards *see* accounting standards
  company size criteria 209, 210
  financial statements *see* financial statements
  offences by directors 212

accounting standards
  application, requirements and options 211
  FRS 102 *Financial Reporting Standard applicable in the UK and Ireland* 210
  FRS 105 *Financial Reporting Standard applicable to the Micro-entities Regime* 210
  International Financial Reporting Standards (IFRS) 210
  large companies, complexities 211
age of directors 27, 36
alternate directors 30, 31
annual general meeting
  agenda 194
  financial statements and other reports 194
  information to be delivered to shareholders 195
  notice of 196, 202
    contents 196
    period for giving 196
    persons notice to be delivered to 196
  period for meetings 194
  points to be covered 194, 202
  private company limited by shares (LTD) specifically 195, 202
  proxies 197, 198, 202
  quorum and attendance 197
  requirement for 16, 193, 194, 202
  shareholders' powers 195
  timing of 194

317

annual return
    audit exemption criteria 245
    delivery to Registrar 104, 114, 200
    Company Secretary's duty 149, 150
    striking off, requirements 306, 307
appointment of directors
    board's considerations and company requirements 34
    consent of appointee 34, 37
    contract of service 34, 35
    due diligence process 32, 33
    fitness and probity requirements 33
    nomination committee see *nomination committee*
    non-executive directors 146, 147
    removal of directors 35, 36
    term of appointment 34
Articles of Association 23, 24
asset finance 84
attachment against directors 59
audit committee
    effectiveness of internal audit 180
    experience and skill requirements 178
    financial reporting process 179
    financial statements, integrity of 179
    good faith reporting 177
    internal controls, report on 179
    membership 178, 179
    report by statutory auditor 180
    reporting to the board 181
    responsibilities 189
    risk management 179
    role and responsibilities of 176, 177, 178
auditors
    appointment of 236, 248
    definition 235
    ethical standards 180, 237
    going concern 294, 295
    independence of 180, 236, 248
    internal auditors 246, 247
        terms of reference 247
    key points 248
    matters to be considered in choosing 236, 237
    potential threats to independence and objectivity 237
    procedures 238
    prohibited from being director 27
    removal of 239
    report see *auditor's report*
    resignation of 239, 240
    rights of 240
    role of 80, 237, 238
    statutory auditor, meaning 235
auditor's report
    adverse opinion 241
    banking and finance, failure to comply 244
    clean or standard opinion 241
    company law, failure to comply 244
    competition 244
    consumer protection 244
    corruption 244
    cybercrime 244
    deficiency in internal financial controls 243
    disclaimer of opinion 242
    emphasis of matter 242, 243
    format and content 240, 241
    fraud 244
    material respects 240
    money laundering 244
    opinion of and what it means 241–243, 248
    qualified opinion 242
    responsibilities to third parties 244, 248
    suspected breach of Companies Act 243
    taxes, incorrect or failure to pay 243

INDEX

audits *see also* auditors
    exemption 244, 245
        application for 245, 248
        charities 245
        criteria for 245, 248
        not-for-profit organisations 245
        objections to 245
    financial statements 221, 235, 236
    internal 246, 247
        definition 246
        key function 248
        terms of reference 247
    key points 248
    purpose of 235, 248
    rotation of 238, 239

balance sheet 216, 217, 226–228
bank payment instructions
    counter-signatures, risk management 94
bank reconciliations
    risk management 94
bankrupts
    notice off general meeting 196
    prohibitions
        auditor 236
        directors 27, 35
        receiver 299
benefits in kind 275, 276
board committees
    audit committee *see* audit committee
    key points 188, 189
    membership 176
    non-executive directors
        participation and role 146
    nomination committee
        see nomination committee
    overview 175
    purpose of 175
    remuneration committee
        see remuneration committee
    terms of reference 176, 189
    types and numbers of 157, 158
board of directors
    accountability 136, 137
    agency theory 132
    allocation of responsibilities 157, 158
    authority of 132, 133
    away days 166
    behaviour 159, 160, 171
    binding the company 158
    chairman *see* chairman of the board
    chief executive officer *see* chief executive officer (CEO)
    composition
        balance and diversity 156, 157
        size and structure 155, 156, 171
        succession planning 156, 171
    confidentiality 166, 171
    ethics and values *see* ethics and values
    entrepreneurial leadership 135, 136
    evaluation of 168–171
        boardroom discussion 170
        external evaluation 170
        interviews and feedback 169
        self-assessment questionnaire 169
    executive management, versus 133–135
    financial resources, ensuring 136
    functions 131
    human resources, ensuring 136
    induction and development of directors 137, 138
    information to be provided to 166–168, 171
    key points 151, 152
    matters reserved for 158, 171
    meetings *see* board meetings
    non-executive directors *see* non-executive directors (NEDs)

board of directors—*cont.*
    obligations to shareholders and other are met 136
    overview 116
    power over the company 133
    review management performance 136
    role 131, 132, 134
    set company's values and standards 136
    stewardship theory 132
    strategic aims 136
    team, functioning as 159
    theoretical perspectives 132
    titles 134
    UK Corporate Governance Code 135, 136
    workplan 162, 171
board meetings
    agendas for 162, 163
    chairing 163, 164
    conducting 163, 164
    conference calls/video links 161
    emergency meetings 161
    general procedures relating to notice/voting and resolutions 160, 161, 171
    location of 161, 162
    minutes 164, 165
bonuses
    award of 276
    clawback 278
    Investment Association support for 276
books and documents
    accounting records *see* accounting records
    inspection, availability for 200, 201
    offences by directors 212
    Office of the Director of Corporate Enforcement (ODCE), powers to require 106

breach of director's duties
    account to company for any direct/indirect gain made 56
    attachment against directors 59
    compliance orders 59
    considerations on 56
    damages, claim for 56
    disclosure orders 60
    enforcement of orders and judgments 59
    equitable relief, grant of 56
    exclusion clause, prohibition 55
    indemnify/compensate for loss or damage incurred 56
    officers in default 58, 59
    penalties
        civil penalties 58, 62
        criminal penalties 56–58, 62
    protection orders 59, 60
    prudent and effective controls 136
    remedies for 55, 56
    sequestration 59
bribery and corruption 109
bullying 261, 262

cars
    benefit in kind 275
cash-flow statement 216, 229, 230
chairman of the board
    appointment 138
    board's behaviour, key role 159, 160
    board's collegiate and productive approach to work, ensuring 159
    chief executive officer (CEO), relationship between chairman and 139–141, 152
    confidentiality, insistence on 166
    evaluation of the board 169, 170
    Higg's Report 139

majority/significant shareholder,
    relationship with 141
  responsibilities 138
  UK Corporate Governance Code
    138, 139
  workplan 162, 171
charges
  financing business 86–88
  fixed 86
  floating 86, 87
  registering, procedure for 88
  retention of title 88, 89
charitable organisations
  Code of Governance for Voluntary,
    Charitable and Community
    Organisations 8
charities
  audit exemption 245
  filing accounts 22
  Statement of Recommended
    Accounting Practice (SORP) 22
chief executive officer (CEO)
  relationship between chairman
    and 139–141, 152
  report, categories of information
    and delivery to board 167
  responsibilities 141
civil penalties *see* Penalties
close companies 223
code of ethics
  adherence to, recognition and
    reward 121
  breaches of 121
  Chartered Accountants Ireland
    Professional Standards 122, 123
  communication of 120
  contents 121, 122
  monitoring and reporting 121
  training 121
  written code 120, 127
Code of Governance for Voluntary,
  Charitable and Community
  Organisations 8

Code of Practice for the Governance of
  State Bodies 7
Common Reporting Standard
  (CRS) 112, 113, 114
community organisations
  Code of Governance for Voluntary,
    Charitable and Community
    Organisations 8
companies
  accounting records, obligations
    16, 24
  annual general meeting,
    requirements 16
  company limited by guarantee
    see company limited by
    guarantee (CLG)
  conversion and change of name
    of old companies to LTD or
    DAC 22, 23
  designated activity company
    see designated activity
    company (DAC)
  documentation, delivery of 16
  key points 24
  private company limited by
    shares *see* private company
    limited by shares (LTD)
  public limited company *see*
    public limited company (PLC)
  registers of directors, secretaries
    and members 16, 24
  separate legal entity 15, 16, 24
    obligations 16
  shareholders' role 16
  types of 17–22
  veil of incorporation 16, 17, 24
Companies Act 2014 10, 11
company limited by guarantee
  (CLG) 17
  audit exemption 245
  financial statements,
    requirements 22
  key characteristics 19

company limited by guarantee (CLG)–*cont.*
  liability of members 22
  name, requirements 22
  outline 21, 22
Company Secretary
  appointment 149
  company seal, custody and control of 150
  compliance 150
  duties 148–151
    delegated by board 149
    filing returns and forms 150
    statutory 148, 149
  letterhead stationery and websites 150
  minutes of board meetings, record of 164, 165
  personal liability 149
  preparing and supporting general meetings 150
  registers, maintaining 150
  removal 149
  skills required 149
  statutory position 148
  supporting meetings of the board and its committees 150
Competition and Consumer Protection Commission (CCPC)
  penalties under competition law 107, 114
  role and responsibility of 106, 107
compliance orders 59
conflicts of interest
  areas of 65
  awareness 74
  company contracts, disclosure of interest in 51, 65, 66
  competing with the company 68, 69
  disclosure of interest in shares or debentures 69
  duty to avoid conflict between director's duties to the company and his/her own interests 47, 48
  key points 75
  loans *see* loans
  restricted activities *see* restricted activities
  substantial non-cash asset transactions 66, 67, 75
  use of company property or information for profit 68
connected persons
  loans *see* loans
  meaning 70
contracts
  disclosure of interest in 51, 65, 66
contracts of employment 251, 252
corporate governance
  background to 5
  Cadbury Report 10
  characteristics of good governance 7
  Companies Act 2014 10, 11
  comply or explain, concept of 9–11
  definition 6, 7, 11
  governance codes in Ireland 7, 8
    Code of Governance for Voluntary, Charitable and Community Organisations 8
    Code of Practice for the Governance of State Bodies 7
    Corporate Governance Code for Credit Institutions and Insurance Undertakings 7
    Irish Development NGOs Code of Corporate Governance 8
  hard law requirements 8, 11
    Companies Act 2014 10
  Irish Corporate Governance Annex 6
  key points 11

INDEX

soft law approach 8, 11
    comply or explain, concept of 9, 10
    UK Corporate Governance Code 6, 8–11
Corporate Governance Code for Credit Institutions and Insurance Undertakings 7
corporate manslaughter 260, 261
corporate plan *see* strategic development plan
credit institutions
    Corporate Governance Code for Credit Institutions and Insurance Undertakings 7
    registration as designated activity company (DAC) 20
creditors
    categories 52
    directors' duties to 52–54, 62
        distribution of company assets 53
        insolvency 52–54
    unfair preference 288, 289, 302
creditors' voluntary winding up 309
    creditors' meeting 309, 310
criminal penalties – see Penalties
crowdfunding 84

damages
    breach of directors' duties 56
data protection 96, 97
death
    corporate manslaughter 260, 261
debentures
    beneficial ownership, disclosure orders 60
    disclosure of interest in 69
debt
    source of finance 82
declaration of solvency
    directors' personal liability 74, 308
    summary approval procedure 73

de facto directors 30
designated activity company (DAC) 17, 24
    conversion and change of name of old companies to 22, 23, 24
    credit institutions, registration as 20
    directors 21
    key characteristics 18
    liability of members 21
    name, requirements 21
    outline 20, 21
Director of Corporate Enforcement *see* Office of the Director of Corporate Enforcement (ODCE)
directors
    age requirement 27
    alternate directors 30, 31
    appointment of *see* appointment of directors
    board *see* board of directors
    breach of duties *see* breach of director's duties
    conflicts of interest *see* conflicts of interest
    contract of service 34
    de facto directors 30
    definition 28
    disqualification orders 60, 314, 315
    due diligence process 32, 33, 36
    duties *see* duties of directors
    executive directors 28, 29
    insurance cover 98, 99
    key points 36, 37
    loans *see* loans
    nominee directors 31
    non-executive directors 29
    owners of their company 27
    personal liability *see* personal liability
    primary function 28
    prohibited persons 27
    public record of 28

directors—*cont.*
   removal *see* removal of directors
   remuneration *see* remuneration of directors
   report *see* directors' report
   residence requirement 27
   responsibilities *see* responsibilities of directors
   restricted activities *see* restricted activities
   restriction orders 36, 58, 312–314
   shadow directors 29, 30
   substantial transactions in respect of non-cash assets 52, 222
   types of 28–31
directors' report
   approval 218
   audit information, statement on 219
   business review 218
   general matters 218
   interest in shares and debentures 218
   obligation to prepare 218
disclosure notices
   interest in shares or debentures 69
disclosure orders 60
disqualification orders
   civil penalties 58
   enforcement of 314, 315
   period of 314
   vacating office 35
dissolution of company 312
documentation *see* accounting records; books and documents
due diligence process
   board and executive 32
   constitution 32
   financial and operational performance 32
   financing 32
   legal status and shareholding structure 32
   other considerations 33
   purpose of 33
   regulatory environment 32
   risk appetite and key risks to which company is expose 33
   strategy and current business plan 32
   structure 32
duties of directors
   accounting records *see* accounting records
   audit of financial statements 51
   auditor's report 51
   books of account 52
   breach of *see* breach of director's duties
   Company Secretary's necessary skills, ensuring 51
   corporate social responsibility 55, 62
   creditors, to 52–54, 62
   directors' loans 52
   directors' report *see* directors' report
   disclosure of any interest in contracts entered into by company 51
   disclosure of directorships in other companies 52
   disclosure of payments in connection with share transfers for loss of office/retirement from office 51
   extraordinary general meetings 52
   fiduciary duties
      acting honestly and responsibly in relation to conduct of company affairs 45, 46
      acting in accord with company's constitution 46
      acting in good faith and in interests of the company 43–45

avoiding conflict between director's duties to the company and his/her own interests 47, 48
codifying 43–51
compliance with Companies Act 2014 42, 61
exercise care/skill and diligence 48–50
exercise powers only for purposes allowed by law 46
first duty of director 42
legal duties and obligations 42, 61
list of general duties 43
meaning of fiduciary 41
not to agree to restrict director's power to exercise independent judgement 47
not to use company's property/information/opportunities for own/anyone else's benefit 46, 47
owed to company 41, 42, 61
regard to interest of company shareholders/members and employees 50, 51, 61
financial matters 211, 212
financial statements *see* financial statements
health & safety 259
key points 61, 62
non-executive directors 147, 148
political donations 52
promotion of success of the company 54
stakeholders 55
substantial transactions in respect of non-cash assets 52, 222
tax compliance 222

emergency meetings 161
employer's responsibilities
  contracts of employment 251, 252, 263
  discrimination, prohibition of 253, 263
  employee handbook 251
  health & safety *see* health & safety
  equality, promoting 253, 263
  pensions *see* occupational pensions
  personal retirement savings accounts 256
  redundancy 255, 263
  transfer of undertakings 255, 263
  unfair dismissal 253, 254, 263
  working time 252
employment law
  complexity 263
  contracts of employment 251, 252
  equality 253, 263
  health & safety *see* Health & safety
  personal retirement savings accounts 256
  redundancy 255
  transfers of undertaking 255
  unfair dismissal 253, 254
  working time 252, 253
Environmental Protection Agency (EPA)
  director's liability 110, 114
  environmental liability 110
  EU Directives, aim of 109
  insurance cover 110
  risk management 109, 110
  role and responsibility of 109, 102
equality in the work place 253
equitable relief
  breach of director's duties 56
equity
  source of finance 82, 83
  statement of changes in 216, 231

ethics and values
  code of ethics 120
    breaches of 121
    Chartered Accountants
      Ireland Professional
      Standards 122, 123
    communication of 120
    contents 121, 122
  ethical challenges
    employee matters 123
    executive director
      remuneration 123
    financial reporting 123
    gifts/hospitality 123
    information technology 124
    insolvency 124
    safety 124
    tax 124
  good faith reporting
    (whistleblowing) 121, 124–127
  in practice 120, 121
  key points 127, 128
  monitoring and reporting 121
  person responsible for 121
  protected disclosures 124–128
  raising concerns 121
  recognition and reward for
    ethical behaviour 121
  resolution of ethical dilemmas
    122, 123
    Chartered Accountants
      Ireland Professional
      Standards 122, 123
  role of the board 119, 120
  training 121
  whistleblowing 121, 124–127
examinership 297–299, 302
executive directors 28, 29
executive remuneration
  see remuneration of directors
extraordinary general meetings
  convening 196
  notice of 196
    contents 196
    period for giving 196
    persons notice to be
      delivered to 196
  proxies 197, 198
  quorum and attendance 197
  reasons for holding 195, 196

fees and expenses
  non-executive directors 146
fiduciary duties
  acting honestly and responsibly
    in relation to conduct of
    company affairs 45, 46
  acting in accord with company's
    constitution 46
  acting in good faith and in
    interests of the company 43–45
  avoid conflict between
    director's duties to the
    company and his/her own
    interests 47, 48
  breach of see breach of directors'
    duties
  codifying 43–51
  compliance with Companies
    Act 2014 42, 61
  exercise care/skill and diligence
    48–50
  exercise powers only for
    purposes allowed by law 46
  first duty of director 42
  legal duties and obligations
    42, 61
  list of general duties 43
  meaning of 'fiduciary' 41
  not to agree to restrict
    director's power to exercise
    independent judgement 47
  not to use company's property/
    information/opportunities
    for own/anyone else's benefit
    46, 47
  owed to company 41, 42

INDEX

regard to interest of company shareholders/members and employees 50, 51
financial difficulties
  adequate accounting records, importance of 287, 288
    personal liability of directors 288, 302
  creditors *see* creditors
  examinership 297–299, 302
  fraudulent acts 296
  fraudulent and reckless trading 295–297
  full disclosure to liquidator 296, 302
  going concern, company considered as 289–291, 302
    assessment of 291–293, 302
    auditors 294, 295
    guidance on 293, 294
  professional difficulties 302
  receivership 299–301
  stress of 287
  striking off *see* striking off
  unfair preference 288, 289
  winding up *see* winding up
financial forecast 81
Financial Reporting Standard applicable in the UK and Ireland *see* FRS 102
Financial Reporting Standard applicable to the Micro-entities Regime *see* FRS 105
financial responsibilities
  accounting requirements *see* accounting requirements
  duties of directors regarding financial matters 211, 212
  importance of 209
  statutory accounting requirements 209–211
financial service providers
  fitness and probity requirements 33, 37

financial statements
  approval and signature 219, 221
  audit obligation 221, 222
  balance sheet 216, 226–228
  cash-flow statement 216, 229, 230
  charities 22
  company limited by guarantee, filing requirements 22
  compliance with Companies Act requirements 215, 216, 217
  directors' compliance statement 220, 221
  directors' responsibility statement 219, 220
  disclosure of accounting policies adopted 217
  notes to 217
  primary statements 216
  profit and loss account 216, 225
  Registrar, delivery to 114
  requirements 219, 220
  statement of changes in equity 216, 231
  'true and fair view' requirement 216, 217
financing business *see also* loans
  charges 86–88, 100
    fixed 86
    floating 86, 87
    registering, procedure for 88
    retention of title 88, 89
  common lending ratios 84
  conditions precedent 85
  long term
    asset finance 84
    crowdfunding 84
    equity 83
    term loan 83
  personal guarantees 86, 100
  representations 84, 85
  risk management *see* risk management
  short term
    invoice discounting 82, 83

financing business—*cont.*
    loans from shareholders 83
    management working
        capital 83
    overdraft 82, 100
    sources of finance 82
    warranties 84, 85, 100
fines *see* penalties
fixed charges
    financing business 86
    registering charges, procedure
        for 88
floating charges
    financing business 86, 87
    registering charges, procedure
        for 88
Foreign Account Tax Compliance
    Act (FATCA) 111, 112, 114
foreign legislation
    Common Reporting Standard
        (CRS) 112, 113
    Foreign Account Tax Compliance
        Act (FATCA) 111, 112
    Sarbanes–Oxley Act (SOX) 110,
        111
fraud or tax evasion
    lifting the veil of incorporation 17
fraudulent acts 296, 297
fraudulent or reckless trading
    fraudulent trading 296, 302
    lifting the veil of incorporation 17
    personal liability 295, 297, 302
    reckless trading 297, 302
FRS 102 *Financial Reporting*
    Standard applicable in the UK
    and Ireland 210
FRS 105 *Financial Reporting Standard*
    applicable to the Micro-entities
    Regime 210

general meetings
    annual general meeting *see*
        annual general meeting
    extraordinary general meeting
        see extraordinary general
        meetings
    key points 202, 203
    notice of 196
        contents 196
        period for giving 196
        persons notice to be
            delivered to 196
    proxies 197, 198
    quorum and attendance 197
going concern
    assessment of 291–293
    auditors 294, 295
    company considered as 289–291
    disclosures 293, 294
    guidance on 292
good faith reporting (whistleblowing)
    121, 124–127, 177
governance codes in Ireland 7, 8
    Code of Governance for Voluntary,
        Charitable and Community
        Organisations 8
    Code of Practice for the Governance
        of State Bodies 7
    Corporate Governance Code
        for Credit Institutions and
        Insurance Undertakings 7
    Irish Development NGOs Code of
        Corporate Governance 8

harassment 261, 262
health & safety
    bullying 261, 262, 264
    corporate manslaughter 260, 261
    employee's duties 259, 260
    employer's duties 258, 259, 264
    harassment 261, 262, 264
    key consideration for
        directors 257
    offences and penalties 258
    risk assessment 262, 263
    stress 262

victimisation 261, 262
violence 261, 262
Higg's Report 139, 144, 185, 267
human resources
  ensuring adequacy of 136

indemnities 98, 100
information *see also* books and documents
  accounting records *see* accounting records
  Common Reporting Standard (CRS) 112, 113
  directors' duty concerning use of 47, 48
    conflict of interest 68
  financial statements *see* financial statements
  protected disclosures 124–127
information communications technology (ICT)
  board's role 95
  data protection 96, 97
  development of strategy 95
  director's responsibilities 95, 96
  e-mail accounts 97
  internal controls 96
  risk management 91, 95
insolvency *see* financial difficulties; receivership; striking off; winding up
insurance cover
  directors'/officers' (D&O) insurance 98, 99
  environmental protection 110
  indemnities 98, 100
  risks that need to be covered 97
insurance undertakings
  Corporate Governance Code for Credit Institutions and Insurance Undertakings 7
International Financial Reporting Standards (IFRS) 210

invoices
  approval, risk management 94
  discounting, short-term finance 82, 83
Irish Development NGOs Code of Corporate Governance 8

key performance indicators 81, 215

letterheads 201, 203
limited liability partnerships (LLPs) 23
liquidators *see* winding up
loans *see also* financing business
  charges *see* charges
  directors and connected persons
    conflict of interests 70–72, 75
    connected persons, meaning 70
    loans from director 72
    loans to 70, 71
    prohibitions and exceptions 70, 71
  overdrafts 82, 100
    common lending ratios 84
    conditions precedent 85
    personal guarantees 86
    representations 84, 85
    warranties 84, 85, 100
  term loan 83
    common lending ratios 84
    conditions precedent 85
    personal guarantees 86
    representations 84, 85
    warranties 84, 85, 100

management accounts *see* accounting records
managing director *see* chief executive officer (CEO)
meetings
  annual general meeting *see* annual general meeting

meetings—*cont.*
   board meetings *see* board meetings
   creditors' meeting 309, 310
   extraordinary general meetings *see* extraordinary general meetings
members' voluntary winding up 307
   appointment of liquidator 309
   declaration by directors 308
   procedure for 308, 309
   resolution, publication of 308
   Summary Approval Procedure 308
Memorandum of Association 23, 24
mergers
   Summary Approval Procedure 74
minority shareholders
   oppression 36, 133, 200
   resolutions 198
mission statement 81
money laundering
   designated persons 108
   directors' due diligence 108, 114
   EU Directive, implementation 108
   meaning 108, 114
mortgages *see* charges

nomination committee
   board and senior management appointments 182, 189
   considering candidates 182
   external search consultants 183
   induction of new members 183, 184
   membership 183
   non-executive director appointments 182
   reporting 184
   responsibilities 182
   role of 181
   rotation and renewal of directors 182

nominee directors 31
non-executive directors (NEDs)
   accounting records *see* accounting records
   appointment 146, 147
   audits, responsibilities regarding 237, 248
   board committees, participation in 146
   board members
      challenging but supportive 143
      engaged but non-executive 143
      essential characteristics 143, 144
      independence 142, 144–146
      independent but involved 144
      role 142, 143
      skills and input 142, 143
      UK Corporate Governance Code 142, 144, 145
   confidentiality clause 147
   duties under company law 147, 148
   exercise care/skill and diligence 50
   fees and expenses 146, 147
   financial responsibilities 209
   letter of appointment 35
   outline 29
   outside interests 147
   remuneration 280, 281
   role 146
   senior independent directors 148, 152
   term of office 146
   third-party advice 147
   time commitment required 146
notice of meetings
   contents 196
   period for giving 196, 202
   persons notice to be delivered to 196

INDEX

occupational pensions
    contributory schemes 256
    defined benefit schemes 256, 264
    defined contribution schemes 256, 264
    directors' remuneration 274, 275
    non-contributory schemes 256
    overview 256
    trustees 257
    underfunded schemes 257, 264
offences
    accounting records 212, 288
    books and documents 212
    bribery and corruption 109
    competition law 107
    corporate manslaughter 260, 261
    Data Protection Acts 97
    directors, financial matters 212
    health & safety 258
    investigations initiated by Office of the Director of Corporate Enforcement (ODCE) 105, 106
    money laundering 108
    penalties *see* penalties
    protected disclosures 125
Office of the Director of Corporate Enforcement (ODCE)
    investigations initiated by, powers and responsibilities 105, 106, 114
    publications 105
    role 104
    suspected breach of company law, auditor's report 243, 244
overdrafts 82, 100
    common lending ratios 84
    conditions precedent 85
    personal guarantees 86
    representations 84, 85
    warranties 84, 85, 100

partnerships 23
penalties *see also* offences
    breach of director's duties
    civil penalties 58
    criminal penalties 56–58
    competition law 107
    financial statements, directors' compliance statement 220
    health & safety 258
    protected disclosures 125
pensions *see* occupational pensions
personal liability
    adequate accounting records 224, 288, 302
    Company Secretary 149
    declaration of solvency 74, 308
    environmental law, breaches of 110, 114
    fraudulent and reckless trading 295, 297, 302
    insolvency, compromising creditors 291
    legal responsibilities, breach of 36
    restriction and disqualification orders, acting in contravention of 315
personal retirement savings accounts 256
private company limited by shares (LTD) 17, 24
    annual general meeting 16
    conversion and change of name of old companies 22, 23
    directors, number of 19, 24
    key characteristics 18
    liability of members 19
    name, requirements 19
    outline 19, 20
    unlimited legal capacity 19, 24
profit and loss account 216, 217, 225
property or interest in property
    substantial non-cash asset transactions, conflict of interest 66, 67

protected disclosures 124–128
protection orders 59, 60
proxies
    attendance and voting at meetings 197, 198, 202
public-interest entities
    audit rotation 238, 239
public limited company (PLC) 17
    key characteristics 18
    'listed', meaning 21
    outline 21
purchase by company of own shares
    financial assistance, declaration of solvency 73, 74

quorum at meeting 197

receivership
    appointment of receiver 299, 300, 302
    realisation of assets 300, 301
    role of receiver 300
reckless trading *see* fraudulent and reckless trading
records see accounting records
redundancy 255
registers
    companies, striking off 58, 62, 306, 307
    directors/secretaries and members 16, 24
    inspection, availability for 200, 201, 203
Registrar of Companies
    annual return, delivery to 104, 114, 200
    compliance order, application for 60
    constitution, delivery to 42
    disqualification of directors 314
    dissolution of company 312
    financial statements, delivery to 200
    information to be provided to 104, 114
    key events to be notified to 104
    liquidator's notice of appointment 311
    objectives 103, 113
    registration of charges 88
    resolutions to be files 198
    returns to 104, 114, 200
    role of 103, 104
    Summary Approval Procedure, filing 73
    summary proceedings against directors 57
regulation and compliance
    bribery and corruption 109
    Common Reporting Standard (CRS) 112, 113
    Competition and Consumer Protection Commission *see* Competition and Consumer Protection Commission (CCPC)
    Environmental Protection Agency *see* Environmental Protection Agency (EPA)
    key points 113, 114
    money laundering 108
    Office of Director of Corporate Enforcement *see* Office of the Director of Corporate Enforcement (ODCE)
    Registrar *see* Registrar of Companies
    US legislation
        Foreign Account Tax Compliance Act (FATCA) 111, 112
        Sarbanes–Oxley Act (SOX) 110, 111
removal of directors
    absence from board meetings 35
    bankruptcy 35
    compensation for loss of office 280

disqualification orders 35, 58
inadequate decision-making due to ill health 35
oppression of minority interest 36
ordinary resolution, by 35, 37
   notice of 35
resignation in writing 35
restriction orders 36, 58
severance agreements 280
share qualifications, failing to acquire 35
termination payments 279, 280
terms of imprisonment 36
vacation of office 35, 36
written representation by director 35
wrongful termination 35
remuneration committee
   chairman's role 187
   induction of new members 187
   membership 186, 187
   policy development 183–186, 189
   principal duties 185
   reporting 188
   role of 184
remuneration of directors
   base pay 274
   benefits and allowances 275
   benchmarking 272, 273, 282
   bonuses 276, 278, 282
   components of 273
      base pay 274
      benefits and allowances 275
      bonuses 276, 278, 282
      pensions 274, 275, 282
      share-based incentives 276, 277, 278
      taxation 278, 279
      termination payments 279, 280
   corporate risk appetite, link to 270, 271, 282
   corporate strategy, link to 270

executive pay
   emergence of concerns over 267
   issues surrounding 267–269
   focus on long-term success of the company 269, 282
   non-executive directors 280, 281, 282
   pensions 274, 275, 282
   performance-based pay 267, 271, 272, 282
      agency theory perspective, based on 271, 272
      argument for/against 271
   share-based incentives 276, 277, 278
   taxation 278, 279
   termination payments 279, 280
   UK Association of British Insurers and performance-related pay 269
   UK High Pay Commission findings 267, 268
      accountability 268
      fairness 268, 282
      transparency 268, 282
   UK Investment Association proposals for remuneration policies 268
representations
   loans 84, 85
resolutions
   amendments to the constitution 132
   instructions to the directors via 198, 201
   mergers 74
   ordinary resolutions 198, 202
      removal of director 35
   special resolutions 198, 202
      adoption of new constitution 23
      summary approval procedure, restricted activities 73

resolutions—*cont.*
   written resolutions 199, 202
      majority written resolutions, use of 199, 200
      unanimous requirement 199
responsibilities of directors *see* also duties of directors
   financing business *see* financial responsibilities; financing business
   information communications technology (ICT) *see* information communications technology (ICT)
   insurance cover *see* insurance cover
   key points 100
   risk management *see* risk management
   strategy, developing and implementing *see* strategic development plan
restricted activities
   Summary Approval Procedure 72, 75
      declaration of solvency 73
      information and statements required 74
      list of restricted activities 72, 73
      mergers 74
      special resolution 73
restriction orders
   enforcement of 314, 315
   insolvent companies 58, 312–314
   non-compliance with Companies Act 36
retention of title 88, 89
rights of members 200
risk management
   appetite for risk 89, 100
   approval of invoices 94
   bank reconciliations 94
   brand and reputational risks 91
   consideration of risk 89
   counter-signature for payments 94
   directors' report 90, 91
   environmental protection 109, 110
   financial risks 91
   good risk management 93
   human resources risks 91
   information and technological risks 91, 95, 100
   insurance cover *see* insurance cover
   internal controls 93, 94, 100
   joint-venture risks 91
   mitigating risk 93, 100
   operational risks 91
   principal objective of board 90
   risk appetite, meaning 89
   risk impact and likelyhood matrix 92, 93
   role of directors 90
   segregation of duties 94
   sovereign risk 91
   strategy of company 90
   tax 91
   types of risk 91
   UK Corporate Governance Code 94

Sarbanes–Oxley Act (SOX) 110, 111, 114
secretary *see* Company Secretary
sequestration 59
severance agreements 280
shadow directors 29, 30
shareholders
   directors' decisions against 133
   directors' disclosure of share holding 69
   loans from 83
   long-term share-based incentives, approval of 277
   majority/significant shareholder, relationship with chairman 141

price-sensitive information 166
role in a company 16
shares
  beneficial ownership, disclosure orders 60
  disclosure of interest in 69
  investigations by Office of the Director of Corporate Enforcement (ODCE) 105, 106
  long-term share-based incentives 276, 277
    approval by shareholders 277, 278
  raising equity 83
  remuneration of directors 276–278
side letters
  awareness of 280
small companies
  owner director/shareholder 27
sole traders 23
state bodies
  Code of Practice for the Governance of State Bodies 7
statutory audits and auditors *see* auditors; audits
statutory financial statements *see* financial statements
strategic development plan
  allocation of resources 80
  components of 80
  developing strategy 80
  finance, sources and types of – see Financing business
  financial forecasts 81
  implementation plan 82
  information communications technology *see* information communications technology (ICT)
  key performance indicators 81
  key role of director 79
  mission statement 81
  process for development 80
  review and approval 100
  risk management *see* risk management
  strategic objectives and supporting actions 81
  strategic planning 79
  typical contents of 80
  vision statement 80, 81
stress 262
striking off
  civil penalty 58, 62
  involuntary strike off 307, 315
  voluntary strike off 306, 315
Summary Approval Procedure (SAP) *see* restricted activities

taxation
  compliance 222
  corporation tax 222, 223
  ethics 124
  remuneration of directors 278, 279
  risk management 91
termination payments 279, 280
transfers of undertakings
  employees' position 255

UK Corporate Governance Code
  audit committee 178, 181
  board evaluation 168
  board committees 175
  board of directors and its role 135, 136
  chairman 137, 138
  chief executive directors 140
  Company Secretary 149
  comply or explain 9
  composition of the board 155, 156
  directors' and officers' insurance 98
  director's role 2
  going concern 290
  induction and development of directors 137

UK Corporate Governance Code—cont.
   minutes of meetings 165
   nomination committee 181–184
   non-executive directors 142, 144, 145
   remuneration committee 186
   remuneration of directors 269, 272
   risk management 90, 94
   senior independent director 148
   soft law 8
   underpinning corporate governance in Ireland 6, 10, 11
unfair dismissal of employees 253, 254
United States of America
   Foreign Account Tax Compliance Act (FATCA) 111, 112, 114
   Sarbanes–Oxley Act (SOX) 110, 111, 114

victimisation 261, 262
violence 261, 262
vision statement 80, 81
voluntary organisations
   Code of Governance for Voluntary, Charitable and Community Organisations 8

warranties
   loans 84, 85, 100
whistleblowing 121, 124–127, 177
winding up
   court, by the 310
   creditors' voluntary winding up 309, 316
      creditors' meeting 309, 310
   dissolution 312
   duties of directors 311
   liquidators, role of 311, 316
   members' voluntary winding up 307, 316
      appointment of liquidator 309
      declaration by directors 308
      procedure for 308, 309
      resolution, publication of 308
      summary approval procedure 308
   priority of debts 305, 315
working capital
   management of, financing business 83
working time of employees 252, 253